Governing London

Ben Pimlott and Nirmala Rao

OXFORD
UNIVERSITY PRESS

This book has been printed digitally and produced in a standard specification
in order to ensure its continuing availability

OXFORD
UNIVERSITY PRESS

Great Clarendon Street, Oxford OX2 6DP

Oxford University Press is a department of the University of Oxford.
It furthers the University's objective of excellence in research, scholarship,
and education by publishing worldwide in

Oxford New York

Auckland Bangkok Buenos Aires Cape Town Chennai
Dar es Salaam Delhi Hong Kong Istanbul Karachi Kolkata
Kuala Lumpur Madrid Melbourne Mexico City Mumbai Nairobi
São Paulo Shanghai Taipei Tokyo Toronto

Oxford is a registered trade mark of Oxford University Press
in the UK and in certain other countries

Published in the United States
by Oxford University Press Inc., New York

ISBN 0-19-924492-8

Cover illustration: Front . © PA Photos.

Back panel. © Photodisc.

PREFACE

LONDON is a puzzle. Logically, 'that monstrous tuberosity of civilised life', as Thomas Carlyle called it, ought by now to have settled down. Mysteriously, it hasn't.

London has presented a problem in urban management for a long time. Ancient in origin, the capital expanded massively in the seventeenth and eighteenth centuries, and by 1750 its population was more than a tenth of the nation's as a whole. In the Victorian era it swelled into the modern sprawl which, 'huger by the day' (in the words of a poet laureate), 'O'er six fair counties spreads its hideous sway!' The city of the Great Exhibition was seen as the new Rome: a place of opportunity, refuse heap for the social dregs, haven for the oppressed. Disraeli described it once as 'a nation, not a city', but on another occasion as 'a roost for every bird'.

Indeed, London as it had become was not merely a place where large numbers of people lived and worked. It was an object of awe, a model. It was the locus of a political system that was copied or adapted in the majority of countries in the advanced world, at the same time providing the most sophisticated network of imperial administration that had ever existed. Partly because of the stability the British government offered at home and aboard, the City of London developed into the world's clearing-house: the leading centre of international finance.

Meanwhile, there was a contrast. For a couple of hundred years, London was—in some respects still is—the world's most pivotal city. Yet it remained conspicuously and embarrassingly backward when it came to managing its domestic affairs. Until the setting up of the Metropolitan Board of Works in 1855 and the London County Council (LCC) in 1889, it was almost as if its leading citizens had failed to notice that the Middle Ages were over—and that its real boundaries had left the limits of the square-mile City far behind.

The new, 117 square-mile LCC provided a structure and a concept, but little agreement. How far should London extend, what were its defining features, who were genuine Londoners, what powers should they or their representatives exercise? The history of London since the 1880s is one of sorry failure to find durable answers to these questions, and of successive experiments—each reflecting the political flavour of its time, and each relapsing into the conflicts and mental habits of its predecessor. Indeed, if the House of Commons has been the mother of parliaments, London local government has been the Fourth Republic of municipal management: an urban quagmire, marked by suspicion, insecurity, and lack of popular authority.

This book is narrow in focus: a question-asking, rather than conclusive, study. It is about the background to, and opening chapter of, the latest attempt to supply a viable structure. It aims to set the scene. In the process, it points to examples across the Channel and the Atlantic. In one sense, such comparisons are inappropriate. In contrast to federal systems where individual regions make their own local arrangements, Britain is a unitary state where local authority powers are determined centrally: a point made starkly clear by Margaret Thatcher. Hence, until and unless London is given entrenched powers, Sidney Webb's dream of a 'self-governing community' can never be a reality. This, of course, is apart from the problem of determining whether such a 'community' would consist of the population of Inner London, the 7 million in Greater London, or the 20 million in the 'Greater South East' within easy commuting distance.

Today, as ever, London government remains local and contingent, subject to the approval and ultimately the whim of an administration in Westminster. This is a limitation, but it does not necessarily stand in the way of a substantial advance. Is the new system working? Will it prove happier and more rooted in consensus than its predecessors? As Chou En-lai remarked of the French Revolution, it is much too soon to tell. Nevertheless, the legitimacy provided both by direct election of the Mayor and by the preliminary referendum make the 2000 reform the most important—and potentially the most exciting—since 1889.

As an interim assessment, this study has necessarily been conducted within a short period of time. Partly for this reason, we have been especially reliant on help and advice. In particular, we would like to thank the Economic and Social Research Council, and the Council's Institutional Change and Development Initiative, for a grant towards research costs; the officials, politicians, and others involved in the new government of London for agreeing to be interviewed, and for their insights; and Kennedy Stewart, researcher on the project, for his work in conducting interviews and collating published materials. We also wish to thank the many officials interviewed who have allowed their views to be expressed—though of course without attribution—in the book.

We are extremely grateful to Dr Bob Chilton, former head of the Greater London Authority (GLA) transition team, for his invaluable comments on a part of the book; Professor Ken Young, whose encyclopedic knowledge of London politics was a much-tapped source, and whose encouragement greatly helped the project; Professor Vernon Bogdanor and Professor George Jones for reading the whole manuscript in draft and making a number of helpful suggestions; and Michael Jones for hosting an immensely stimulating London Government seminar at Bucks Club in December 2000. We would also like to thank the seminar participants, Rodney Brooke, Simon Jenkins, Susan Kramer, Bob Neill, Martin Pilgrim, Barry Quirk, Jean Seaton, John O'Brien, and Lord Tope for sharing their reflections with us.

The book is a collaborative effort. Nirmala Rao carried out much of the research and wrote an initial draft. Ben Pimlott has redrafted, suggesting changes and additions. The authors are jointly responsible for what has been written.

Ben Pimlott
Nirmala Rao
New Cross, London, December 2001

CONTENTS

LIST OF FIGURES

LIST OF TABLES

LIST OF ABBREVIATIONS

ACPO	Association of Chief Police Officers
ALA	Association of London Authorities
ALG	Association of London Government
AMS	Additional Member System
APA	Association of Police Authorities
CBI	Confederation of British Industries
CLD	Commission for Local Democracy
CRE	Commission for Racial Equality
CSU	Community Safety Unit
DES	Department of Education and Science
DETR	Department of the Environment, Transport, and the Regions
DHSS	Department of Health and Social Security
DoE	Department of the Environment
DTI	Department of Trade and Industry
EDIC	Economic Development Investigative Committee
EDS	Economic Development Strategy
EIP	Examination in Public
ES	*Evening Standard*
GLA	Greater London Authority
GLC	Greater London Council
GLDP	Greater London Development Plan
GLEB	Greater London Enterprise Board
GLTB	Greater London Training Board
GOL	Government Office for London
HMIC	Her Majesty's Inspectorate of Constabulary
ILEA	Inner London Education Authority
LAC	London Advisory Council
LAMS	London Area Mobility Scheme
LBA	London Boroughs Association
LBGC	London Borough Grants Committee
LBL	London Buses Limited
LCC	London County Council
LDA	London Development Agency
LDDC	London Docklands Development Corporation
LEU	London Ecology Unit
LFCDA	London Fire and Civil Defence Authority
LFEPA	London Fire and Emergency Planning Authority
LPAC	London Planning Advisory Committee
LRB	London Residuary Body

LRC	London Research Centre
LRT	London Regional Transport
LSPU	London Strategic Policy Unit
LT	London Transport
LU	London Underground
LVSC	London Voluntary Services Council
MBW	Metropolitan Board of Works
MPA	Metropolitan Police Authority
MPC	Metropolitan Police Committee
MPS	Metropolitan Police Service
NEDO	National Economic Development Office
OMOV	One Member One Vote
PCCG	Police and Community Consultative Group
PFI	Private Finance Initiative
PPP	Public Private Partnership
RPG	Regional Planning Guidance
SCLSERP	Standing Conference on London and South East Regional Planning
SDS	Spatial Development Strategy
SERPLAN	South East Regional Planning
TEC	Training and Enterprise Council
TfL	Transport for London
UDP	Unitary Development Plan
WARS	Westminster Against Reckless Spending
WRAG	Westminster Residents Against Gridlock

1

Introduction

IN May 2000, Londoners went to the polls—in disappointingly small numbers—to vote for the first time for a directly elected executive mayor and assembly to represent and govern them. So began the latest episode in the recurrent experiment that is the government of London. The novelty of the new arrangements lay in the attempt to provide a concentrated focus, and above all a single voice, for the British capital. How did it come about? Is it likely to work? Can the mayor provide the political leadership necessary to rebuild a metropolitan community?

To put the matter in this way is to presuppose that there was once a London political community. There has indeed been a widespread belief that this was the case. Thus, the heyday of the former London County Council (LCC), from its inception in 1889 to the run-up to the Great War in 1914, has been seen by historians as a period in which the capital was a recognizable entity with its own democratic and well-supported government (Davis 1989: 33–4). More than half of the electorate went to the polls at each successive fiercely contested election before 1918, a significantly higher proportion than in 2000. Yet it was a transient 'community'. What subverted London's unity was suburban growth beyond the LCC boundary. By the late 1920s it was no longer possible to ignore the fact that 'London' was merely the core of a vast and rapidly growing metropolitan sprawl. There were repeated attempts to integrate London with its suburbs: fiercely resisted locally, largely on the ground that they had no shared interest with the LCC area. Yet, significantly, when the Centre for Urban Studies gave evidence to the Royal Commission on Local Government in Greater London in 1959, it argued for continuation of the LCC on the grounds that it represented, spoke for, and corresponded with a genuine and tangible community: the people of inner London.

What followed—the London Government Act 1963 and the creation of the Greater London Council (GLC)—dropped all pretence of embodying a metropolitan community in favour of an ambitious attempt at regional strategic planning. In so far as communities could claim to be represented, it was through 32 new borough councils, covering almost the entire population of the built-up area. Not all residents, of course, considered themselves truly Londoners. Those on the metropolitan fringe strove to maintain their independence. The sense that the suburbs were technically in London but not psychologically of it was one reason why the GLC never aroused much warmth among the people of Greater London. Regarded with general indifference, it succeeded in winning the loyalty of a proportion of the Greater London population only when facing abolition at the hands of Mrs Thatcher's government.

The abolition of the GLC in 1986 was to leave London without an overall government for 14 years. The Labour Party pledged itself, first, to reinstate the GLC, and second, in the guise of New Labour, to find a new solution to the age-old problem of governing London. Thus, the 1997 manifesto set out an approach to the problem that was not just a response to abolition but also a great step forward from the unthinking restoration of the GLC. 'London', it declared,

is the only Western capital without an elected city government. Following a referendum to confirm popular demand, there would be a new deal for London, with the strategic authority and a mayor, each directly elected. Both will speak up for the needs of the city and plan its future. They will not duplicate the works of the boroughs, but take responsibility for London-wide issues—economic regeneration, planning, policing, transport and environmental protection. London-wide responsibility for its own government is urgently required. We will make it happen. (Labour Party 1997)

Following its election to office in May 1997, the Blair government acted swiftly to ensure that the new bodies would assume their powers within three years of it taking office. After circulating a consultative document *New Leadership for London*, the new administration published its White Paper, *A Mayor and Assembly for London*, in March 1998, holding its promised referendum in the spring of the following year.

The Greater London Authority Act 1999 established for the first time the office of executive mayor for Greater London which, together with a Greater London Assembly, constitute a new Greater London Authority (GLA). This body covers the same area as, but has differently constituted powers from, those of the former GLC. The elections for the Mayor and the Greater London Assembly took place in May 2000. Their assumption of office two months later on 3 July marked the beginning of a new era in the governance of Greater London.

This book is about a British problem, but one that exists in the global context. London's problems are not *sui generis*. Great cities of the Western world share many common characteristics: social and economic diversity, political fragmentation, and persistent tensions and conflicts over who gets what, where, and how. Mayors and city leaders wherever they are need to provide vision and leadership if they are to surmount these problems, and building coalitions is essential to their success.

Governing London will consider this key aspect. In particular, Chapter 2, 'Governing Great Cities', considers the diversity of metropolitan communities and the contrasting styles of mayoral leadership. Chapter 3, 'London: The Elusive Community', deals with the desire to achieve a metropolitan form of government which was realised with the creation of the London County

Council in 1888 and eventually led to the establishment of the Greater London Council. It also deals with the short history of the GLC as it sought to become a strategic authority for the metropolitan region.

During the interregnum which followed the abolition of the GLC in 1986, the felt need for 'one community, one government' remained. This was a phase, explored in Chapter 4, 'London Dismembered', in which metropolitan government was abandoned and power passed to central government and to a maze of unwieldy joint arrangements. The same chapter examines the new approach to London governance provided by New Labour, in an attempt to find a fresh expression for London's identity.

The incoming administration fine-tuned its initial proposals and secured their endorsement with a London-wide referendum before piloting the new legislation through Parliament. Chapter 5, 'A New Government for London', considers the politics of setting up a new system of metropolitan government, while Chapter 6, 'London in Transition', deals with the setting up of the new London-wide arrangements. This process was not only entirely novel but was accomplished with notable speed. Moreover, the experience was shrouded in electoral uncertainty, first about the candidates, then about the outcome of the election itself. When, on 6 May 2000, it became clear that Ken Livingstone would lead London as its first mayor, the political stakes were raised both for Londoners and for the government.

Three key issues provide the context for the next three chapters of the book. Chapter 7, 'London on the Move', reviews the significance of traffic and transport in metropolitan politics, showing how the policy debates shaped, and were in turn shaped by, the form of London's government. These issues were central in the pre-election and election period for the new Mayor and Assembly: this chapter examines how the new mayoral politics has influenced London's transport policies. Policing has been the second major issue of public concern since the 1980s. Chapter 8, 'London's Crimewatch', assesses the impact of the radical changes involved in transferring policing powers to a new authority on which the mayor's nominees exert considerable influence. Economic development and the promotion of the capital city as a site for investment have been matters of concern since the oil crisis of the early 1970s. Under the GLA, the responsibility for developing London as a world city lies with a new authority accountable to the Mayor. Chapter 9, 'Renewing London', accordingly assesses the initial strategies of the Mayor in regenerating the London economy and promoting its development.

The final chapter, 'The Mayor and Metropolitan Government', takes stock of the early experience of Livingstone's London. The success of any system of metropolitan government lies in its ability to manage a complex network of relationships: local, regional, and national. This chapter assesses how such relationships have been shaped by the Mayor's coalition-building tactics and his political style and personality.

Our treatment of the issues has been selective. While the legislation necessarily set the boundaries of the new authority's remit, the events of the first year were shaped by political factors and by the Mayor's own dynamism—personal and political. Just how London will continue to be governed, and how well, is another matter. Necessarily, this book is a snapshot of the opening phase: the first scene of the third act in a drama that began more than a century ago with the establishment of the LCC. How the capital will be governed in the long run—whether, indeed, the new arrangements will last longer than either the GLC or the protracted interregnum—remains to be seen. It is likely, however, that the future shape of the present authority will, to a large extent, be determined by the events and emerging tensions described in this book.

2

Governing Great Cities

THE assumption behind the creation of the Mayor and Assembly was, and is, that London can 'learn' from other cities and that a new model can be grafted onto London without undue regard for its governmental history. Given the record of London's arrangements, the case for striking out in a new direction, making use of examples drawn from elsewhere, is a clear one. The validity of the assumption, however, depends on the answer to a question: can successful experiments elsewhere be translated into a British context, or do they depend on local traditions and circumstances?

Whatever the verdict, today London is coming to terms with a form of urban government—the directly elected mayor—that is recognizably derived from the experience of several other countries and from the United States in particular. The great differences between patterns of urban leadership in the United States, France, and Germany on the one hand, and Britain, with its council-based structure, on the other, might be thought to vitiate any comparison. In reality, however, great cities in all developed countries face analogous problems, suggesting that perhaps some solutions, be they specific policies or governmental arrangements, might indeed be transferable.

In considering whether this particular example of policy transfer is likely to prove successful, the starting point must be to identify the problem accurately. To focus on the ability of London's new government to resolve problems of, for example, public transport, or crime and disorder, would be to narrow the question unduly. It is more appropriate to take the broader view and to see the London mayoralty as an experiment in *political* innovation, against which any assessment must be made.

The Metropolitan Community

In the pre-1997 election debate about a 'new deal' for London, there was extensive discussion about the need not just for better local government in the capital but for arrangements that provide or foster a 'metropolitan community'. This much-used phrase, however, was seldom defined. What exactly is 'metropolitan'? The term has been used in different senses. Certainly, in policy-making usage the dictionary definition of 'metropolis' as a country's chief or capital city has been blurred. Los Angeles may be regarded as more 'metropolitan' than Washington, for example, and Glasgow than Edinburgh. Current usage may denote scale: a metropolis is a highly populated area. It may also, more specifically, denote function; thus, many writers see the metropolis as a major centre of urban activities, a gathering place of people and ideas and the centre of political and intellectual processes. This is to attribute to the metropolis an influence over an extensive hinterland, conceived 'not just as the built-up area but as a more abstract phenomenon with extensive spatial influence' (Miles 1970: 495). This sense derives from the original meaning of 'metropolis' as mother-city.

Yet another usage of the term 'metropolis' is one that denotes a city plus its suburbs. This has become increasingly common, and the 'metropolitan problem' is today frequently understood in terms of the sometimes fraught relations between the local governments and agencies of the different communities that make up the metropolitan area. Considerable attention has been given to these inter-governmental relations, almost to the extent of obscuring other substantive issues that arise in great cities. On this view, the metropolitan problem is a problem of local inter-governmental relations.

Taking all three senses together, we can see that big cities are characterized by common problems of population concentration, polarization, heterogeneity, and transience. They have a political and cultural significance that flows from their influence over an area much wider than their own territories. They may well be plagued by jurisdictional conflicts arising from the plethora of locally based governments and functional agencies. From any perspective, the fundamental problem of big cities lies in the challenge they pose to the governmental process.

Generally speaking, the response to this urban challenge has been to see the city as a problem of administration. Issues of service delivery and citizen satisfaction were to be addressed by administrative reform and enhanced management capacity. At the same time, reformers have characteristically overlooked the fact that great cities are also political entities infused with conflicts, strategies, competition, cleavages, turf wars, and bargaining. As Banfield and Wilson showed in *City Politics* (1965), their path-breaking analysis of the American city in the mid-1960s, big cities are indeed political systems in their own right. But the politics that they sustain is the politics of urban problems, of meeting the needs of housing, movement, jobs, education, and welfare of its diverse population. The city can be understood neither as an administrative problem alone nor simply as a political arena devoid of real tasks and challenges. The politics of the city *is* the politics of the city's problems.

Managing diversity

Inescapably, metropolitan politics centres on the features of diversity and fragmentation. Differentiation by land use, by the socio-economic characteristics of the residents, or by ethnic and religious clustering, establish the diversity of the modern city. Such differentiation encompasses office centres, industrial parks, ghettos, red-light districts, municipal housing estates, gentrified areas, and comfortable and leafy suburbs. The larger and older the city, the greater the degree of differentiation—or specialization—of neighbourhoods and thus the greater the degree of diversity to be found among the people of the city and the areas in which they reside.

An important feature of this diversity is that it arises, in large part, from the choices of many individuals. People cluster where they can access the facilities they value, the quality of life they seek, and the company of people like themselves. For some, this will mean settling in the vibrant and fashionable areas of young singles. For others, settlement is a matter of living within a community of common interest, served by cultural and religious facilities and an extended family structure. For many, the ideal is to bring up a family in spacious, peaceful, and well-protected residential districts. The city is a 'social cafeteria' from which choices congenial to an individual's style of life may be made (Williams *et al.* 1965): 300 languages are spoken by schoolchildren in London today (Baker and Eversley 2000). Yet the metropolis is not just a kaleidoscope of cultures. It is also an ecology of opportunity and choice.

This diversity of choice is also one of conflicting outlooks and expectations, leading to entrenched alignments. When major issues arise, they commonly divide people holding one set of expectations from those who hold another. For the businessmen, the city is the source of commercial opportunity, something to be protected at all costs. For some residents it is the source of social and cultural experience the loss of which would be regretted, for others the site of their employment. For all, urban change may be a threat. Diversity is compounded by urban growth, spilling over boundaries to be incorporated—and expressed politically—in the 'patchwork quilt' of community government. New suburbs value their municipal privileges, and maintain a defensive posture towards any encroachment from the city that becomes entrenched over time (Young and Kramer 1978). The result is political fragmentation. Los Angeles provides the classic example of the problems of achieving political order without a common government (Warren 1966). Fragmented government, and the intractability it brings, is *the* metropolitan problem. Fragmentation was characteristic of London before the creation of the Greater London Council in 1965, when a long campaign to overcome it by establishing a single authority for the metropolis finally succeeded (Smallwood 1965; Rhodes 1970). In time it would become clear, however, that the persistence of diversity and its corollary, the politics of territorial defence, remained a powerful constraint upon GLC policy.

Creating a metropolitan community

Against the evident realities of diversity is pitched the presumption of an underlying unity. The long campaigns for metropolitan reform, both in London and in many American cities, were based on the belief that beneath the surface, conflict was to be found an inherent common interest: a metropolitan community. The idea that such a community must exist, if only in nascent form, was a simple extrapolation from the evident economic and physical unity of the city. The reality is more complex:

Communities and to an even greater extent, various Londons, are planners' and administrators' concepts. The fundamental unit of London, and of any other city, is the individual citizen. Communities are the expression of his [sic] gregariousness and of the consequent concentration of all the things that supply his [sic] needs . . . (Carter 1962: 80)

Indeed, if 'metropolitan' defies an easy definition, 'community' is more elusive still. 'Metropolitan' is not a politician's word. Crucially, and perhaps disastrously, 'community' is. As such, of course, it has many contexts, but if there is a core understanding of the term, it relates to a shared sense of identity and attachment. Thus, the patterns of community in a great city are necessarily complex and operate with different intensities at different levels:

Every resident of a metropolis occupies space, but not everybody feels the sense of community contained in the neighbourhood, the city, or even the whole metropolis. Yet many do. Perhaps for a few, the neighbourhood is the pre-eminent experience in their lives and they can be considered urban villagers, but most metropolitan residents are part of more than one community in the spatial sense and may also be part of one or more communities without a precise geographical base, such as a racial, ethnic, or religious community. (Hallman 1977: 160)

Although the encompassing of a 'community' is reckoned to be a prime value for local government structure, it is attainable only at the most local level, if at all. The search for community in London has always been chimerical. As one writer almost a century ago commented, London 'is not only too big for herself—so big, indeed, that she has no civic consciousness—but she is far too big for England' (Barlow 1991: 48). In the case of London and other English metropolitan areas, a series of committees and royal commissions on local government organisation have sought to deal with this problem by identifying local communities that may be grouped together on the basis of common interest (Barlow 1991: 13–16). In this way, the term 'community of interest' came to be commonly used, based usually on the examination of commuting, shopping, and leisure patterns. Defining the boundaries of metropolitan areas then became a matter of defining a significant community of interest.

Defining the 'objective community' in this way enabled political arrangements to be brought into correspondence with the social and economic community. As Warren (1966: 5) put it in his summary of this—flawed—'one community-one government' thesis:

Metropolitan areas represent a single community linked by social and economic ties, but are artificially divided governmentally; the public needs of such a community cannot be satisfactorily met by the collective action of numerous units of government, rather chaos and breakdown result; and the welfare of the metropolitan community can only be realised through an integrated governmental structure in which municipal decision-making authority is formally centralised in a single jurisdiction.

Metropolitan government, then, represents an attempt to incorporate in its entirety a perceived community that may or may not be felt by the residents to exist. This was the object of the London government reforms of 1963 which created the GLC. Whether it succeeded in achieving that aim during its brief 21-year life is debatable. The GLC's history is, for whatever reason, one of repeated shortfalls in achievement. Above all, the intense conflicts that its policies engendered, so far from uniting Londoners, had the frequent and corrosive effect of dividing them. Hence, the search for a means of bringing London together as a 'political community', is one which continues.

Models of Community Leadership

The cities of the Western world are replete with attempts to represent the urban community through political leadership. Different national systems have developed a wide variety of different mechanisms for managing the city, reflecting their cultural, historical, and constitutional circumstances. It has been against such a cacophonous background that the British debate about institutions at the end of the twentieth century came to be dominated by the urge to import ideas from other countries. Thus, the United States has provided the most influential model of the elected mayoral system—but by no means the only one. We need now to consider this and other experiments and their potential applicability in the UK context.

The US mayor

Historically, the mayoral form of government in the US owes its origins to the colonial period, when the mayor was commonly appointed by the governor and given wide police powers (Goodnow 1969: 70). It also, critically for any British comparison, derives from a system that interposed the power of the State between that of the town or urban administration and that of the federal government. As Tocqueville pointed out at the beginning of the nineteenth century, the United States singularly lacked an interventionist central government. Local authority, he observed, 'has been carried further than any European nation could conduce without great inconvenience', (Tocqueville [1835] 1994: 87). Mayors declined in significance with the diffusion of power to appointed or elected boards, only to recover in the late nineteenth century. A new era of municipal charters at the turn of the nineteenth and twentieth centuries empowered mayors in many cities to appoint new heads of executive departments without first obtaining the consent of the council. The driving force in bringing about these changes was the National Municipal League, which proposed in 1897 a programme of model State constitutional amendments and a model State Municipal Corporations Act. These proposals served to insulate the city from excessive State interference, to establish a more uniform system of city government, and to provide for a mayor-council system which concentrated executive power and responsibility in the hands of the mayor (Fox 1977: 51–62).

Today, city government in the United States is enormously varied in both size and institutional form. Around 30,000 local government units exhibit three principal forms of government: the council-manager form, the mayor-council form, and the commission form—this last is now in long-term decline and is no longer much employed in American cities. The council-manager type of urban government arose from the reform campaigns against corruption and partisanship in the 1920s. Promoted by the non-partisan National Municipal League, the council-manager scheme centred on the ideal of a professional chief executive accountable to a small council elected city-wide—'at large'—on a non-partisan ticket. The city manager heads the administration and appoints the departmental heads, enjoying far more power than a British chief executive. He or she is accountable to the council, which itself consists in many cases of prominent local businessmen working part-time.

This type of urban government, however, does not provide clear and identifiable political leadership. Although city managers are inescapably prominent figures in their communities, they lack the authority that comes with election to leadership. Instead their position is such that they defer to the collective authority of the council. The directly-elected mayor system was designed to give political leadership to both the council and its manager. An important variant is one in which the directly elected mayor has administrative authority over the departmental heads. This is the so-called 'strong mayor' model in which the council—which is also elected—has a weaker mandate. Early experience of the strong mayor model was that it threatened to eclipse in significance the elected council. Accordingly, there were moves to bolster the role of the council and protect it from political extinction as a representative body. The strong mayor system favoured by reformers was intended to eliminate the jobbery of a locally based system of council election. The National Municipal League feared, however, that a strong mayor system threatened to 'throttle' the council, 'eliminating the "representative" principle, the essence of the democratic process' (Fox 1977: 120–2). The strong mayor today, as found in Baltimore for example, is in effect an elected chief executive with considerable administrative powers, including responsibility for preparing the budget, for running the bureaucracy, and for appointing departmental heads. He may also veto council decisions.

The second variant of mayoral government is the so-called 'weak mayor' system in which the council itself generally appoints the chief officers and holds them to account. The mayor in such cases is usually directly elected, leads the city and speaks for it, but has limited formal powers to ensure his political will, and must rely upon networks of influence and processes of negotiation. Authority is fragmented under this system, with power dispersed among the mayor, the council, and the professional departmental heads. The source of the mayor's weakness is twofold: the limited power of appointment, and an inability to determine budgetary allocations in a way that expresses his policies.

The power structures in many American cities have been characterized as 'spherical', with major participants orbiting around the mayor and his close associates with interest groups, community organizations, the press, and local politicians more loosely connected (Savitch 1988: 248 ff.). The image is one of free-floating actors circulating around the core beyond which political connections are fluid and changing. No longer are top politicians selected by party leaders; mayoral candidates win their nomination by running in primary elections, a system which opens up influence to interest groups and lobbies who can contribute the necessary money to mayoral campaigns. Most mayors win office by building coalitions among business, labour, and community groups.

In the debates on London, New York is frequently held up as a model, partly because many problems—crime, transport, overcrowding, ethnic diversity, difficulties associated with a global status—are shared. The precise nature of New York's governmental arrangements are therefore worth considering. In America's premier city, the mayor shares power with a number of other elected officials. Two officials hold city-wide office: the comptroller and the president of the city council. There are also five borough presidents elected from each of their respective boroughs. In recent years, the borough presidents have lost much of their power and have been reduced to acting as the voices of their boroughs and local communities. Their power as members of the city-wide Board of Estimate gave them the ability to shape the budget, vote on contracts, and reconcile city policy with borough and community issues. The abolition of the Board, following a Supreme Court ruling that its composition was unconstitutional, left the mayor and city council sharing power.

New York's 51-member city council is elected from single-member districts for a four-year term. The council long had little effective power and was not well placed to challenge the mayor, although during the 1990s it made a number of attempts to make its presence felt. Under the city charter the mayor has sole power to set revenue estimates which spending cannot exceed. His budgets have to be adopted by the council and are subject to their amendment, but he has veto power over council budgets and over local laws. He is the political chief executive of the city and appoints members of the several boards and commissions that manage city services. According to a British local government study, these extensive formal powers

are matched by his role as a political leader, his visibility, his capacity to attract media attention, and his recognition as a major national figure . . . No other local New York City official, elected or appointed, commands so much attention. The tradition of charismatic, elected political executives is endemic throughout United States, and especially so for large City mayors. (Greater London Group 1992: 12–13)

European continental mayors

If the US model has been the primary, and most often-cited, example in recent British discussions, it is not the only one. In Europe too there have been a number of interesting and relevant examples of elected mayors. The most important are to be found in Germany. In particular, in reunified Germany, which has adapted its federal system to meet post-Communist needs, there is a range of parallel systems. Thus, the North German council form resembles the version developed in England and Wales, and originated under the British administration of North-Rhine Westphalia and Lower Saxony. Here the *mayor* is a figurehead, elected by the council, who also appoints a chief official to implement their decisions. On the other hand, the *Magistrat* form, which prevails in Hessen, in Schleswig-Holstein, and in parts of Bremen, consists of an elected municipal assembly which selects and supervises a decision-making executive, the *Magistrat*. Here the *mayor* chairs the *Magistrat* and heads the executive. In the Rhineland and the Saar, as well as in the rural parts of Schleswig-Holstein, the *mayor* heads the administration, but is voted into that position by the council. Only in the south German states of Bavaria and Baden-Württemberg does the *mayor* enjoy powers comparable with those of a US mayor. Directly elected, he or she chairs the municipal assembly and heads the administration, although the assembly retains formal powers. This, however, is becoming a more common model.

As in the United States, actual power in the German cities depends as much on configurations of politics and personality as on constitutional formalities. In south Germany, where a strong *mayor* coexists with a weak assembly, it is possible for the office-holder to become a dominant figure in city politics. Meanwhile, the directly elected mayors of larger cities enjoy greater public visibility and the possibility of building a strong base of public support. Thus in Stuttgart *Oberburgermeister* Manfred Rommel won 70 per cent of the popular vote in 1990 despite the weakness of his party, the Christian Democratic Union (CDU). His administration consisted of three figures from the CDU itself, three from the Social Democratic Party, one from the Free Democratic Party, an Independent, and, later, a Green.

If Germany presents a patchwork quilt, the system in France follows a relatively consistent pattern throughout the country, reflecting the unitary nature of the state as a whole. Typically, the French mayoralty stands at the centre of the complex system of actors varying in nature and status, but all looking to the mayor as the locus of local power and decision: as such, he is an apparent exemplar of the maxim that urban government is about negotiating, influence, and bargaining. The mayor of any sizeable city controls the administration through a chief administrator, the *secrétaire générale*, to whom the various departmental heads are accountable, and through the appointment of deputy mayors with specific portfolios. A mayor may work primarily through the *secrétaire générale* or, if he doubts the official's ability to control the administration, through his deputies, who relate directly to the various service heads.

Overall, the mayor's power stems from the influence the office holder wields in Paris. Indeed,

French local government cannot be understood without reference to the central state. Conceived from the start as a level of state *déconcentration*, the mayor is both an elected official and an agent of the state, particularly in matters of police and civil status. He is also the main interlocutor of the local representative of the state in the *département*, the prefects. It is from this position that French mayors derived most of their power. (Borraz 1994: 12)

However, the power of the mayor in France has traditionally not been unqualified (Lagroye and Wright 1979). The intimate relationship between the mayor and *préfets* that characterized the 1950s and 1960s has been modernized in the last generation by the participation of local groups and associations that sprang up in response to the pressures of urban growth.

These new social groups agitated and organized, achieving considerable local electoral success and displacing many sitting mayors. The common thread in the new urban politics was the desire for greater local autonomy to tackle local problems. The resulting pressures for decentralized government came to fruition after Socialist victories in the legislative and presidential election of 1981. Decentralization reinforced municipal status, tempering the hitherto extensive powers of the *préfets* and greatly increasing the scope of local initiative. The role of the mayor has been changed by these developments in that the mayor no longer represents the state to the city but instead represents the city to the state.

Paris, however, remained insulated from participatory politics. In contrast to provincial France, the capital was governed for most of the twentieth century by a council, with no mayor. Power over the city was vested in two central government officials: the *préfets* of Paris and the *préfets* of police. During this period, the city's administration was divided into 20 districts—*arrondissements*—and the activities of the council remained very much subordinate to the executive power of the *préfets*. In 1975, a statute was passed granting Paris the right to have its own mayor. Two years later Parisians acquired their first mayor: Jacques Chirac, a leading Gaullist and subsequently President of the Republic. Major powers were intended to be shared between the mayor and the *préfet* of Paris but Chirac had no intention of sharing power with the official. Chirac's popularity and power was boosted by his advocacy of the city especially after he defeated a Socialist move in 1984 to undermine his authority by dividing Paris into 20 self-governing neighbourhoods based on the *arrondissements*.

Power in Paris has been characterized as a pyramid, with top politicians and technocrats at the apex. Key players in central and local government 'put the decisions together, leaving little room for outside competition', and Parisian decision-makers have been presented as a law unto themselves (Savitch 1988: 249). The mayor can be a dominating figure in national as well as in metropolitan politics: Chirac, for example, combined the positions of Mayor of Paris and Prime Minister. The power of the mayor flows from his influence with national government and is compounded by his ability to appoint members of the city council as deputy mayors to hold particular portfolios—transport, urban development—and thus become extensions of mayoral authority. After 1986, a number of Parisian deputy mayors also held seats in the national legislature.

Such are the concentrations of power in Paris that there is scarcely any room for local people and community groups to influence events. The political and technocratic decision-makers see themselves as representing the public interest and 'the idea of making policy around the wishes of interest groups or a narrow segment of the public strikes them as bizarre' (Savitch 1988: 255). Strong central government and *préfectoral* tradition combined to make decisive action easier to achieve in France than in almost any other national system.

Mayors as City Leaders

Thus the American, German, and French systems presented a variety of possibilities, and no single mayoral structure for a reforming British government to copy. However, the variation goes beyond structures. The different systems and their historical legacies have produced a range of styles, often within the same polity. How do mayors seek to lead their communities and shape their cities? The answer is that mayoral power depends, critically, on two factors: the political—and financial—resources at the mayor's disposal, and his or her own ambition to make key decisions and innovate. Thus, a 'powerful' mayoralty may, in practice, carry little effective power, while to a greater extent than is often true of central government, a dynamic personality can often stretch the formal powers of an office that is inherently weak.

Power resources

Obviously, mayors or other city leaders or regimes vary greatly in the resources they are able to command. Different national systems at different points in time bestow greater or lesser statutory powers on those responsible for governing cities. Beyond this, the actual exercise of powers may or may not be circumscribed by the political realities of having to forge alliances and win consent. The capacity to enforce the mayor's will through statutory means may in practice prove too expensive in terms of the withdrawal of cooperation on the part of those against whom it is exercised. Real power is usually far more diffuse than statutes suggest. In any event statutes are frequently blind to the existence of political parties. Particularly where a political party is in a dominant position, power within that party—which may or may not coincide with formal office—can be used to resolve disputes and enforce decisions.

Power may also have a financial basis. A well-placed city leader may have large sums—whether raised by local taxation or by grant-in-aid—at his disposal with which to make things happen. By contrast, a city leader who is financially circumscribed and over-dependent on other levels of government is likely to find it harder to buy policy outcomes. Finally, strength of personality may be another important resource for a city leader. City leaders are in the public eye and provide a focal point for the media. An attractive or controversial personality will seek coverage on the front pages in the hope that visibility will translate into popular support. At the same time, a mayor with a strong and persuasive personality is better able to build coalitions, win allies, and exact promises: the stuff of urban political leadership.

Leadership style

As well as personality, public mood also bears directly upon mayoral style. Thus, the urban public has become more demanding, even vociferous, requiring the modern mayor to listen, to respond to public concerns, and to demonstrate a greater concern and commitment in that response. Public opinion, indeed, is often more tangible in urban than in national politics because it relates to physical needs—transport, for instance, or housing. To be successful, a mayor has to accept this expectation of accountability, be prepared to answer, and mayors that misjudge the public mood have to take responsibility when things go wrong.

However, responding to the general mood is complicated in the modern metropolis because the contemporary city is typically a place of not one but of many publics. Public opinion is often fierce, but the cosmopolitan nature of the city makes it textured, with no single or undivided issue to which a city leader might tailor a response. Thus, a mayor may be confronted with apparently contradictory and incompatible demands, and pressed to accommodate as many of them as possible at the same time. Even at the level or rhetoric, let alone concrete action, this is not possible. The result is to make 'community leadership' a delicate balancing act to achieve a broad-based coalition and to carry the myth that the mayor speaks for the city as a whole.

In practice, the rhetoric is seldom convincing. Cities are places of conflicting interests, not common ones. Where a mayor is identified with a political party capable of pulling in the votes, this matters less. On the other hand, where a mayor is dependent upon his own personal standing to be re-elected—as in the case of non-partisan, independent mayors—there are choices to be made about which groups to align with. One mayor might aim to please the affluent middle classes in the suburbs by identifying with their issues and aligning himself with their concerns about the quality of their lives. Another might see electoral success lying in regeneration, aligning himself with those business interests that can be encouraged to invest, and so create an improved physical fabric and a forward-looking economy. It is a rare—and visionary—mayor who stakes his fortunes on the articulation of some overarching vision of the city and its future, hoping thereby to mobilize support on the basis of the widest common interest. More often, a mayor will represent as the public interest a fragile compromise put together from day-to-day relations with important groups within the city.

At the same time, style has to be adapted to the particular character and conditions of the city. A mayor whose core constituency lies in the urban heartland has little choice but to align with a 'rainbow coalition' of minority groups, celebrate the diversity of the city, deliver tangible benefits to significant groups, and so sustain their support. The changing character of cities has produced a fragmentation of urban politics in which the old option of building a secure political base among the white working-class majority is no longer available. Instead of identifying with such an obvious majority group, a mayor has to court diverse minority and sectional groups, and secure their goodwill, doing as much as possible to avoid antagonisms and conflict. Thus, the growing heterogeneity of the city of New York in the middle years of the twentieth century led to a succession of mayors, among whom Robert Wagner was the consummate artist, who built their constituencies on a patch-work of micro-interests rather than on an undifferentiated appeal to the mass.

The contemporary city is also highly diverse in a geographical sense: different places have markedly different characteristics, needs, and demands. The ecology of the city becomes more complex as areas become more specialized in terms of the spatial division of labour. Business and residential uses congregate and concentrate. In the London context, suburban sub-centres spring up, prime office locations attracting new office development— Croydon— industrial estates re-emerge as retail parks—Hounslow—while the conversion of disused industrial building into spacious flats and penthouses attract more young singles in search of similar conversions—Clerkenwell. The needs of those areas have to be accommodated, not least for the implications that the pressures of change may have for business fortunes and, ultimately, employment and the quality of life.

Types of mayoral leadership

In his seminal *Ungovernable City*, Douglas Yates (1977) drew together these two dimensions to create a neat typology of mayoral leadership. He began with the proposition that mayors differ along these two dimensions of (1) the amount of political and financial resources they can bring to bear on the problems they face and (2) their style: the degree of activism and innovation they display in their daily work. Thus, he identified four ideal types that correspond closely to patterns of mayoral leadership in the largest American cities, termed *crusader*, with high activism and low resources; *boss*, with high resources and low activism; *broker*, with low resources and passive style; and finally *entrepreneur*, with high resources and activist posture. Figure 2.1 illustrates these four types which, as we shall see, continue to have a resonance in US and European styles today.

Yates was pessimistic about the future of urban politics, pointing out that mayors often overestimated the power resources available to them, failing to notice that power was steadily flowing from City Hall. The picture was one of transfer both upwards to the federal government, creating a state of increasing dependence, and downwards to groups and communities, creating a condition colourfully described as 'street-fighting pluralism', which few mayors can hope to manage. Although mayors might have gained some formal authority,

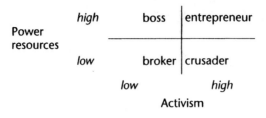

FIGURE 2.1: Mayoral leadership

their net influence would be less than in former times. Accordingly, Yates predicted that entrepreneurs would lose ground to 'frustrated crusaders' while 'confident bosses' would be replaced by 'cautious political brokers'. The tendency was, in his view, for urban leadership to refashion itself to take account of its increasing weakness.

What Yates—and many others—called the *boss* system remains the most powerful and enduring image of American urban government, though its heyday is long past. Personified by the first Mayor Richard Daley of Chicago, the 'boss' is seen as having great power but little vision about using it for the good of the city. The boss symbolized a regime which was opaque to outsiders and closed to their influence, working through a political party and sustained by the spoils system. The influence of the boss permeated all the key institutions of the city, with power used primarily to sustain the regime in office: the quintessential political machine. The machine was typically based on majority support from a homogeneous blue-collar work force, a population that has today dissolved into a *mélange* of highly differentiated groups clustered around competing identities. The administrative strategy of the boss reflected

his need to maintain the strength of his political machine, and the strength of his machine gives coherence and loyalty to his administration. The boss fills his administration with party workers, and he has strong control over their work because he can replace them at will. In turn he has a strong incentive to stay in close touch with and be responsive to his bureaucrats because his political strength depends on having large numbers of satisfied loyal party workers. (Yates 1977: 156)

In the United States, the boss system fell victim not merely to changes in the social structure of the city but to a change in the public mood towards accountability and transparency, which materialized in some States in new countervailing powers of referendum and recall. The tradition of boss politics typified American cities when they were the bastions of heavy industry and ethnic politics. In industrial cities, political bosses 'traded ambiguous favours' whereas their post-industrial successors stress the 'cooler politics of interest accommodation . . . Charisma is important, bargaining is a primary tool, and making the big deal is the main objective' (Savitch 1988: 257–8).

In fact, the mayor as a *broker*—having neither resources nor innovative ambitions—is perhaps more typical of the actual American experience of the system today. In contrast to the stereotype projected by the media and by fiction of the US mayor as a powerful distributor of key decisions and patronage, such a mayor frequently does little more than ratify agreements reached by competing interest groups. An example was the mayor of Minneapolis in the 1960s, who appears not to have actively sponsored any initiative at all. Instead,

he waits for private groups to agree on a project. If he likes it, he endorses it. Since he has no formal power with which to pressure the Council himself he feels that the private groups must take the responsibility for getting the plan accepted. (Banfield 1969: 54)

The decline of the boss system has made the broker style of leadership a more common one. Expectations of effectiveness are much lower than for the entrepreneur or crusader. On the other hand, the broker style may be seen as a form of protection against political disasters. The broker mayor will be receptive to proposals that are well supported and while 'he may be impressed by the intrinsic merit of the proposal . . . he will be even more impressed at the prospect of being well regarded by the highly respectable people whose proposal it is' (Banfield 1969: 390). Unlike the classic boss, the broker-mayor has little patronage to dispense in support of his own programmes.

The third category, that of *crusader*, represents a quite different type of leadership, in which visionary ambition is unconstrained by the absence of the power needed to attain it. The mayor as crusader is typically represented as charismatic, a popular—and populist—spokesman for change, intervening at will on a broad front in support of a few reformist slogans that capture the imagination and inspire enthusiastic followers. Crusade politics came to be seen as a response to the urban crisis of the 1960s, an era of protest and political turbulence. Crusader mayors like John Lindsay in New York were the products of a shift in public mood towards intervention and 'solving' urban problems. Lindsay entered city hall with few political resources, no machine, and no overwhelming electoral mandate:

From Lindsay's perspective the parts of the bureaucracy that were not controlled by hostile Irish or Italian clubs or by political hacks were likely to be dominated by old-line bureaucrats—another scourge of liberal reformers . . . Lindsay (and many other reformers) centralised power in the hands of a few mayoral aides, attempted to introduce strong administrative control through scientific management, and, in general, tried to shake up the outmoded, recalcitrant bureaucracy through guerrilla raids from city hall . . . through the deployment of 'whiz kid' assistants, highly professional budgeters, and scientific managers such as the McKinsey Corporation and the New York City Rand Institute . . . (Yates 1977: 153–4)

Over time, however, Lindsay came to discover that the need merely to survive had to take precedence over the elusive goal of reform. The Mayor and his team found their ambitions for change frustrated and the challenges they presented to existing bureaucratic interests ineffectual. The rhetorical commitment to the poor and apparent disdain for the white middle class led to a bitter political polarization. The result was a loss of popularity within the city and of reputation outside it.

Many will recognize the fourth category, the *entrepreneur*, as the idealized image of a successful mayor. The combination, however, of political resources and political activism, the necessary ingredients of the successful entrepreneurial model, is rarely found. An example of the entrepreneurial system of leadership in London was that of Herbert Morrison, Labour leader of the London County Council from 1934 to 1940, and often mistakenly seen as an archetypal 'boss'. Morrison's initial power base lay in the party machine itself, which he had effectively built up from scratch. His dominance enabled him to control the selection of candidates and thus the likely composition of the Labour group of councillors. As leader of the council, he worked through a presidium of close associates, selecting his committee chairmen and getting his nominations approved by the party meeting, but dismissing them at will on occasion (Donoughue and Jones 1973:189–210). His method was to consult key chairmen and officials, listen to their views, and then give a decision. It was a style calculated to gain consent for strong leadership. Morrison's goals, in pursuit of which he devoted extraordinary energy, were to rebuild and modernize London's services. In practice, however, the Morrisonian model proved highly personal: it did not translate to his successors. Charles Latham and Isaac Hayward, who followed him, inherited Morrison's formal powers but, lacking his authority, were unable to capitalize on the position he had built up.

In the United States, the mayor as entrepreneur was a product of the years of urban renewal during which lavish federal funds were spent on regeneration. New money, deployed through new programmes, called for the creation of new agencies and structures which provided opportunities for patronage and the targeting of capital expenditure. Large-scale projects required a different type of management skill and a new type of administrator. Urban renewal generated a need for staff expertise to build a bureaucratic machine whereby the city could work through redevelopment agencies. The political order based on urban renewal empowered the mayors of the rust-belt cities. It provided a potent political resource when directed by a mayor of the energy and ambition of Richard Lee of New Haven. Renewal provided 'the dramatic, highly visible, and tangible issue that allowed [Lee] to dominate a city for almost two decades' (Yates 1977: 49–50).

A Mayor for London

If London needed to learn from foreign experience, it was not at all obvious what the main lesson should be. Indeed, international examples provided a variety of different approaches, with little indication that any was particularly successful in practice or self-evidently applicable to British conditions. What problems should be addressed? In the late 1980s and early 1990s a key issue in urban leadership appeared to be the ability of metropolitan government to promote and project a city's image and maximize its attractiveness as a location for global business. City-wide governments and mayors were judged internationally on their ability to provide such a focus. London seemed to lack one after 1986. Its absence was seen as giving other cities a competitive edge. 'Whether or not this perception is correct', according to one study, 'London is certainly taking a risk by not having in some way to promote itself and also of providing outsiders with a view of the City's future development' (Greater London Group 1992: 4).

This was seen as a primary challenge: if London was to remain in the same league as the major cities of North American, Europe, and the Far East, it needed the political arrangements to facilitate it. Such a logic led to what was seen as the nearest or most compatible model at hand. However, transposing a US-style mayor into the British local government context was bound to be a radical move. It was naive to assume that this would make the politics of London more akin to the politics of New York, even on the assumption that such a change, overall, was desirable. A new structure does not, in itself, produce new habits. Whereas the mayoral system was both long-standing and widespread in US cities, reflecting the separation of powers at the federal level, the British tradition had been one of collective responsibility through a council-based system in which mayors, where they existed, were generally figureheads (Rao 2000). However, in the case of London, circumstances—and traditions—were sufficiently different from the rest of Britain to make the importation of a foreign system more acceptable than elsewhere. Not only did London have no overall government since 1986, so there was no existing structure to be displaced, but the British capital also had a tradition of strong and personalized leadership not to be found in many other towns and cities.

At the same time, the social and economic problems of London were, at least in some respects, comparable to those of American cities. Hence, not only is the London experiment derived principally from US practice, there is at least some basis for comparing the outcome with American experience. Whether the new London will turn out to be a success or failure depends, critically, on the first few mayoral incumbents—and, most of all, on the first. Ken Livingstone's effectiveness, in turn, will depend on his ability to work within the institutional and political constraints. The formal political resources at his disposal are limited, while his own political style is interventionist, flamboyant, even charismatic. Time will show whether Livingstone turns out to be a 'crusader' or is forced to retreat to a 'broker' role.

In speaking for London, and mobilizing popular support to address London's problems, Livingstone faces a challenge that differs in degree, but not in kind, from that facing the mayors of New York, Paris, or many other great cities. In attempting to recreate the sense of metropolitan community for London that existed at the turn of the century under the Progressive LCC, the Mayor must confront the range of groups and interests bidding for consideration. This he must do against the backdrop of central government's continuing control of key London issues and the localization of power within the London boroughs, where a strong tradition exists of resisting area-wide government.

3

London: The Elusive Community

IS there, or can there be, a genuine London community? To deny the possibility would be to reject the combined rhetoric of left and right for more than a generation. Yet the assumption that such a community—whether of interests or of sentiment— exists can be seen to be, if not entirely false, then over-simplified.

All government has roots. In Britain, this political truth, keenly appreciated in central administration, has been repeatedly ignored in the handling of local affairs. Where the centre has evolved incrementally, the tendency in dealing with the periphery has been to tear up existing arrangements and start again. Yet the repeated experience has been that, sooner or later, old patterns reassert themselves. Indeed, the history of British local government, which is medieval in origin and was radically adapted and developed in the nineteenth century, is fundamental to any understanding of contemporary practice and needs. This is particularly true in the case of the capital city, where the story has long been one of conflict, of interplay between central government, campaigners, and recalcitrant local authorities. Thus, the late twentieth century attempt to create a 'metropolitan community' scarcely took account of the historical absence of such a concept in relation to urban management.

For most of the twentieth century, communitarian emotions were challenged by local—chauvinist—ones. Thus, 'Greater' London, as it came to be known, emerged as an arena of entrenched territorial conflict in which the concerns of the old LCC area ran counter to those of the more affluent and spacious suburbs. The creation of the Greater London Council as a mega-authority for London inflamed rather than calmed such conflicts. There was no longer a pretence of a London community, but rather an acceptance of social and political difference and a reluctance by many to accept that they were 'Londoners'. The GLC's existence was challenged from an early date, and GLC politicians of both main parties frequently found themselves on the back foot. It remains one of the ironies of London history that the decision by the Thatcher government to terminate the GLC's life in 1986 did more than any action of that council to unite Londoners behind it.

London Before the LCC

The problem of metropolitan government is partly a problem of scale. By the start of the nineteenth century, London's population was already almost a million; and the world's first 'metropolis'—the term entered popular usage in the 1830s—had come into being. In the course of the century, expansion was exponential. By 1855, the total was already three times that of New York or Berlin. There was still, however, no formal definition of London beyond the tiny population living in the City of London's square mile, which, in governmental terms, was distinguished from the vast and rapidly growing settlement outside the city wall: the place 'where London ends and England can begin'. Not until 1851 was a stable boundary delineated for census purposes which survived as the boundary of 'inner London' for a century and a half.

Already in the 1830s there was a sense of London needing a system of administration adequate to serve its growth. The second report of the Royal Commission on Municipal Corporations in 1837 was devoted to London. The commissioners were reluctant to confront the question of the City of London, the stumbling block of all reforms. One apparently plausible proposal was to divide the populous area surrounding the City into a set of contiguous boroughs coinciding with their existing parliamentary constituencies, recognizing the pre-eminence of the City by formally granting it powers as a metropolitan authority to oversee the whole. On this the Commission could not agree, while apparently regarding the alternative—that the City's boundaries should be so extended as to make it *the* metropolitan authority—as too radical for them to contemplate. Lacking concrete proposals, the Commissioners' report was no more than a staging post in the definition of the metropolitan predicament.

Anxious to preserve its boundaries and privileges unchanged, the City Corporation won a second reprieve when London government was considered again by a royal commission in 1852. The incorporation of the parliamentary constituencies was again proposed, but with the City and the new boroughs sending representatives to an area-wide body which would attend to the common interest in public works. On this occasion it was the responsible minister, President of the Board of Works Sir Benjamin Hall—he gave his name to the clock tower at the Palace of Westminster—who rejected the creation of seven large boroughs, instead reconstituting some of the vestries as local authorities and amalgamating others into district boards. This solution, though mocked at the time, reflected the reality of London's diversity, in which a myriad of locally based trades and occupations gave London the political fragmentation that sustained the administrative maze of vestry London. 'London', commented the *Spectator* in 1849, was 'a constellation or cluster of cities, each having its separate district and conditions of existence—physical, moral and political' (cited in Young and Garside 1982: 20).

Hall's Metropolis Management Act 1855 created the Metropolitan Board of Works (MBW) to engage in the construction of major projects (Davis 1988). Indirectly elected, it held little attraction for radical reformers whose voices were increasingly heard on the subject of London government. At the same time, the larger and richer vestries were inspired by the example of the great provincial towns to seek municipal status for themselves. Thus, contrary forces pulled towards both a stronger London-wide government and more powerful and dignified boroughs. While the case for London's rationalization was barely contested, the form of rationalization was politically bound to be one that, while reflecting the realities of metropolitan unity, would recognize the distinctively local conditions and the domains of the locally powerful. London was too large and too socially diverse for any unitary civic ethos to be plausible, and its metropolitan awareness 'was too weak to be invoked with confidence; civic pride was still primarily parochial, and if anything divisive in its effects' (Davis 1989: 34). Indeed, London was an inherently *federal* polity (Young and Garside 1982: 21).

The reform movement, which developed in opposition to the MBW, at first reflected London's federal nature, favouring strong local government. John Stuart Mill was only the most prominent of those who lent their name to the 'municipalities movement'. In time, though, a preoccupation with municipal government at the local level came to be eclipsed by a demand for representative government at the metropolitan level. Reformers turned their sights upon the indirectly elected and unresponsive MBW, which they portrayed as an undemocratic body in the grip of the City Corporation and the conservative vestries. By 1880 they had succeeded in winning the support of the incoming Liberal government for its replacement by a directly elected council for London.

The Liberal government's bill, which would have created an elected council on the MBW boundaries, failed through lack of real support at Cabinet level and because of Gladstone's querulous insistence on including provisions to bring the metropolitan police under the control of the council. This Sir William Harcourt, Home Secretary and minister responsible for the bill, could not accept, for reasons of 'public safety'. The argument in the Cabinet delayed the bill so long that it ran out of parliamentary time and was eventually withdrawn. The main effect of this inconclusive episode was to make the government of London a party matter, with the Conservatives as spokesmen for local authorities and the radical Liberals the advocates of strong metropolitan authority.

It was ironic that it should have been the Conservatives who created a metropolitan government for London, and one which totally overshadowed the local authorities. Lord Salisbury's government—supported after 1886 by the dissident Liberal Unionists—took up the London question as a part of the wider reform of county government. Radicals were taken by surprise to find London included in the county councils bill and delighted that no attempt was made to strengthen the local authorities to provide a countervailing power. Instead, an all-powerful London County Council was created on the existing MBW boundaries, and brought into being even earlier than expected when the MBW collapsed under the weight of allegations of endemic corruption.

For ten years, from 1889 to 1899, the LCC enjoyed complete dominance of London government issues (Davis 1988). The reform of the local authorities when it came in 1899, was bitterly contested by the Liberals, and resolutely opposed by their majority on LCC itself. Yet the 28 new metropolitan borough councils established by the Conservatives' 1899 Act were never strong enough, individually or collectively, to mount a serious challenge to the LCC's authority. It remained the predominant representation of 'London', a vast urban and suburban sprawl that by the 1880s had some 4 million inhabitants, four times its size at the beginning of the century.

The LCC and the Political Community of London

Popular support for the LCC as a metropolitan authority was premised on the idea that there existed a body of Londoners for whom it could provide a voice. Yet it was very much an imagined community, a vision rather than an actuality. Before the creation of the LCC, attempts to create a metropolitan political consciousness had been an uphill struggle. There was no sign of collective consciousness before 1880 and 'such flickerings as occurred in the following decades reflected the growth of the progressive middle-class opinions of the professional population' (Young and Garside 1982: 20). The tone was set for the heyday of high-minded Progressives. To some extent, the history of the LCC was a history of successive attempts to build a pan-London identity.

Speaking for London

The Liberals, fighting as the Progressive party, won six successive LCC elections, presenting themselves as the voice of London, speaking for its unity and the common interest against the fragmentation and vested interests of localism. The LCC, to which they had an almost proprietorial attachment, 'was the capital's first democratic metropolitan authority . . . invested by many with the task of bringing to London the sort of energetic administration that had transformed Britain's provincial cities since the 1840s' (Davis 1989: 27). They accordingly claimed for their programme

the kind of consensual approval which they believed to have sustained municipal enterprise in the provinces. Their rhetoric was pervaded by the assumption that they spoke for the London community as a whole and that opposition to their policies was prompted by the naked self interest of ground landlords, public utility companies, the City Corporation and its livery companies, the House of Lords, dock owners, the holders of market rights and other metropolitan parasites. Consensus was not entirely illusory. The first council elections were held at the height of the social concern that suffused London in the 1880s, which demonstrated that metropolitan opinion could attain a kind of unity in response to an evangelistic appeal to social duty. (Davis 1989: 33)

The professional classes and their opinions lent a semblance of unity to London, for they were the most articulate among the population. The ruling Progressive group, unlike its counterparts in many provincial cities, included a high proportion of professionals: 42 of the 134 members of the first council were still employed in professional occupations, while others had recently retired from them. This proportion remained constant throughout the life of the LCC, reflecting the strength of the professions in London's occupational mix and thus the distinctiveness of the capital (Clifton 1989: 5–7).

If the Progressive years to 1907 provided a flowering of the idea of London as a community of interest, the period was short-lived (Davis 2001). The 27 years of Conservative rule that followed had no such pretension. London was changing under the pressure of rapid suburbanization. The 'once upon a time London' had become incapable of satisfying modern needs, but had 'exploded and scattered its homes and the loyalties and emotional attachments of its people into hundreds of square miles of un-urban confusion' (Carter 1962: 74). When Labour won control of the LCC for the first time in 1934—a control it never lost, for the duration of that council's existence—something of the rhetoric of community leadership was revived, but for an attenuated London in which the priority was to develop the provision of county services (Jennings, Laski, and Robson 1935). Herbert Morrison, the architect of the London Labour Party, led the Council from 1934 until he joined the wartime government in 1940, putting his stamp on London politics and leaving an enduring legacy as the first 'Mr London'.

Labour's London?

For nearly 30 years—Labour's London heyday—the Labour Party traded on the idea that it had a special relationship with 'Londoners'. This pretension weakened with the seemingly boundless growth of outer London, within which the LCC area remained a largely Labour stronghold in a sea of Conservative suburbia. At the same time, the presentation of London's metropolitan character as founded on an identity of interest did not go unchallenged, and was by no means the only approach to the problems of the capital in the eyes of Westminster politicians.

When a Royal Commission was set up to consider London government in 1957, a study group led by the London School of Economics public administration expert, William Robson, argued for an area-wide elected council for London (Rhodes 1970). Against the idea of London as a cohesive unit was the notion of it as a patchwork quilt. A rival group at University College took a quite different line from Robson, criticizing 'the inadequacy of some of our conventional stereotypes' and rebutting 'certain misconceptions current in discussions about the character and problems of the metropolis':

Greater London is a conglomeration of local communities only partially dependent on each other. These communities together form a large, continuously built up area; and they share a common link with central London as a source of services and employment. But they are far more loosely tied to each other, and even to the centre, than is generally assumed. The image often held of the metropolis as 'a vast sea of inchoate development', a 'morass' of dormitory suburbia surrounding the old economically active core, cannot be maintained. (Westergaard 1961: 93)

Crucially, London had an inner core and an outer ring, with problems and interests that were not identical. The Centre for Urban Studies' analysis of the distinctive character of inner London, and of the case for retaining the LCC on the grounds that it reflected more exactly the realities of London's social structure, was trenchantly expressed. But the tide was flowing in another direction, as 'modern' opinion favoured the integration of the LCC with the outlying suburbs. The sense of having lost an argument and of having failed to win attention was painfully apparent. London in the 1960s was, according to the Centre,

subject to the new fashion of putting the cart before the horse in matters of social policy—of preparing an administrative blueprint as a substitute for a policy programme. This is done on the assumption that shortcomings of national policies (or of resources for implementing such policies) can be *a priori* attributed to defects in the machinery of government, and especially to that of local government. Responsibility is thus shifted from central to local authorities; a new machine is constructed, rather strangely, without knowing (or saying) exactly what it should produce, other than the magic word 'reform'. (Glass 1961: xxvi)

On this analysis—and it is one that was arguably vindicated by subsequent events—twentieth-century London resembled its predecessor in being both highly diverse and unmanageably fluid,

. . . long before the term 'conurbation' was invented, London was a 'real' entity, not by virtue of possessing a definite boundary, but for the opposite reason—just because the city was amorphous, and extended its influences over a wider, and again not clearly delineated area. And we can see that this is still the case . . . Nowadays it is the centre of London with its pull, drawing in people from ever-widening circles and exercising its influences in other ways, which is the maker of a 'Greater London' that neither has, nor can have, a fixed frontier. Hence the current pastime of re-drawing local government boundaries—in the belief that London can be contained by authorising it to be a 'region'—is liable to be futile. It is based on a misunderstanding of the nature of the metropolis and its interdependence with the rest of Britain. Any administrative line is bound to be an arbitrary one, already out of date even before it is established; and so a new line is not necessarily preferable to an old one, nor is a bigger administrative authority for London necessarily a better one. (Glass 1961: xxviii–xxix)

Above all, while the LCC area had some continuing claim to reality as 'London', the proposed Greater London area would be a constellation of competing communities. However, there was no longer a premium on the kind of identity of interest or community that was arguably—but certainly not demonstrably—a characteristic of the doomed LCC. Instead, by 1960 the argument had moved on to the new territory of functional effectiveness and the search for a machinery of government appropriate to planning and coordinating metropolitan development. In doing so, it gave belated recognition to the half-century of suburban growth that had obliterated the LCC.

A Strategic Authority for Greater London

Almost from the time the LCC was created, London's boundless outward expansion was already subverting any attempt at overall government. The 1901 census showed for the first time the extent of suburban expansion outside the LCC area, with more than 2 million 'Londoners' living in the suburbs of Middlesex, Kent, Surrey, or Essex. From that year the LCC's own population began to fall while that of outer London continued to grow rapidly, with a further 2 million added to the outer area in the next three decades. The Second World War emergency accelerated the decline of the LCC's population, while that of outer London stabilized. By 1961, the LCC's population had fallen to its 1871 level of 3.2 million, with 5 million people now living in the outer suburbs.

This outward expansion made imperative the framing of a plan to contain and manage growth, together with some form of governmental reorganization to put it into effect. Following several attempts in the inter-war period to bring the local authorities of the metropolitan region together for that purpose, the planning pioneer Patrick Abercrombie was commissioned to draft a master scheme. Abercrombie's 1944 plan covered a vast area of south-east England, extending far beyond the built-up Greater London and beyond the metropolitan green belt to Luton in the north, Basildon in the east, and the Surrey-Sussex borders in the south (Buck, Gordon, and Young 1986).

There was, however, no attempt—unlike in the pre-war period—to reorganize local government on this scale. Instead, reliance was placed on coordinating development through the county development plans to be produced, under ministerial guidance, in response to the requirements of the Town and Country Planning Act 1947. That act, in effect, gave the central government the strategic oversight of London's regional planning. The process of dialogue between ministry officials and county planners provided a framework for the post-Abercrombie period, and it soon became apparent that many of the assumptions of the Abercrombie plan had been falsified by events. Few—the exception was Robson in his reissued *Government and Misgovernment of London* (1948)—argued for a restructuring of metropolitan government. There were three reasons. First, the sheer geographical scale of the metropolitan problem seemed to make any 'Greater London' authority inappropriate. Second, those who debated metropolitan government—including the question of whether to extend the LCC boundary to the whole built-up area—argued themselves to a standstill in the face of strong suburban opposition. Third, the Labour Party in inner London was content to focus exclusively on its own heartland.

Nevertheless, it was hard to argue that the existing system of local government worked well. The Ministry's civil servants were disenchanted with their limited strategic role, exercised only through the coordination and periodic review of the development plans (SCLSERP 1974). There was some hankering for a strong metropolitan authority that would be able to take forward the planning process and, above all, implement the huge and costly urban motorway proposals of the Abercrombie plan. Thus, it was felt that if decisions on these matters had to remain with central government, then local government in London would be fatally weakened. A broad movement to local government reform preoccupied the Conservative governments of the 1950s, whose series of White Papers representing a new deal for local authorities was published in 1956 and 1957 (Young and Rao 1997). London could hardly be excluded from the proposed changes even if it required special treatment. A review area was marked out, and a Royal Commission under Sir Edward Herbert was established in July 1957 to examine the working of local government in the Greater London area and to recommend what changes, if any, were needed to secure effective and convenient local government (Herbert 1960).

Three years after its appointment, the commission produced a radical and controversial report. This concluded that local government in the review area failed the twin tests of 'administrative efficiency' and 'representative health'. As to the first, the commission concluded that 'with the exception of some of the environmental health services, none of [the] major functions can be discharged best by the local authorities that exist under the present system of local government, and some of them cannot be adequately discharged at all under the present structure' (Herbert 1960: 175). The implication was that the existing authorities—more than 100 of them, including the London and Middlesex county councils—had to be replaced by an entirely new structure.

Excluding some of the review area as not being properly part of Greater London, the commission proposed a metropolitan form of government for what some critics termed the 'bricks and mortar' conurbation. For this area there would be established a Council for Greater London and 52 London borough councils. The metropolitan council—the GLC, as it was soon to become—was to be a new type of authority concentrating on strategic planning and the metropolitan infrastructure. Its area-wide responsibilities would cover planning policy, main roads and traffic, refuse disposal, fire and ambulance services, and—a short-lived proposal—general education policy. The one novelty was the statutory requirement to establish a research and intelligence service to collect, collate, and disseminate information relating to local government services. The GLC would also share some powers with the boroughs, including parks and open spaces, main sewerage and land drainage, and aspects of environmental health and housing.

The boroughs for their part were to be the 'primary units of local government'. As such, they would exercise all the services that were close to the people and raised issues of possible local sensitivity. These included housing, personal health, welfare and children services, environmental health, local roads, libraries, planning applications of local relevance, and the day-to-day administration of education. Foremost among the metropolitan functions was to be the preparation of a Greater London Development Plan (GLDP). This would go beyond the existing planning authorities' approved proposals to provide a structure plan for the metropolis and so carry forward Abercrombie's vision, particularly as regards the urban motorways and patterns of land use. The key characteristic of the proposed strategic authority was its ability to distance itself from traditional local authority practice and operate as a truly regional body.

Accordingly, the GLC, once created, liked to refer to itself as a 'regional authority' as opposed to a local authority, a description that to some extent reflected the historic distinctiveness of the old LCC, which had always stood outside the local authority associations. Nevertheless, the difference was more apparent than real. Constitutionally, and in its internal organization, the GLC was essentially a local authority writ large. Its 147 members operated through a traditional committee and departmental structure that was modelled closely on that of the LCC itself. It stood apart, as had the LCC, from the representative structures of the local authority associations and enjoyed its own system of pay bargaining. At the same time, while it was intended as a slim, analytically competent strategic authority for the coordination of land-use planning and transport, it employed a total operational staff of 37,000. The significance of this continuity of organization was that it reflected a continuity of approach, the origins of which lay in the LCC's 60 years' dominance of London politics and policy. The impact of tradition was striking: not only did the GLC's own committee structure closely resemble that of the LCC, but 11 of the 14 chairmanships were taken by former LCC councillors, while 13 of the 17 chief posts were filled by former LCC officers (Rhodes and Hastings 1972).

Some critics later claimed that the GLC's eventual failures could be attributed in part to this conventional organization and continuity of purpose. In an interim verdict, the GLC was characterized as 'a body rooted in and developing out of local government as it has been traditionally understood in this country . . . It has not yet satisfactorily resolved the problems of its own distinctive range of functions' (Rhodes and Hastings 1972: 431). Arguably, the blame lay at the door of the government, which failed to think through the need for a new type of body to be freed from traditional local authority statutory requirements. Yet the responsibility might equally well be placed upon the Herbert Commission itself, for not fully thinking through the requirements of the strategic role which it perceived but did not fully articulate. As the planning expert Peter Hall (1963: 191) commented at the time:

The English have an extraordinary knack for devising pieces of administrative machinery for London that are admirably suited to the conditions of a quarter-century back. The important question about the Herbert Commission's report is not: Why did they create the system of government they did?—the logic behind that was almost inescapable—but: Why did they refuse to carry that logic to its 1960 conclusion?

The effect of these continuities and half-hearted departures from the past was more than superficial. Labour won the first GLC election against the odds, aided by a temporary borough-wide electoral system that favoured the leading party (Rhodes and Young 1972). The impression of continuity which that victory conferred had profound effects. The early GLC treated the London boroughs—now only 32 in number and with greatly enhanced powers—in much the same patrician spirit as its predecessor had approached the comparatively weak metropolitan boroughs of the LCC area. It would soon discover that the outer London boroughs, many of which had enjoyed the respect and cooperation of their former county councils, and some of which had formerly enjoyed county borough status—more having aspired to do so—could not be handled so disdainfully. The initial conflicts came early, and their apparently trivial nature merely served to underline the gulf between GLC perceptions and those of councillors and officers in the boroughs.

These conflicts did not arise from the GLC's major strategic responsibilities but rather from the concurrent powers that recognized both the boroughs and the GLC interests. Some 560 miles of 'metropolitan' roads were initially vested in the GLC, with a further 390 miles a few years later. Responsibility for most of the remainder—some 6,900 miles of 'local' roads—lay with the borough councils. Among the more irritating of the GLC's habitual interventions concerned the location of pedestrian crossings on metropolitan roads, with both purely local and wider 'strategic' considerations brought into play. An even more potent recipe for conflict existed in relation to the handling of planning proposals, where the GLC had the power to call in for its own decision a wide range of applications which borough councillors and officers would have regarded as properly within their own sphere. Fewer conflicts arose from those decisions which were clearly the direct responsibility of the GLC: the nine LCC comprehensive development areas and Covent Garden; cases relating to major transport centres, educational institutions, or public meeting places; and larger mineral workings.

Another source of conflict concerned decisions which had to be referred to GLC for advice and which then became subject to GLC direction whenever the borough proposed to grant planning permission. These decisions included shops of more than 250,000 square feet, factories over 5,000 and offices over 2,500; the erection of buildings over 150 feet high in the central area or 125 feet elsewhere; development within 220 feet from the centre or existing or proposed metropolitan roads; car parks for more than 50 cars; development in the green belt and the demolition or alteration of listed buildings. A third type of planning application promised still further disagreements. These included potential redevelopment areas, applications relating to certain important amenity areas such as the South Kensington museums, the area around St Paul's, and the Hampstead-Highgate area. Here the GLC had to be notified by the boroughs of any planning application and, while it could not directly intervene, it could request the minister to call in the application for his decision with the benefit of GLC advice (Self 1971).

The GLC's rationale was the coordination of land-use planning and transport. Arguably, in order to perform that role effectively it needed the authority to override the boroughs and give binding direction on the boroughs' own plans and on the planning applications they considered. But even the limited powers the GLC actually possessed led it into corrosive disputes with the boroughs. More extensive powers would simply have deepened the conflicts. Here lay the paradox, as one commentator on the abolition of the GLC observed: it was either too weak to be effective or too powerful to be acceptable (Young 1986: 44). But there was a deeper issue. The GLC justified itself as a 'strategic' authority, yet the conception of strategy was—and perhaps remains today—essentially vacuous:

At best a metaphor, strategy belongs to that vocabulary of politics wherein a maximum of appeal is combined with a minimum of substance, and in political life tends to manifest itself in rhetoric or incantation . . . It was seen as axiomatic that a distinction between strategic and non-strategic functions could be made, and that the metropolitan policy vacuum could be filled simply by the attribution of a 'strategic responsibility' to the new GLC. When the crucial decisions were taken, between 1960 and 1965, few dissented from the proposition that 'strategy' needed to be 'done'. But there was little grasp even within academic circles of *what strategy might look like*. So, with a convenient and glib circularity, strategy became 'what the strategic authority will do', in an unconscious echo of Herbert Morrison's dictum that 'Socialism is what the Labour Government does'. (Young and Kramer 1978: 214)

The Road to Abolition

The GLC is remembered as a comparatively short-lived experiment in urban governance; and, indeed, the writing was on the wall within ten years of its inception. In 1973 Conservative borough leaders were lobbying within the party for the abolition of the GLC and, in 1974, Geoffrey Finsberg, Hampstead MP and long a critic of the LCC, was appointed as Opposition spokesman for London affairs. One of his first tasks was to prepare proposals that would severely circumscribe the GLC's powers or abolish it altogether. Labour's general election victory in October 1974 seemed to guarantee the GLC's future for the time being. However, Margaret Thatcher's accession to the Conservative leadership could be seen retrospectively as a portent, for she was on record as a fierce opponent of 'unnecessary' tiers of local government. Moreover, under her leadership Geoffrey Finsberg was further promoted to be vice-chairman of the party with responsibility for London affairs.

These developments created a new sense of uncertainty about the future of London government. The GLC Labour group in opposition after May 1977 found itself on the defensive. Sensitive to Conservative demands for greater—and possibly, total—devolution of GLC powers to the boroughs, the Labour group denied that they were jealously protective of their own detailed planning powers. They offered devolution to the boroughs 'as the appropriate authorities for the execution of local functions' wherever it could 'be clearly established that the GLC has no strategic role to play'. However, with the special exception of housing management, Labour thinking was that there were in fact very few such areas and that it was 'foolish to believe that the problems of one of the major capitals of the world can be solved by 33 individual authorities with conflicting interests.' The GLC must have a strategic role in housing, employment and industrial development and act as 'a body directing resources to the areas of greatest deprivation.' It was 'sheer nonsense' to suppose that London's transport system could exist independently of the democratically accountable strategic body. Overall, 'the devolution of GLC powers to the boroughs would be a retrogressive step which ignored the need to maintain the cohesiveness of Greater London as a political and economic unit' (Labour Party 1977: 1.3.2).

The sharpening of Conservative knives was not the only source of uncertainty for the GLC. The Labour government was flirting with regionalism and had published in December 1976 a White Paper entitled *Devolution: The English Dimension.* The discussion that followed showed little support for regional government and, in particular, highlighted the special problems of London within a south-east region. Parallels were drawn with New York City, which enjoyed a similar dominance within New York State while being financially dependent to some degree on the upstate capital Albany. The future debate would seem to turn on how the GLC's truly strategic role could be strengthened while issues of more local import were devolved to the boroughs. In other words, 15 years after the London Government Act the search for a surer meaning of the terms 'strategic' and 'local' was to continue.

The Conservative election victory in 1979 had few immediate implications for the GLC, for at that stage County Hall was under Conservative control and a Conservative government was unlikely to dissolve its own stronghold in the capital. However Horace Cutler, Conservative leader at County Hall since 1977, had been under considerable pressure to respond to the concerns of his borough colleagues. The borough leaders forced from him an agreement that there would be a fundamental review of the GLC, which Cutler commissioned from Sir Frank Marshall, former Conservative leader of Leeds City Council. The Marshall inquiry was a milestone in the history of metropolitan government. Instead of the expected slimming down, Marshall produced in 1978 a densely argued case for a powerful and strategically effective Greater London Council. Aided by his panel of expert advisers, he produced the definitive case for metropolitan government, a testament to the idea of a metropolitan authority as a strategic planning, resource-allocating, and redistributive body. The GLC should be concerned with the reconciliation of London's various needs. It should have the power to allocate resources across a complete and fully integrated range of government activity. It should assume responsibility for the public management for change (Marshall 1978). The GLC should inherit central government's role in the allocation to the boroughs of rate support grant, approval of capital projects, and such special funds as the urban programme.

Marshall's starting point was that a metropolitan authority for London was necessary, for 'the total interest of London as a whole transcends that of its constituent parts, their local needs and individual aspirations. It must be cared for by a corporate body charged with taking an overall view of issues and events in Metropolitan terms'. Only by strengthening the GLC's powers could it act as 'the recognised guardian of the interests of the community as a whole'. Marshall recognized that such a role implied a wide-ranging devolution of power from central government to what would in effect be an elected regional government. Equally, he recognized the corollary: that such a devolution would hardly be accepted for one part of the country only. It should occur 'nation-wide or not at all' (Marshall 1978: 105), a point which, as the London Boroughs Association (LBA) observed, fatally condemned the plan.

The Marshall report sank like a stone, having had no influence on policy. Opposed by the boroughs and ignored by central government, the report was, ironically, attacked by Ken Livingstone, then a leading left-wing Labour GLC councillor, as too academic. He regretted 'that Marshall did not push on and say "abolish the GLC", because I think it would be a major saving and would have released massive resources for more productive use' (Forrester, Lansley, and Pauley 1985: 43). Elsewhere, opinion was moving towards rethinking the future of metropolitan government.

Meanwhile, as expected, Labour won control of the GLC in May 1981—a victory that was immediately followed by the overthrowing of Andrew McIntosh's leadership of the Labour group and the gaining of power by Livingstone and his associates on the left of the party. Livingstone had lost the leadership election by one vote to McIntosh in 1980, and the Conservatives had made much of his declared intention to renew the challenge after the election. With Livingstone as leader of the GLC, and with the left taking almost all of the committee chairmanships, London was divided. One result was to give the abolitionist tendency a new stimulus.

The Livingstone regime

The acquisition by Ken Livingstone of the GLC leadership marked a watershed in London politics. The dispute between Livingstone and his left-wing supporters on the one hand and the Labour right on the other was part factional, part ideological, involving a view of politics and of the potential for municipal socialism. The ideological stance of the new regime manifested itself in a distinctive political style—campaigning, confrontational, polarizing, and rhetorical—and in a range of novel policy positions that characterized the GLC for the remainder of its life.

One striking signal that the world of London politics had changed was the use made of the GLC as a platform for a wide range of causes. These ranged from promoting gay rights to highlighting pensioners' needs, from anti-racism to nuclear-free zones, and from cheaper public transport to improving workers' rights and conditions. Livingstone had worked to organize the left to take control of the GLC for two years before its election victory, arguing that the GLC could become a model of local socialism. The post-1981 GLC policy positions were, however, more than just Livingstone's personal predilections. Power was diffused among the Labour left members, and Livingstone himself could be upstaged and outflanked by his colleagues. The leader's own flamboyant personality added further colour to the GLC's controversial positions, making him a natural target for press comment. His flair for publicity and relaxed public persona gave him a popularity that was almost independent of the policies he and the GLC espoused. However, some of the causes he promoted—troops out of Northern Ireland, the IRA saluted as 'freedom fighters'—ensured long-lasting suspicion within and beyond the Labour Party. At the same time, his instinct for a headline-catching stance made him a star. Populist, articulate, and witty, the more controversial his position was, the greater the attention he attracted.

Transport was the most important of all GLC responsibilities. The early GLC's pretensions to be a strategic authority were hampered by its failure to match its responsibility for highways with any corresponding influence over public transport. In 1969, Barbara Castle's Transport (London) Act had placed the London Transport Board with its bus and Tube services under the control of the GLC. The 1973–7 Labour GLC was committed first to freezing fares and ultimately to free travel but was unable to progress its policies. In opposition after 1977, London Labour prepared a new transport strategy, which found expression in the 'Fares Fair' policy introduced in 1981. The basis of Fares Fair was a 25 per cent reduction in bus and Tube fares, the cost of which—an estimated £100 million—would be met by a supplementary rate of five pence in the pound.

The GLC had not, however, calculated the effect of the grant penalties applied to expenditure above the government targets, which had the effect of doubling the cost to ratepayers. This brought a legal challenge to the policy from Bromley, one of the few London boroughs that did not benefit from the underground system. The GLC was confident of winning on the basis that the 1969 act empowered it to determine the level of subsidy to London Transport. This interpretation was thrown out by the Court of Appeal and the House of Lords, which determined that the fares cut and the supplementary rate were unlawful on the grounds that the act required London Transport to be run 'economically'. Forced to abandon the policy, the Labour group split and in January 1982 a coalition of Labour, Conservative, and Alliance members defeated Livingstone and the Labour left, who proposed to defy the courts and provoke a showdown with the government. Instead, bus and Tube fares would be doubled. Labour's central policy had collapsed, and Livingstone became the focus of widespread attack, although not from his own, left-wing, power base or from the London public, which, on the contrary, seemed to regard him with increased respect as their defender. It was not until 1983 that London Transport fares were safely reduced and restructured without legal challenges, although in the meantime GLC spending on transport almost doubled.

A second key initiative of the Livingstone regime was in the area of social and economic development. The new social objectives, which ran as a common thread through the proposed alterations to the GLDP, were among the more spectacular of the Livingstone initiatives. A women's committee had been established to tackle discrimination against women and improve their position throughout London. A support unit was created to service the committee and expanded rapidly to 70 staff. Dogged by internal dissension and pilloried by the press, the women's committee seemed to feed the popular view of the GLC as committed to extremism and gesture politics. A parallel ethnic minorities committee was established to reverse the under-representation of black and Asian people in jobs—within the GLC's workforce and beyond—to improve access to services, and to provide them with greater opportunities to influence the policy-making process. Both the women's and the ethnic minorities committees operated in large part by combining campaigns with the bestowal of grants to groups and projects. The GLC's approach to pursuing its objectives by direct funding of groups and projects to which it was sympathetic aroused widespread disquiet as funding rose from £6 million in 1980, the last year of Conservative administration, to over £50 million in 1984. One fear was that by means of such lavish support, the GLC left was bolstering its own political position outside mainstream politics.

In fact, 'Livingstonianism' represented a new form of local government politics that was as much about symbolic stances aimed at a national audience as about specifically London issues. Thus, in contrast to his predecessors, the new GLC leader was accused of using 'the council machinery as part of a political campaign both against the government and in defence of socialist policies' (*The Times*, 6 May 1983). It was also, of course, about building up a power base. In the words of Anne Sofer, a former Labour GLC councillor who defected to the Social Democratic Party, the approach and style of the Livingstone regime had extensive parallels with the American mayoral system 'whereby one person, backed by a party machine, wins control of a city, and can then use its resources for his or her own propaganda and patronage for the next four years' (Sofer 1987: 21). Meanwhile, Ken Livingstone's approach was seen by the government as particularly dangerous because of his alleged exploitation of causes relating to ethnic and other minorities, the so-called 'rainbow coalition'. Kenneth Baker's speech to the 1984 Conservative Party Conference was intended to impress upon his listeners the seriousness of this threat. Livingstone, he warned,

is not a loonie member of the lunatic fringe, though his closest friends are to be found there. He is a dedicated, determined, extreme socialist who has control of a municipal cheque book, to spend Londoners' money to achieve his Socialist plan. He has turned County Hall into Tammany Hall. (Baker 1984)

The Livingstone phenomenon was not confined to County Hall. Left-wing activists were taking power in local Labour parties in a number of London boroughs, as well as other cities. Within a year of Labour's GLC victory, similar regimes were established in such boroughs as Southwark, Haringey, Camden, and Islington. Lambeth already provided its own model of vigorous anti-racist strategies, which were imported into the GLC. Outside London, local political circumstance intersected with the new 'urban left' movement, giving rise to a distinctive local politics: employment and regeneration initiatives in Sheffield; financial brinkmanship in Liverpool; support for the miners against the police in Derbyshire. Thus, the political outlook identified with Livingstone, but extending beyond the GLC and London politics, transformed the landscape of local politics in the 1980s, giving the Conservative government an opportunity for confrontation.

 With the help of his enemies Livingstone came to enjoy a remarkable status among Londoners, even when excoriated by the press. In fact, however, the GLC leader was less interested in public opinion, broadly defined, than in the attitudes of committed followers. To be pilloried by the media—'the most odious man in Britain' according to the *Sun*—was to be exalted by the faithful (Pimlott 1994: 136). To Livingstone at the GLC, the only electorate that really mattered was the intra-party one. Livingstone came to stand for the more resilient, less deferential, breed of socialist then coming on to councils in large numbers. But was this left-wing icon himself of the left? His tactic was to organize and mobilize the London left, run with the left, and yet stand somewhat apart and aloof from the left. A centrist at first, Livingstone never quite lost his bearings in the maelstrom of London politics. His lack of a settled political anchorage was to stand him in good stead when, two decades later, he skilfully engineered his return to the leadership of London.

Abolition gathers momentum

In a number of ways the Livingstone regime set off a sequence of political events that, as they gathered momentum, contributed to the government's decision to abolish the GLC. In essence, the Council's majority group sought to undermine government policies and to oppose the interests of the government's friends. Cutting London Transport fares by one third under the Fares Fair policy and levying a supplementary precept to meet the deficit thereby created, represented a transfer of the burden from users to ratepayers. The City of Westminster responded first by proposing to Michael Heseltine, Secretary of State for the Environment, the abolition of the GLC and the transfer of its functions to the boroughs, and second by forming a campaigning group—Westminster Against Reckless Spending (WARS)—to campaign against the GLC's 'alleged profligacy'. Meanwhile, the Fares Fair policy itself was challenged in the High Court by the London Borough of Bromley, and in December 1981 the House of Lords ruled the precept illegal. In response, the GLC doubled London Transport fares and sought the support of the boroughs in campaigning for a restoration of its former power to subsidize London Transport. The Conservative London Boroughs Association would not lend its support to the Labour GLC and called instead for a general review of transport organisation in Greater London. In July 1982 the House of Commons transport committee supported this call, proposing the creation of a Metropolitan Transport Authority for an area wider than the existing GLC, and signalling the tendency towards more fundamental thinking about London's problems.

These events encouraged those who wished to see the GLC dissolved, a broad front that now included the Institute of Directors and the Confederation of British Industry. In the summer of 1982 John Wheeler, Tory MP for Paddington, organized his fellow London Conservatives to press the case for abolition upon the government. Within the Party itself a policy group on London had been set up, and it was here that the GLC's fate was effectively sealed. The Conservative GLC members on this group argued for replacement of the GLC by a directly elected metropolitan regional strategic authority—a proposal which looked set to become Conservative policy until a revolt by suburban borough leaders successfully led a move against it. The demand was now for outright abolition. By January 1983, London's leading Tory MPs were confident that abolition would be included in the coming general election manifesto.

Meanwhile, the LBA had again rebuffed the GLC's attempts to increase its transport powers and voted instead for its abolition. There were clear signs that the vote on abolition would split London local government, and Livingstone had taken legal advice on the possibility of setting up a Labour-only local government association for London. Most Labour boroughs now withdrew from the LBA to form the Association of London Authorities (ALA), and a publicity campaign against abolition was launched.

For the time being, Whitehall and the Cabinet remained cool. Ministers generally disparaged the abolitionist sentiment. Environment Secretary Tom King was deeply opposed, as was his predecessor, Michael Heseltine (Forrester, Lansley, and Pauley 1985). Patrick Jenkin and Kenneth Baker, who were in turn to succeed King, had earlier argued before the Marshall inquiry in favour of a stronger, albeit 'strategic', GLC. When a Cabinet committee in the winter of 1982–3 discussed the options, splits were publicly aired, with the Prime Minister now rumoured to be pressing for abolition. Yet as late as April, Tom King denied the existence of a planned White Paper and dismissed hopes that abolition would be in the Conservative manifesto. When the draft manifesto was looked at by the Cabinet, the proposed abolition of the GLC and the metropolitan counties was not considered, and manifesto proposals for local government had yet to be tabled. Nevertheless, immediately after the meeting Mrs Thatcher met with two of her allies outside the Cabinet and drafted a passage for inclusion in the manifesto criticizing the GLC as a 'wasteful and unnecessary tier of government' and giving an unequivocal commitment to abolish it. Members of the Cabinet were furious at having been bypassed in this way. King, hearing the news while on a train, was apparently 'aghast'; as responsible minister he had spent four years arguing against abolition (Forrester, Lansley, and Pauley 1985: 66). On the other hand, many of the party's backbench MPs and borough leaders were delighted (Young 1994: 435–40).

The GLC Conservatives, having been defeated in the party's policy group on London, decided to fight on, not least because they now expected to defeat Livingstone's embattled and by now unpopular Labour group at the 1985 GLC election. Their response was to resuscitate their earlier plan: conceding that abolition was likely to happen and proposing as an alternative a new London assembly for strategic purposes. Their presentational problem lay in showing that their proposed Greater London Assembly really differed from the GLC itself. They argued that it would not be a local authority but a new type of body with specific functions and strictly limited spending powers. As far as possible, existing GLC powers would be passed on to the boroughs and the assembly, a 'slim-line' authority with a small staff, would do no more than lay out 'working parameters' to guide the boroughs. The assembly would be responsible for London-wide services of fire and waste disposal but, where possible, these would be privatized or delegated to boroughs for day-to-day purposes. Although this scheme won some support, it failed to appeal to the Prime Minister as it promised little hope of a final disposal of the GLC.

Protests from County Hall Conservatives notwithstanding, the Tory manifesto promised the abolition of the GLC and the metropolitan county councils, proposing instead that area-wide services would be run by joint boards of borough or district representatives. The GLC was accused of gross mismanagement of London transport, and the manifesto pledged that a new London Regional Transport Authority would be created at an early date.

On 9 June 1983 the Conservatives won the general election with a decisive majority. Patrick Jenkin was appointed Secretary of State for the Environment to replace Tom King. It now fell to Jenkin to oversee the GLC abolition process and to chair the Cabinet committee established for that purposes. The task was a dramatic one, and symbolized—as much as the government's response to the miners' strike in 1984—Thatcherism at its most unrelenting. In the government's eyes, the GLC and the metropolitan counties had been profligate, consistently exceeding government expenditure targets and placing a heavy burden on ratepayers. The GLC's 1983 budget of £867 million was 53 per cent above the government's target of £566 million and, together, the GLC and Inner London Education Authority accounted for as much as 40 per cent of the national overspend. The system of grant penalties had failed to influence the GLC's behaviour, for Livingstone and his colleagues had chosen to forgo grants and to finance their activities solely through imposing precepts upon the boroughs.

Published in October 1983, the White Paper *Streamlining the Cities* portrayed the two-tier system in London and other metropolitan areas as a 'recipe for conflict and uncertainty'. The GLC and metropolitan counties were obliged to search for a 'strategic' role in order to justify their existence, which led them into an inevitable conflict with the boroughs (DoE 1983). The government's criticisms of the GLC centred on the futility of its search for such a strategy. The GLC had been created during 'the heyday of a certain fashion for strategic planning, the confidence in which now appears exaggerated'. Expected to behave 'strategically', it engaged in 'a natural search for a "strategic" role which may have no basis in real needs' (DoE 1983: 3). This search, argued the government, underlay the conflicts which the GLC had generated with other levels of government. The White Paper maintained that

a strict interpretation of the upper tier role, as envisaged in the [1963] legislation, would leave members of these authorities with too few functions. The search for a wider role brings them into conflict with the lower tier authorities. It may also lead them to promote policies which conflict with national policies which were the responsibility of central government. (DoE 1983: paras 111–12)

Some independent commentators were sympathetic. In the words of one, 'the GLC's failure can be summed up thus: it did the things it was supposed to do badly or not at all, and it tried to do too many things it should never have tried to do' (Hall 1989: 170).

Under the White Paper proposals, a wide range of functions would be transferred to the boroughs, including planning, highways, traffic management, waste regulation and disposal, housing, trading standards, and support for the arts, sport, and historic buildings. Responsibility for public transport in London would be transferred to a new authority under ministerial control. Land drainage and flood protection would move to the Thames Water Authority and joint boards of borough representatives would take control of remaining area-wide functions. A series of subsequent consultation papers set out the details of these proposals for particular services. Specifically, London's planning would be the responsibility of a special commission appointed by the Secretary of State to advise him on planning guidance after consultation with the boroughs (Young and Grayson 1987). Almost all of these provisions were fiercely resisted; some did not survive.

The Labour GLC responded vehemently to the White Paper. The government's proposals were attacked as fragmenting and dispersing London-wide services to 'a collection of boards and quangoes none of which would be subject to a direct election by the people of London. Other services would be dispersed to a plethora of ineffective joint borough committees'. Whitehall would assume unprecedented control and abolition would be the 'first time in the history of local government that such major changes have taken place without any prior consideration, analysis or planning by an independent commission or enquiry'. Abolishing the GLC had 'got nothing to do with giving more power to the local boroughs; nothing to do with a cheaper, more efficient management of public affairs; nothing to do with simplifying or streamlining London's local government. The objective is the destruction of the GLC *per se*' (GLC 1984). The Labour-controlled boroughs opposed the proposals with almost equal vehemence, falling readily into line behind the GLC leadership. Conservative boroughs, on the other hand, whether the expensive central London Westminster, Kensington and Chelsea or the suburban boroughs—Barnet, Bexley, Bromley, Croydon, Enfield, Harrow, Hillingdon, Kingston, and Sutton—supported and welcomed the principle of abolition though sometimes with reservations about the lack of financial detail. Tories on the GLC, on the other hand, robustly advocated the retention of an over-all authority.

The battle for London

The various proposals for abolition depended on the successful passage of leg-islation through Parliament for them to be realized. The earliest possible date for royal assent was the summer of 1985, with the appointed day for abolition 1 April 1986. Meanwhile, GLC elections were scheduled for May 1985, raising the prospect of Labour fighting them on the single issue of the GLC's contin-ued existence, with the probable result that they would be successful, thereby claiming a mandate for resistance and severely embarrassing the government. Unpalatable as it was, not least to the Prime Minister herself, cancellation of the elections appeared the only way to avoid an electoral impasse. For that purpose preliminary legislation was required. Hence, Patrick Jenkin, the environment secretary, brought forward the Local Government (Interim Provisions) Bill—the so-called Paving Bill—in order to cancel the elections and appoint an interim board of borough councillors to run the GLC for the remaining months of its life.

It was not just the GLC or the Labour Party that was outraged at this move to stifle a democratic process, solely on the grounds that its outcome was likely to be disagreeable to the government. The Paving Bill attracted the most intense opposition, not least from many Conservatives. In the event, a total of 19 Tory MPs, led by the former prime minister Edward Heath, voted against the second reading in the Commons. Described as 'a dangerous precedent', it barely survived the second reading in the Lords. Then on 28 June cross-party opposition in the Lords succeeded in wrecking the bill at the committee stage with an amendment to delay the election cancellation provisions until after the main abolition legislation was passed. The constitutional argument was unassailable, but the effect was to sabotage the government's strategy. A humiliated Jenkin was forced to fall back on extending the life of the GLC. In a ministerial statement on 5 July he announced that the government had agreed to drop its election cancellation provisions and allow the existing councils to continue in office for a further eleven months, thereby leaving Livingstone and his colleagues in power to campaign with impunity against the government.

At the same time, restrictions on the GLC's freedom of action were intro-duced, including a ban on the disposal of land without ministerial consent and a requirement for ministerial consent for all new contracts worth over £100,000. The GLC responded by rushing through some £140 million of con-tracts before the bill became law at the end of the month, and subsequently flooded the Department of the Environment with some 250 contracts a week requiring ministerial approval. Meanwhile, Livingstone and three of his colleagues decided to force by-elections—and hence provide an immediate demonstration of sympathy for the GLC cause—by resigning their seats. Unwilling to be drawn into a tactical trap, the Conservatives did not contest them, allowing the Labour candidates to win all four by-elections with large majorities but low turn-outs.

Between them, the apparent heavy-handedness of the government and the energetic campaign against abolition mounted by the GLC served, if not to unite Londoners, to generate an increasing body of opinion against abolition, and at the same time an unusual degree of pan-London camaraderie. The GLC campaign began immediately after the 1983 general election, with an increase in the staffing of the GLC's public relations branch and the production of an information pack arguing the case against abolition. Roland Freeman, a former GLC Conservative who had argued before the Herbert Commission for a GLC-type solution, was appointed as parliamentary lobbyist. In February 1984 the advertising agency Boase Massimi Pollitt was appointed to develop a campaign focusing on the cancellation of the 1985 GLC elections with the slogan 'Say No to No Say'. The first posters, promoting the anti-abolition slogan with sharp and telling images, appeared in March 1984. One featured a padlocked dustbin with the title 'Next year all Londoners' votes go the same way'. Another featured the Palace of Westminster—carefully showing both the Commons and the Lords—asking 'what kind of place is it that takes away your right to vote and leaves you with no say?'

With the Paving Bill defeated in the Lords, the campaign concentrated its attack on the prospect of life without the GLC. One poster showed a stereotypical civil servant with a wall of bricks in place of his face, with the caption 'if you have any complaints when the GLC goes, you'll be talking to Whitehall'. Another showed an army of bowler-hatted snails moving onto an empty space, and captioned 'if the GLC goes, Whitehall moves in'. It was by common consent a well-targeted campaign, for which Boase Massimi Pollitt won seven awards. It almost certainly helped to rally opinion behind the Council which, for all its ready access to campaign resources, could be skilfully presented as a plucky David taking on the Whitehall Goliath. In January 1985 Westminster city council was granted an injunction forbidding the GLC from using 'persuasive' publicity and allowing only factual advertising. It was less of a handicap than might have been supposed, as the GLC was able to use public opinion data in its advertising for the remainder of its campaign.

This data was increasingly on its side. Shortly after the publication of *Streamlining the Cities* in October 1983, an opinion poll had shown 54 per cent of the Londoners questioned to be opposed to the abolition of the GLC. In March 1984 this figure had risen to 62 per cent; only 22 per cent favoured abolition. In September that same year, an opinion poll for Thames TV showed the majority against GLC abolition to stand at 74 per cent. A corollary of these shifts was that Livingstone's own standing underwent a transformation. Between the spring of 1983 and the spring of 1984, his satisfaction rating among Londoners leapt from a modest 26 per cent to 43 per cent. Subsequent stages of the battle would see it rise still further, to make him one of the most instantly recognizable and talked about politicians in Britain, in striking contrast to all previous London leaders with the single exception of Herbert Morrison.

In September 1984, Kenneth Baker was appointed local government minister with responsibility for steering the main abolition legislation through Parliament. When the Local Government Bill received its second reading in the Commons in December 1984, ministers were attacked by Tory backbench opponents of abolition. There was cross-party support for attempts to replace the GLC and metropolitan counties with elected strategic bodies, a threat that the government was able to meet, but which severely reduced its majority. At the report stage an amendment by a Conservative backbencher, Patrick Cormack, calling for the GLC to be replaced by a directly elected authority attracted widespread support, cut the government's majority to 23. As the bill faced the Lords, Baker made a point of appealing to the upper house not to vote for a directly elected London-wide authority. Between April and June 1985 the House of Lords debated the bill at great length, discussing both its detail and its broad constitutional implications. The Lords passed several amendments designed to set up strategic authorities for functions such as waste disposal and traffic management, but they were rejected by the Commons.

Throughout this period, the government's case was made more difficult by critics within the Conservative Party, especially Tories on the GLC. Alan Greengross, Conservative leader at County Hall, stood firm for a overall authority to speak and give 'direction for the specific tasks that must be done for London as a whole' (Carvel 1999: 171). Meanwhile, his Conservative group produced a 20-point rebuttal of the abolitionist case. George Tremlett, once a County Hall leadership hopeful, opposed the proposal root and branch and was driven from the party after urging voters to support Labour candidates in the by-elections precipitated by Livingstone and his colleagues. At the same time, the Tory deputy leader Cyril Taylor publicly warned that GLC abolition could increase local rates, jeopardize control of some boroughs, and put a number of Conservative seats at risk. At the end of the day, however, the running was made by the more vociferous advocates of borough government who were not prepared to contemplate any form of Greater London Authority. Sir Peter Bowness, leader of Croydon, the most independent minded of all the boroughs, poured scorn on the faint-hearted, claiming that

the concept of a directly elected authority has credibility only with the GLC members. Londoners know and understand borough government. The existing boroughs may have been created in 1965 but they are all based on units of local government with history and tradition. (*The Times*, 22 January 1985).

Moreover, although some Westminster politicians were critical of the government's policy, others vigorously supported it. Norman Tebbit, in particular, was a staunch advocate, justifying his position on grounds that were unashamedly partisan:

the Labour Party is the party of division. In its present form it represents a threat to the democratic values and institutions on which our parliamentary system is based. The Greater London Council is typical of this new, modern, divisive version of Socialism. It must be defeated. So, we shall abolish the GLC. (Tebbit 1984)

The GLC: A Verdict

Pitted against a government at Westminster which not only had a substantial majority but also had no imminent fear of electoral defeat, the GLC never had any chance of survival. Indeed, the contest was a reminder of another fundamental truth about British politics and about the way local government in the United Kingdom necessarily differed from its equivalent elsewhere. Britain was a unitary state with all constitutional power vested in a national parliament. A Westminster prime minister, confident of House of Commons support, was the most powerful chief executive in the Western world, capable of pushing through virtually any domestic legislation he or she chose, given sufficient determination: an elective dictator, indeed. In Britain, 'local democracy' only ever existed on licence.

The GLC was seen, rightly, as victim of the system. Its defeat was also seen—perhaps rightly—as a blow both to democracy and to the principle of community government. Yet the viability of the authority itself remains arguable. Can the GLC be seen as a success? Whereas the LCC had a glittering record of achievement in housing, education, planning, and the arts, the GLC appeared in comparison a fettered giant. Where its predecessor had been the dominant authority scarcely needing to recognize the presence of the small and weak metropolitan borough councils, the GLC found itself the weaker partner in London's system of government. The boroughs, significantly designated as the 'primary units' by the Herbert Commission, had wide-ranging powers, were large and resourceful, and by 1986 were responsible for 84 per cent of local government current expenditure across London. They were very powerful local governments by any standards. In the space of a few years they developed the political capacities, vigour, and tactical skill to outwit the GLC's sometimes predatory initiatives. Paradoxically, the extent of the threat to borough autonomy posed by the GLC prompted a political response that effectively contained that threat and in time moved to curtail the GLC's powers.

In searching for space that it could claim as its own, the GLC fell prey to the temptation 'to do many things it should never do' while it did things it was meant to do either 'badly or not at all' (Hall 1989: 170). Facing 'the serried ranks of thirty or so of the most powerful local governments in Britain' the GLC seemed 'incapable of comprehending the antipathy felt by the new London boroughs' (Sharpe 1995: 117). Fatally, the GLC lacked political friends. Central government departments saw it as a potential rival in a field—the capital city—where they always claimed a special role. The other institutions in the London area, while not so hostile as the London boroughs, had no special sympathy for the GLC. Even the national leadership of the Labour Party, which viewed Livingstone with the darkest suspicion, was ambivalent.

Two more fundamental problems underlay the demise of the GLC. The first was its inability to identify and express a sense of London's unity. London's size and complexity and internal differences rendered it 'a kind of no-man's land . . . a series of linked urban villages with its centre as more a sort of national territory [lacking] a true local identity' (Sharpe 1995: 114). Related to this was the limited ability of the GLC to capture the imagination of Londoners and command their loyalty and respect on issues other than Fares Fair or its own abolition. It 'never enjoyed the prestige, status, and perhaps that degree of citizen allegiance that ought to have accrued to the country's capital city government. And what status [it] did acquire was always overshadowed by the existence of the City of London which always seemed to command greater public interest' (Sharpe 1995: 114).

A cartoon in the *Observer* (16 April 1967) after the second GLC election of 1967 showed two elderly ladies passing an newspaper placard announcing that 'Tories Win GLC'. 'I know what Tories are', says one, 'But what's GLC?' In terms of actual achievements the Council failed to gain, even to seek, the high public profile that follows from major visible projects, with the exception of the 'motorway box', the impact of which on its standing and reputation was mixed. Ironically, the only point in its history in which the GLC engaged a high degree of public interest was when it was able to turn a death sentence into martyrdom.

4

London Dismembered

GETTING rid of the Greater London council was one thing. Providing a long-term alternative was another. Not only did it not prove easy; the problem was almost entirely ignored. Yet the very failure to tackle it raised an unexpected question. Did it matter?

The abolition of the GLC in 1986 left London's future in the hands of ministers, the 32 London boroughs, and a web of joint arrangements. Decision-making became highly fragmented, with powers drifting to Whitehall. A network of joint bodies struggled to build a basis for the planning of the metropolis, while Labour politicians looked on askance as the London Residuary Body set about its task of disposing of the remaining GLC assets. Yet, despite all predictions, the governance of London continued to function. Although abolition was a massive administrative exercise, the chaos or creeping domination by Whitehall predicted by the GLC did not materialize. Uncertainty there certainly was, and County Hall politicians had the bitter satisfaction of being proved right on one point: that whatever form the new government of London took, it could hardly be termed 'streamlined.' It was instead both centralized and atomized. Gradually, the private sector moved into the vacuum created by the abolition of the GLC. Taking up the lead apparently by default, bodies sponsored by industry and commerce sidetracked the debate about GLC restoration and promoted 'partnership' as a panacea for London's ills. By the mid-1990s, however, the limits of partnership served only to highlight the gaps in the overall management of the metropolis.

The problem was twofold. First, there was an over-dependence on elaborate structures of cooperative joint action developed to coordinate London-wide services. Second, the capital appeared to suffer from the lack of any overall responsibility for formulating and giving effect to a vision for London. The Labour Party had an answer to both. The party had officially opposed abolition and initially took it upon itself to restore the GLC at the first opportunity. Commentators and academics alike condemned London's dismemberment as an act of political vandalism. Gradually, however, outrage died down and was replaced by sober reflection. The lessons of the GLC's two decades had been learnt, and support for the creation of another giant local authority ebbed away. The analysis of the problem of London government became more sophisticated. Opinion moved from the need for a metropolitan-wide service providing local authority towards creating a 'voice for London' that might—or might not—take the form of an elected mayor with executive powers.

Picking Up the Pieces

The abolition period was one of fevered activity and banner headlines. Meanwhile, out of the limelight—and out of the press—the work of adjusting to the new situation went ahead. The London boroughs and the City Corporation were required by the Local Government Act 1985 to set up a joint body, the London Co-ordinating Committee, to make preparations for the abolition of the GLC. Chaired by Sir Peter Bowness, Leader of Croydon, this committee was given the task of exploring whether functions could be undertaken jointly and whether separate joint committees should be set up for research and voluntary organizations. The preferred solution was for joint committees to act as the key decision-making bodies, with services provided by a 'lead borough'.

It was in the interest of the GLC to talk up the problems that would arise following its abolition, regarding both the cooperation required from disparate authorities and the exposure of services, activities, and voluntary bodies to changes in policy. An immediate crisis was generated by the new-found vulnerability of voluntary organizations, some of which the Council had funded generously. The GLC made an eleventh-hour attempt at 'forward funding' of voluntary and other groups whose existence was threatened by abolition. The City of Westminster mounted a legal challenge, and the High Court blocked most of the council's proposals. In March 1986, the House of Lords debated the possibility of serious damage to the voluntary sector arising from funding difficulties following abolition.

The arrangements made to provide continued funding to those organizations that had enjoyed the support of the GLC left decisions in the hands of borough representatives who constituted the London Boroughs Grants Committee (LBGC). The London Boroughs Grants Scheme was one of a number of funding sources established to replace the GLC, with all London boroughs together with the City of London as its constituent members. The LBGC had the key responsibility for all policy and expenditure decisions. Aided by a steering group to advise on policy matters and subcommittees to consider individual funding decisions, its lead borough, Richmond-upon-Thames, established the Grants Unit, which became responsible not only for administering schemes and advising the committee but also for monitoring social needs in Greater London.

Most of the funds were provided by the London boroughs, contributing in proportion to their share of Greater London's population. Accordingly, securing the consensus of all parties in setting the annual budget became a major hurdle, and often involved delays. The problem became acute following the 1986 elections when the committee achieved political balance. Although the funding of individual projects required a simple majority vote of committee members, without referral back to the boroughs, the criteria for defining the nature of projects to be funded remained controversial. Many organizations complained that they were ignored by the scheme, while black and minority organizations, the homeless, women, and the arts were accorded priority. In June, the London Voluntary Services Council claimed that two organizations a week were closing down due to lack of funds, and in July published figures to show that 43 had been shut down and an additional 44 had suffered from greatly reduced funding, insisting that ethnic minority groups were discriminated against under the new funding regime (LVSC Briefing July 1986).

In fact, the expected crisis did not arrive, although the uncertainties of joint decision-making received considerable coverage in the press, and the time taken to reach firm funding decisions led a number of grant-supported voluntary bodies to prepare redundancy notices for their staff (*Guardian* 30 January 1987). One reason for the unexpected reprieve was the unwillingness of Conservative ministers to court further unpopularity in the aftermath of their hard-fought abolition campaign. The rate support grant settlement for 1986/7 was adjusted to divert an additional £200 million to London boroughs to ease the transition. When the LBGC repeatedly failed to achieve the required two-thirds majority needed to give effect to their funding decisions, ministers prevailed upon Conservative councillors on the LGBC to agree a funding settlement close to GLC levels (Carvel 1999: 249). Overall, the scheme developed extensive links with voluntary organizations and worked closely with civil servants from the Department of the Environment, the Home Office, Department of Health and Social Security (DHSS), and the Department of Education and Science (DES). It provided for effective coordination of the various funding arrangements for the voluntary sector, and set up consultation procedures at both officer and member levels.

Research was easily handled, with the remaining parts of the GLC research and intelligence function reconstituted under section 88 of the 1985 Act as the London Research Centre. Accountable to a joint committee of boroughs, Islington took the 'lead borough' role. Research access to the archives was provided by the Greater London Record Office and Historical Library that maintained records of the GLC, LCC, and Middlesex County Council. Far more important and controversial was the arrangement made for London regional planning. Following the abolition of the GLC, primary responsibility for strategic planning was transferred to central government. The proposals in the Local Government Bill not only shifted the administration of London-wide planning from County Hall to Whitehall, but left local elected representatives with little say over policies that went beyond their own boundaries. The government intended that the Secretary of State for the Environment should have exclusive powers to decide on such matters, acting on the advice of an ad hoc commission of his own appointment. The London boroughs protested vociferously and, following a rebellion in the House of Lords, ministers conceded that the right body to advise the Secretary of State was a joint committee of the local planning authorities. Thus the London Planning Advisory Committee (LPAC) was established, with Havering as lead borough.

Advised by a panel of chief officers comprising chief executives, borough planners, engineers, surveyors, and finance officers, LPAC was funded by London local authorities contributing on a per capita basis. The Committee had a budget of £589,000 in 1987/8 which went up to £1 million in 1988/9. LPAC's principal task and statutory *raison d'être* was to make representations to the Secretary of State on behalf of the London boroughs over the periodic strategic guidance, which provided a framework of general policy within which boroughs prepared their own Unitary Development Plans. LPAC's balanced composition, however, reflecting the party distribution across London, did little to facilitate its coordinating role across the city, at least until 1994. But even when Labour took control of many of the boroughs in the elections that year, diversity was still an issue and many boroughs expressed doubts about LPAC's overall role in representing London-wide concerns (Hebbert and Travers 1988).

Another major role of LPAC was to advise, on behalf of London boroughs, on major development proposals before local planning committees and to define criteria for distinguishing major from minor developments. Although a majority of London boroughs agreed to work within LPAC's guidelines, some local authorities, notably including the City of London, chose to notify LPAC of their applications rather than engage in consultative processes. On other planning and policy matters, LPAC's coordination role involved setting up working parties to advise and make recommendations as appropriate. Where disputes or disagreements arose over geographical or party lines, the Secretary of State's intervention was deemed necessary to decide contentious applications.

To some extent, LPAC's role in planning was also constrained by the work of other committees that existed alongside, such as the London Advisory Committee of the Historic Buildings and Monuments Commission, which had responsibility for matters relating to historic buildings and conservation, and the Greater London Advisory and Consultative Committee of the Department of Transport. Likewise, the London Research Centre held much of the strategic information which LPAC had to obtain on a commercial basis. Finally, LPAC's location in suburban Romford on the eastern fringe of London made the involvement of members and officers from elsewhere difficult. Nevertheless, its officers liased with particular effectiveness with the Department of Environment and Transport, the London local authority associations, and other centrally-located agencies (Travers *et al.* 1991). LPAC was to be an important player within the London and South East Regional Planning Conference (SERPLAN) a body which, established some years before, continued its monitoring and advisory role on major transport and planning issues affecting the region and coordinated joint policies on waste disposal, regional shopping centres, maintenance of open land in the green belt, and the allocation of building land for housing.

Housing lettings, as distinct from development, was another one of GLC responsibilities involving boroughs across London, and one which the demise of the Council passed back to them. The London Area Mobility Scheme (LAMS) was established to facilitate household movement within local authority and housing association dwellings. With staff of 55 and Camden as its lead borough, its numerically most important scheme—the London Mutual Exchange Bureau—handled some 2,000–3,000 lettings annually. As with LPAC and LBGC, its members were derived by nomination from all the London boroughs and the City Corporation. In addition, other specialist committees were set up, including the London Boroughs' Children's Regional Planning Committee, supporting the boroughs in developing policies for children, and the London Advisory and Consultative Committee that provided a London-wide forum to discuss policies for highways and traffic management.

With a budget in excess of £150 million, the London Fire and Civil Defence Authority (LFCDA) was one of the major authorities that undertook a number of important functions such as firefighting, fire precaution and regulation, civil defence, and petroleum licensing. LFCDA's 33 members, appointed by each of the London boroughs and the City Corporation, were accountable to their constituent local councils. Some, however, felt that its membership was too numerous to be effective and that the principle of indirect election rendered the nature of its accountability cumbersome. Other schemes that came into effect on abolition included the London Advisory Panel on Transport Schemes, set up by the London Co-ordinating Committee to advise London boroughs on taxi-card schemes and concessionary transport fares scheme for pensioners and disabled people.

The post-GLC period also witnessed the emergence of other local government bodies for parts of London. A key issue for the post-GLC capital was the future, if any, of the Inner London Education Authority (ILEA). Prior to GLC abolition, ILEA had existed as a Council subcommittee, the members consisting of the GLC councillors from inner London constituencies together with representatives from the inner London boroughs. As such, it was the largest education authority in Britain, with 300,000 pupils, 21,000 teachers, and an annual budget of around £800 million. After GLC abolition in 1986, it became an independent authority in its own right, with directly elected members who were responsible for providing education in the twelve inner boroughs and the City. At the same time, it took on a number of comparatively minor additional responsibilities, including the Geffrye and Horniman Museums, the London-wide supplies purchasing arrangements, and the direct labour building and engineering functions.

Based mainly at the County Hall, the education service was administered in ten divisions, each covering one or two boroughs. The authority was one of the highest-spending authorities in the UK, with expenditure per pupil almost twice as that in outer London. The high cost, together with the allegedly low quality of education ILEA offered in inner London, provoked much criticism. GLC abolition also spurred some enthusiastic Tories to go further, and in their

1987 election manifesto the Conservatives promised to give individual boroughs an opportunity to leave ILEA. In autumn 1987 the legislation to facilitate opting out was introduced in Parliament. A group of powerful Conservative backbenchers, including Norman Tebbit and Michael Heseltine, pressed the government to abolish ILEA altogether, encouraging Kenneth Baker, the Education Secretary, to move amendments to the Education Reform Bill of 1987. The outcome was the abolition of the Authority and the transfer of education services in their entirety to the boroughs in 1990.

The disappearance of ILEA marked the high point for abolitionists, who saw existing forms of pan-London government as implicitly subversive. Other bodies were far less controversial, and several continued their work virtually unchanged by the wider trauma. The Lee Valley Regional Park Authority had been established in January 1967 as a statutory body to manage the area that covered the three counties of Essex, Hertfordshire, and Greater London. Its membership of 28 indirectly elected councillors was altered following the GLC's abolition to include additional representatives nominated jointly by other London boroughs, in order to achieve a balance between London and non-London authorities. The precept paid by the GLC was substituted by a direct levy on the London boroughs that amounted to 80 per cent of the Authority's running costs. The long-standing Thames Consultative Planning Committee which brought together river interests for consultation was replaced by the London Rivers Authority so as to provide for better coordination on the basis of a core membership of six boroughs, river users, trade unions, and recreational and community groups. Its main task was to prevent damage to the Thames that might result from expanding private residential development along the waterfront. One of the largest functions of the GLC—waste disposal—was also transferred to the newly established Waste Disposal Authority (WDA), which comprised four statutory joint authorities covering Western Riverside, East London, West London, and North London. Twelve London boroughs linked together into three voluntary groups covering Central, South London, and South East London worked alongside the joint authorities to form the WDA.

Inevitably, there were attempts to provide for a 'GLC in exile'. The London Strategic Policy Committee, set up as a voluntary committee of eight sympathetic London boroughs with Camden as the lead, was intended to provide continuity in the work of various policy teams of the GLC. A reconstituted London Policy Strategic Unit absorbed the work of the policy teams specializing in issues concerning women, race, police, transport, planning, local economic policy, and recreation. The Committee and the Unit, however, were abolished in March 1988 because of financial difficulties and a lack of effective political backing.

Alongside these arrangements for continuing GLC services were some unique provisions for ensuring that the controversial authority was well and truly buried. If the Council had a publicly recognized successor, it was the London Residuary Body (LRB), whose members were appointed by the

Secretary of State and charged with managing the GLC's loan debt and deal-ing with other legal liabilities. Led by anti-GLC critic 'Tag' Taylor of Sutton, the LRB also assumed responsibility for a broad range of the former GLC's tasks that were not transferred to other bodies, and for making pension, redun-dancy, and compensation payments to the ex-GLC staff. More specifically, LRB was given the task of selling GLC's assets involving some 9,000 properties. Most GLC housing had been sold off during the 1970s and by the mid-1980s the Council had effectively ceased to be a major housing authority within the capital. The LRB transferred its housing in the counties outside London to housing associations. Major issues arose over Thamesmead, the GLC's large 'new town in town' development on the reclaimed marshlands adjacent to the Thames barrier. Despite continuing financial concerns, the development was eventually transferred to a tenant body, Thamesmead Town Ltd. The GLC's industrial properties were sold to Inner City Enterprises, while the sale of com-mercial properties centred upon office accommodation at County Hall. Statutorily, the LRB had a duty to 'use its best endeavours to secure that its work is completed as soon as practicable' and to submit plans for winding up its affairs by 1990.

Finding a Vision for London

Meanwhile, the Conservative government sought to pre-empt any possible revival of the case for a Greater London Authority by strengthening its own administrative arrangements for London affairs. When John Major succeeded Margaret Thatcher as Prime Minister in 1990, he brought Michael Heseltine back into the Cabinet as Environment Secretary with particular responsibility for finding a politically acceptable replacement to the poll tax. Heseltine brought to the DoE a fresh drive and enthusiasm, not least for new decision-making structures for local government. He had a number of proposals. The most radical was one he had developed as a backbencher—which Peter Walker had advocated as early as the 1960s—and which he now pressed with renewed vigour: the introduction into the British system of the directly elected execu-tive mayor. What Heseltine could not do, however, was link this idea to the need to develop arrangements for governing London. John Major specifically rejected an elected mayor for London in January 1992 as 'too fundamental' a change to local government and one which would cede too many powers from central government, although this firmness was somewhat undermined when Lord Howe, the former Chancellor, expressed in a radio interview his regret that the government of which he was a member had abolished the GLC.

Instead, the official Conservative line on London was to stress the need for coordination, directed by central government itself. Thus John Major estab-lished a Cabinet subcommittee to link up separate Whitehall departments; and when, in the following year, John Gummer was appointed Secretary of State for Environment he was also given a new and significant designation as

Minister for London. In 1994 the Government Office for London (GOL) was
set up as one of ten regional offices in England. The machinery was now in
place to enable Whitehall to function effectively as a strategic authority for the
metropolitan area. Accountable to Gummer's Cabinet subcommittee, GOL
was an inter-departmental entity bringing together the regional offices of the
Departments of Environment, Transport, Trade and Industry, and Education
and Employment. A fuller integration came about in 1996 when the various
departmental offices were brought together at Millbank, location of the
Labour Party headquarters.

From its inception, GOL was responsible for allocating the Single
Regeneration Budget and the Competitive Challenge Fund to a total value of
around £1 billion, as well as promoting London's interests within Whitehall.
GOL also coordinated the London Training and Enterprise Councils (TECs)
and Business Link, the small business advisory network, and became the vehicle through which the strategic planning guidance for London and indicative
strategies were published. From 1996 two representatives of the private sector
joined the management board of GOL. Yet, despite this elaborate structure,
GOL was in no sense a monolith, as its component parts continued to report
to their own sponsoring departments (Travers and Jones 1997).

By the mid-1990s, the London boroughs, working with GOL, had consider-
ably increased the part they played, individually and collectively, in London's
government. This was itself partly a reflection of the emerging role of private
sector-led bodies. A new organisation, London First, brought together London
borough leaders, the voluntary sector, and leading private-sector interests, and
took the lead role in shaping the debate on the future of London government
(Newman and Thornley 1997). Launched in 1992 to fill the gap left by the abolition of the GLC as a London-wide promotion and development body,
London First merged with the existing promotional agency, London Forum,
in 1993. Chaired by Lord Sheppard, London First enjoyed the support of more
than 300 businesses, and latterly, the London boroughs. For promotional purposes it established the London First Centre, which acted as a conduit for
inward investment.

The London Pride Partnership was launched by London First to assemble
London's response to the City Pride initiative. The City Corporation met the
costs of a secretariat to do a year's preparatory work on the City Pride prospectus. Private sector partners included the CBI, London region, the London
Chamber of Commerce and Industry, and the TECs. London government was
represented by the Association of London Government (ALG), by LPAC, and
by the Cities of London and Westminster, and the chair alternated between
Lord Sheppard and Councillor Toby Harris of the ALG. In his role as Minister
for London, John Gummer set up a Joint London Advisory Panel in 1996 com-
posed of the twelve ministerial representatives on the Cabinet subcommittee
and eleven private sector representatives of the London Pride partnership.

The initiative was to promote the locational advantages of London as a
world city and business centre and to demonstrate that the 'abolition of the

GLC and the lack of a firm planning and investment framework created the space for business and the City to promote their priorities' (Newman 1995: 118). But the Partnership did not escape divisions. The business partners were keen to concentrate on London's central area, while the borough members insisted on taking a broader view and including the suburbs. Considerable energy was expended in trying to get agreement on the relative importance of economic growth, infrastructure improvements, and social cohesion. The partnership focused on topic and area task forces to advance its agenda, but inescapably this coalition of uncomfortable partners could not avoid highlighting the problems arising from the fragmentation of London government. The Conservative boroughs vetoed any reference to the need for a strategic authority for London in the Partnership's prospectus, which instead limply recorded that London was 'unusual' among major cities in not having an elected city-wide government.

The entire thrust of the London Forum/First/Pride initiatives was to avoid the question of London's governmental integrity and to advance issues at a sub-regional level. Not only did this express the pragmatism of a business-led organization seeking specific and targeted interventions in preference to structures of governance; it also reflected the origins of such bodies as London First in the local partnerships promoted by Business in the Community. The Thames Gateway, the central area, the Lee Valley, and the A40-A4 corridor were seen as the areas of opportunity in London's development, a perception supported by LPAC and reinforced by GOL's allocation of the single regeneration budget. The partnership promoted sub-regional initiatives and cross-sector alliances as an implicit alternative to the new greater London authority sought by the Labour boroughs. GOL appeared to view the partnership as the optimal framework within which London's problems were to be addressed. Labour's involvement, in turn, was seen as conditional and probably short-term.

As a result of these initiatives, promoting London internationally received a major boost, with efforts focusing on the creation of a new 'environment for sale'. This became a government theme. Internationalism and economic liberalism were joined to a new concern for urban ambience stressing the 'look and feel' factors that were key to locational attractiveness. In policy terms, the initiative had material effects in moving infrastructure improvement, urban design, and transport in particular up the policy agenda and in introducing new concerns such as cultural quality (Chevrant-Breton 1997). The aim was to end the effective neglect of London's status as an international city. Nevertheless, the proliferation of organizations that sprang up following the abolition of the GLC, threatened disruption through lack of coordination despite the best efforts of Gummer's Joint London Advisory Panel. The CBI London regional director warned that it was 'axiomatic that inward investors—vital to the future economic success of London—could well be confused with such a plethora of agencies' (*Property Week*, 19 June 1998: 26). The need to tackle fragmentation with a greater degree of coordination was increasingly recognized as the 1990s advanced.

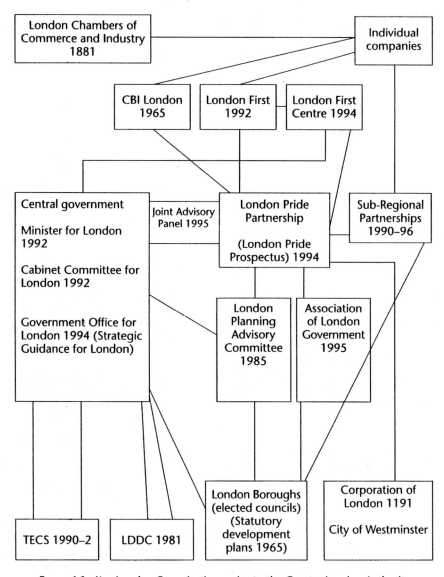

Figure 4.1: Key London Organizations prior to the Greater London Authority
Source: Adapted from Newman and Thornley (1997)

The split in the London Boroughs Association over GLC abolition had led to the formation of two rival associations, institutionalizing the differences that then existed between the parties over the future of London, with the ALA speaking for London boroughs and the LBA largely for the Conservatives. Rumours abounded of initiatives to seek a rapprochement between the two organizations, in London's interest. Leading politicians on both sides steadfastly refused to be drawn about private discussions on the subject. In 1994 the two associations reached preliminary agreement to set up a coordinating committee to consider London-wide policy issues. The ALA leaders intended that this should pave the way for a single association for the capital. The two political parties, so long opposed to each other on London issues, had now begun to draw together in recognition of the need for a bipartisan approach to some aspects of London governance. The outcome was a new single Association of London Government (ALG). Even so, some Conservative borough leaders feared that this single association would be a Trojan horse, designed to bring a strategic authority for London back onto the agenda (Biggs and Travers 1994).

Rethinking London Governance

None of these developments and initiatives, however, solved—or was thought to solve—the 'London problem'. Despite the Conservative government's victory at the end of its strenuous campaign to abolish the GLC, scarcely anyone believed that a permanent solution had been found. In the final months of its existence, the GLC had sponsored a major exercise to review and identify options for the future government of London. Its key areas of concern became the basis for a consultation in which the vast majority of responding organizations favoured the re-establishment of some kind of democratically elected strategic authority for the capital. A policy review presented to the 1989 Labour Party conference advocated far-reaching reforms of local government, prompting a refocusing of thought on London (GLC 1986). The party had entered the 1987 general election promising what looked rather like the re-establishment of the GLC. For the 1990 borough council elections the party's manifesto promised 'a new kind of democratically-elected strategic authority for London to plan, co-ordinate and promote the development of the capital as part of Labour's plan for a new national arm for regional government': an authority that could be lean and tightly managed (Labour Party 1990). The Labour group on the ALA sought to put flesh on the bones of this idea, insisting meanwhile that 'a new strategic authority for London should not simply replicate the GLC'.

Two years later, Labour's manifesto for the 1992 election promised a new metropolitan authority with responsibility for strategic planning, police, fire, and public transport for the existing area of Greater London. Labour thinking had moved on, and the party now eschewed the reinstatement of the GLC itself as involving too large a bureaucracy. Instead, it argued for a streamlined body to provide accountability for London-wide services and to articulate the views of Londoners.

It was an important shift. Labour now acknowledged that the greater degree of integration at the central government level, coupled with the deliberate involvement of London business that would characterize the post-1992 period, was in some respects an improvement on previous arrangements. It recognized that promotion was handled with new vigour, while cross-sector links had improved mutual understanding. Meanwhile, the London boroughs had in some respects become much more effective than they had been in the days of the GLC, and were starting to form their own partnerships across local boundaries on common issues. For the future, as even GOL officials conceded, something different would be needed. Recognizing the new realism in the Labour Party, one official recalled: 'We couldn't go back to the GLC structure—and what is the right structure that will provide enough leadership without the bureaucracy?'

That was the question to which almost all London's players were addressing themselves. Meanwhile, the Labour Party was rethinking its approach to regional government and urban regeneration. In 1995, Keith Vaz set up the City 2020 initiative, which proposed the recasting of the Single Regeneration Budget and the establishment of a Civic Forum bringing together local business and political leaders in each city. Such a Forum would prepare a Civic Plan for the allocation of funding on the basis of objective indicators of need. A Minister for Urban Regeneration was proposed to take overall responsibility for such arrangements.

In parallel with this initiative, Labour launched a major study of regional policy under the chairmanship of Bruce Millan, a former European Commissioner for Regional Policy. The remit of this study was

To discuss how regional economic and social policy can be integrated within a democratically accountable regional government framework, building on Labour's commitments to devolve power to a Scottish Parliament and Welsh Assembly, and to regional government for England. (Labour Party 1996a: 2)

The Regional Policy Commission recommended the establishment of regional development agencies as the 'executive arms' of the regional assemblies, with responsibilities for economic development, regeneration, and promotion of regional competitiveness and business efficiency. There was a strong preference for elected bodies in the place of a plethora of non-elected quangos. The Commission said nothing about London, but it was implied that London would be treated as a region in its own right.

As the general election expected in 1996 or 1997 approached, Labour was bound to place new proposals for London government in its campaign showcase. With public attachment to the GLC fading, the time seemed ripe for fresh thinking about London. The Labour manifesto for the 1994 London borough elections, *Working Together for London,* had made the point that London was the only capital city in Western Europe that lacked city-wide government and an overall strategy. The same document castigated the Conservatives for their inability to deal with London's problems, something which was attributed to an alleged unwillingness to 'trust Londoners'. In fighting on such a platform Labour promised to turn back the 'tide of decline' and carry out the tasks that had been vested in 'bureaucratic quangos' since the abolition of the GLC.

'London needs a voice', the manifesto declared, 'a body that speaks for all of London to carry weight in Whitehall. Only a directly elected body can have this legitimacy.' Meanwhile, London's new single association, the ALG, claimed that rationalization and central service provision could deliver substantial savings and

In the longer term establishing the strategic authority could offer scope for much larger savings on service delivery by major London-wide devolved services . . . by allowing them to improve co-ordination, acquire facilities jointly, and share core administrative functions. (ALG 1996: 12)

Opponents, however, argued that such a proposal for a strategic authority for London could result in a 'London Tax' which would have a negative impact on inward investment and promote relocation of London-based companies.

A number of prominent Labour politicians including Tony Banks, a former close associate of Livingstone and chairman of the GLC, and Margaret Hodge, the former leader of Islington Council and newly elected MP for Barking, had picked up Michael Heseltine's proposal for a directly elected mayor and advocated such a solution for London. So too had Simon Jenkins, former *Times* editor, *Evening Standard* journalist, and influential writer on London affairs. Approaching the issue from different angles, they succeeded in linking Michael Heseltine's shelved proposal for directly elected mayors to the idea, by now universally supported in Labour circles, that Greater London needed a democratic government. The mayoral bandwagon had begun to roll. How far it travelled would depend on the response of the party leader. Tony Blair was believed to be temperamentally sympathetic to US-style city management. He was certainly no friend of the old Labour tradition in local government, and was seeking an alternative, non-Tory approach. Thus he was open to suggestions made in a report by the Commission for Local Democracy, chaired by Simon Jenkins, which set out some advantages of having a directly elected executive mayor:

The post would be highly visible and thus highly accountable. Local decisions would be more readily identified with one person than with the more abstract notion of a party group. We accept that this might increase the role of 'personality' in British local government. We see this as no bad thing in boosting public interest and turnout at elections. Local elections might be dragged back from being national opinion polls to show more concern for local issues. . . . A network of elected Leaders/Mayors would provide a more powerful voice for local government in Whitehall and Westminster. Their visibility and elected status would give them the opportunity and the authority to speak, negotiate and make demands on behalf of their communities. The innovation offers a means of bridging together the fragments of central-local government relations and attracting media attention to local government. In particular it would help restore the political self-confidence of the big cities and re-identify local leadership with local democratic institutions. (CLD 1995: 22)

Jenkins claims that his advocacy was decisive. 'The great battle was to get it into the manifesto', he recalled. 'I saw Blair for an hour and he got out a bottle of whisky and said "persuade me"' (D'Arcy and MacLean 2000: 8). No doubt there were also other influences, including a visit made by Blair and Gordon Brown to the United States shortly after the 1992 Labour defeat, to view Clinton's 'New Democrat' experiments.

At any rate the idea swiftly became identified with Blair after his election as Labour leader. Blair first floated the idea of a directly elected mayor for London in his John Smith memorial lecture in February 1996 (Carvel 1999: 254). Britain, he argued, had 'the most centralised government of any large state in the world . . . None has such an extraordinary degree of power held in the hands of central government'. He conceded that the proposal was controversial, and had yet to become party policy, but threw his personal weight behind the idea, exposing himself as an enthusiast for a New York-style executive mayor. He wanted to see local government reorganized around small executives, with most councillors relegated to a representative and scrutiny role. Impressed by Mayor Rudi Giuliani's achievements in New York, and hostile to the English municipal traditions, he was contemptuous of the committee system and suspicious of what he saw as the endemic failings and inefficiencies of local government. A mayor would provide a clear 'voice' for the local area. Focusing authority would establish clearer lines of accountability locally by making it explicit who should be held responsible when things went wrong. At the same time, through bypassing the traditional committee cycle, mayoral power would expedite decision making and make it easier to take action.

Meanwhile, Blair recognized—up to a point—that a directly elected mayor for London would have a powerful mandate and would pose a potential challenge to central government. However he saw this as a creative tension. Behind this kite-flying lay a sharp division of view between the party leader and his shadow environment secretary Frank Dobson. While Blair may have been persuaded, many colleagues were not, arguing that an elected mayor would reduce the role of elected councillors. Whereas Blair had no roots in local government and had an unabashed antipathy towards it, Dobson had many years of local government service, including a period as leader of Camden council. Dobson was opposed to the idea of an elected mayor on the grounds that such a system put too much power in the hands of one individual and hence was an unacceptable departure from a tradition of local democracy that made councillors collectively responsible for decisions. He also argued, with good reason, that there was little support within the Labour Party for such an innovation. Hence he was reportedly determined to defeat Blair's plan, arguing instead for an *indirectly* elected mayor, without the popular mandate of a directly elected one, drawn from the members of a Greater London Authority. Thus, Dobson seems to have used his position as environment spokesman to delay the drafting of the long-awaited policy document on London, and to ensure that the proposals for a London mayor eventually put forward within it were couched in general terms. In his hesitancy about the mayoral proposals, Dobson represented the view of a great number of Labour councillors who had little interest in losing their power to a single individual either in London or elsewhere in the country. Meanwhile, Simon Jenkins claimed that his own advocacy was directed against precisely these kind of people, as 'a frontal assault on the old politics, on the clubs, cliques and cabals that have blighted Labour and local government alike' (*ES*, 9 February 1996).

In April 1996 Labour published *A Voice for London* (Labour Party 1996*b*), the consultation document on the election manifesto that Dobson had been working on. For the first time, the proposal was put forward for a Greater London Authority (GLA)—not Council—which would take an area-wide view but which would not be directly responsible for the provision of services. Instead, the GLA would promote economic, transport, planning, environmental, and policing strategies as well as inward investment. Those services for which it would be responsible, such as fire and police, would be run at arms length through appointed boards. While this framework was entirely new, it was arguably a logical extension of the post-abolition thinking. Politically, it reflected the prevailing New Labour view that few votes were to be gained by proposing the restoration of the GLC, an institution which had come to be regarded by the public at best with ambivalence. That the authority might be complemented by an elected mayor was put forward only tentatively. 'Such an approach', it said, would 'be quite new in Britain, changing the role of the elected assembly and its individual members and leaving one person in a much more powerful position than had been customary. We invite Londoners' views' (Carvel 1999: 253–4).

Those Londoners whose views were to be heard, however, were mainly the constituency and trade union delegates who came together to discuss the proposals in June 1996. The half-hearted proposal for a directly elected mayor evoked little enthusiasm, but no vote was to be taken (Carvel 1999: 255). The *Voice for London* was attacked as ultra-cautious, Dobson having significantly watered down plans for a powerful elected mayor for London (D'Arcy and Maclean 2000: 9). Although the party's National Executive had approved the plan, Blair was clearly embarrassed, his spokesman briefing that there was no split with Dobson on the issue. Meanwhile, Dobson predicted that Londoners would in due course get an elected mayor. From the Tory side, John Gummer, the Environment Secretary, attacked Labour's plan for 'son of GLC', exploiting the disagreement between Blair and his environment spokesman (*ES*, 9 July 1996). In fact, the Conservatives were themselves split, with Michael Heseltine identified as the original author of the fashion for executive mayors. Heseltine fended off his Conservative critics by arguing that a mayor for London was a step too far: his own 1991 proposals, which found little favour within the world of local government, had never mentioned the capital (*ES*, 17 April 1996).

By January 1997 Blair had overcome opposition within his party, promising the creation of a strong executive mayor, apparently believing that the proposal would gain votes in London in the forthcoming general election. Old Labour opponents were reported to be fighting a 'rearguard action' to have the mayor drawn from the largest party on the new Greater London Authority.

Blair, however, was determined to have a directly elected mayor in the election manifesto. Speaking at a second *ES* debate on the future of London, and having tested the temperature the previous February, he now came out more strongly than ever as an advocate of mayoral government for London. 'Strong civic leadership', he proclaimed,

could help restore some of the much needed civic pride in London. It could provide vision and a direction for London's future, someone to drive the development of the city, to pull together the partnerships needed to make things happen. (Carvel 1999: 255)

London needed 'a galvanising powerful vision of its future' and 'for a vision, there does need to be a voice'. Acknowledging the opposition, Blair nonetheless committed himself to creating not just an elected mayor for London but also a similar opportunity for the other great cities across the country as a 'spur for the renewal of local democracy'. Many in the party remained unconvinced, with Labour MPs split along 'Old' and 'New' Labour lines. More important, scarcely any of London's Labour council leaders supported direct election. How could there be an elected mayor against the wishes of London's representatives? New Labour had a legitimizing answer: to widen the debate by promising a London-wide referendum.

The manifesto arguments settled London's future. A GLA would comprise an elected assembly together with a separately elected mayor and would have wide-ranging powers of appointment and direction over the major metropolitan services, including police and transport. In May 1997, the long-awaited general election produced its predicted result, though with an even larger Labour majority than had been anticipated. Blair became Prime Minister with a mandate, and unquestioned parliamentary means, to carry out manifesto commitments. At the same time, it helped that the Chancellor had committed himself to a cautious budgetary programme. Hence, reforms that appeared radical yet involved little increase in expenditure had a high priority. The greater London proposal was one of them. There was also the additional spur that Labour's results in London were particularly favourable. The swing from Conservatives to Labour of 12.5 per cent was by far the largest in Britain (Geddes and Tonge 1997: 11).

Whatever the view in the Labour Party, there was wider non-party backing. The high-profile business group London First came out in support of an executive mayor or 'governor' for London, although it preferred one untrammelled by an elected assembly. Speaking to the London First conference following his election triumph, Blair acknowledged the business community's role in shaping the agenda and proclaimed the mayor's office to be

an immensely powerful position with the mandate of five million voters. It needs to be, because the challenges London faces are immense . . .What we need is government, business and the new Mayor to work together for the good of all London. That should be our aim so that we can make this city and our country ready to face the next century even stronger than it leaves this one. (*ES*, 9 September 1999)

Meanwhile, arraigned against the Prime Minister and the business community were the local authority leaders. Lord Bowness, Conservative former chairman of London Boroughs Association and Croydon Leader, rushed to the defence of the status quo, dismissing the 'transatlantic' proposal for an elected mayor as containing 'serious ambiguities and contradictions' (*ES*, 9 September 1996). He argued that the dynamic factors in making London well governed were the energy and initiative of the boroughs and the support and the coordination of ministers. The principal problem of London was that of transport, and it was here, he claimed, that Steven Norris, as Transport Minister for London, had been such a success. However, the opponents of a mayor for London were now powerless and isolated, while the proposal seemed to have caught the public imagination. A MORI survey in November 1996 showed 72 per cent of those questioned supporting a Greater London Authority, with 58 per cent in favour of a directly elected mayor.

To avoid any chance of backsliding, Blair did not offer Dobson Environment, his shadow responsibility, but made him Secretary of State for Health instead. Local government reform became the responsibility of the Deputy Prime Minister, John Prescott. This reshuffling of portfolios took away an important source of resistance, but it also reduced the opportunity for informed debates. One result was that the London mayor proposal was not only one of the most emphatic in the government's immediate programme; it was also one of the least considered in advance. The disagreement between Blair and Dobson had prevented the issue from being worked out within the party or becoming the subject of pre-election discussions between shadow ministers and civil servants. When the new ministers took up their posts the government had still to begin its detailed assessment of how London was to be governed.

5

A New Government for London

AFTER the election events moved rapidly. The Prime Minister's office briefed on Blair's determination to act immediately, while the new Minister for London, Nick Raynsford prepared the ground. The first stage was to seek, and get, public endorsement. To achieve this a London referendum bill was included in the Queen's speech, offering Londoners the opportunity to express their view on whether or not to have an elected mayor as the centrepiece of a new Greater London Authority. The referendum was set for May 1998, with a view to inaugurating the new authority, and mayor, two years later.

While the referendum bill was before Parliament, the government published a consultation paper, *New Leadership for London*, and invited responses. These in turn were fed into the proposals in the subsequent White Paper *A Mayor and Assembly for London*, which was also heavily based on recommendations from non-governmental consultants. The drafting of the Greater London Authority Bill in itself gave rise to criticism, and the bill was much revised as it proceeded through Parliament, with the government tabling a large number of amendments of its own. Nevertheless, as the Greater London Authority Act 1999 it completed its passage and became law in the autumn of the same year, bringing the new Mayor and the Assembly into being in two stages, with an election on 4 May 2000 and transfer of power eight weeks later on 3 July.

The Government's Proposals

When the new ministers took office, civil servants had done some preparation on the basis of the party's manifesto and Blair's speeches in particular. They were able, one recalled later, to present the new minister with a series of questions along the lines of 'do you want a strong mayor or a weak mayor? Small assembly or a big assembly?' Raynsford was talked through the list and within the first week or two the main outlines had taken shape, including the nature of the mayor's powers. In this way, the text of the Green Paper was ready for Cabinet approval by the end of June. Encouraged by Raynsford, officials looked abroad for inspiration as they fleshed out the proposals: to New York, Boston, and Washington, to Cologne, Barcelona, and Paris. There were exploratory visits. One civil servant later claimed New York to have been 'absolutely seminal. Both in terms of what we should do and what we shouldn't do. Lots of the issues were decided in our minds by those visits to America'. Yet officials recognized that local government in the US and Britain had very different political roots:

There are lots of elected positions in American cities that don't really seem to contribute. They are mainly there for historical reasons . . . I suppose we came away with a feeling that we wanted to create something that was more inclusive and more likely to work in a consensual way . . . I guess we came up with a sort of hybrid and whether that will work? I don't know.

New Leadership for London inaugurated a consultative process on 61 questions, which by the end of October had attracted more than 1,200 responses, 45 per cent of them from organizations. They showed overwhelming support for the basic approach and were fed into the preparation of the subsequent White Paper. Accordingly, the *Mayor and Assembly for London* proposed a new forum to provide democratic leadership, to continue to promote London as a world city, and to bridge the gap between community-led and national government. 'Elsewhere in the world', it proclaimed, executive mayors 'have made a positive difference to the lives of their citizens and the communities they serve.' Here in Britain 'the capital needs leadership' as well as 'someone who will work with the grain of London, bringing the people, the boroughs, the private and voluntary sectors together to tackle the real issues' (DETR 1998*a*: 2).

The new arrangements for London centred on a new elected body—the Greater London Assembly—and the Mayor. Together, the elective elements would constitute the Greater London Authority. This new authority was to be responsible for strategic planning, transport, economic development and regeneration, environmental protection and culture, media and leisure, the metropolitan police and fire, and civil defence. Although the ultimate responsibility of the new GLA, not all of these functions were to come under its direct day-to-day control. Some would be run through arms-length agencies. Thus, only four of the existing pan-London organizations—the London Research Centre (LRC), the London Planning Advisory Committee (LPAC), the London Ecology Unit (LEU), and the London Pensions Fund Authority (LPFA)—were absorbed into the GLA itself to become key components of the organization.

Other bodies providing the key metropolitan functions were to be kept separate from the GLA, but were to be accountable to it through the Mayor appointing their board members. Transport for London (TfL) was to absorb London Transport and the functions of the Traffic Director for London, together with some of the functions of the highways agencies and the Government Office for London. Transport for London was to be given overall responsibility for roads, buses, trains, and the underground, managing the traffic light system and regulating taxis and mini-cabs. The Mayor would not only appoint the members of the TfL board but also have the right to chair their meetings. His overriding responsibility would be to draw these several modes of transport together through the preparation of an integrated transport strategy for the capital. The London Development Agency (LDA) was to become a major instrument of economic growth policies, taking over from central government funds for inward investment and regeneration—including the Single Regeneration Budget—and the land-acquisition and development powers of English Partnerships. Its creation would parallel that of the Regional Development Agencies elsewhere in England.

Two new bodies responsible for public safety were to enjoy a rather different relationship with the GLA and the Mayor. The new Metropolitan Police Authority (MPA) was the first such locally accountable body in London's history, funded through the Mayor, who was to appoint assembly members to eleven, later twelve, places on the 23-strong Board. The London Fire and Emergency Planning Authority (LFEPA) was to be similarly structured. A number of other bodies, including the London Boroughs Grants—formerly the London Boroughs Grants Committee—the London Ambulance Service, and the Lee Valley Regional Park Authority remained outside. The first of these was eventually taken under the umbrella of the ALG. For their part, the London boroughs and the City of London, with some minor exceptions, would continue to be responsible for the delivery of local services. Although the relationships established by the Greater London Authority Act were complex, the new plan amounted to a substantial streamlining of the government of London.

The Mayor was given significant planning powers as regards both overall strategy and development control. He would be responsible for preparing a spatial development strategy for the improvement of London's physical fabric, housing, culture, recreation, economic regeneration, social inclusion, and London's role as a world financial centre: in effect, a London plan. The boroughs would remain local planning authorities, but where the Mayor considered that an application for a large-scale development contravened the London-wide strategy, he could direct the borough to reject the application. On the other hand he would not be able to direct approval, while any rejected applicant could still appeal to the Secretary of the State. Alongside the spatial development strategies, specific strategies were required for environmental improvement. Here again, day-to-day responsibility remained with the boroughs but the Mayor was to be given some powers to compel them to act in accordance with the strategies.

A New Conception for London

In one vital respect the new government for London was intended to be radically different from its predecessors. The GLC had been created without any clear conception of what a strategic authority might do. Despite the common view of the 1960s as a time when strategic planning was fashionable, little was actually done to achieve a clear conception of what it might mean in a London context. Hence, the GLC pretended to plan without really doing so. Its critics accused it of being no more than 'the LCC writ large'. Not until the 1978 Marshall Inquiry was a serious attempt made to work out a philosophy for metropolitan governance, by which time the GLC's days were already numbered. When Labour came to power in 1997 there was a concern not to repeat what was perceived as the tendency of the GLC merely to drift. Thus, Nick Raynsford drew a sharp contrast between the former authority and the GLA, arguing that the government was proposing not another GLC but a new form of city-wide government, streamlined and strategic, headed by a directly-elected Mayor (*Hansard*, 6 June 1997).

The 'strategic' aspects of the new authority emerged from a vigorous debate involving policy-makers, commentators, and vested interests. Key elements were provided by the Institute of Public Policy Research (IPPR), whose joint report with KPMG was published by the City Corporation (IPPR and KPMG 1997). The government's Green Paper *New Leadership for London* prompted the IPPR to develop its case in the context of the consultation exercise. The IPPR was emphatic in its espousal of a new direction for London. Although it acknowledged that there had been 'no immediate and obvious disaster which could be attributed to the lack of a pan-London governance structure' it nevertheless identified an important missing element, that of an overall coordinating body. The capital, the IPPR argued, 'does not need a general city-wide service provider. Plugging the gaps in London's governance does not amount to a call for the reinstatement of the GLC.' Such a return to the past 'would be against the principle of making a service delivery body responsive by keeping them as close as possible to the community they serve' (IPPR and KPMG 1997: A3, A10).

The most important novelty in the IPPR's proposals concerned the political accountability of the Mayor and Assembly. The IPPR's authors looked back to the Commission for Local Democracy's proposals for a separation of powers between an assembly and the directly elected mayor. Unlike the CLD, however, the IPPR was sceptical of the notion that there was much to be learnt from mayoral government in other countries. In particular, it pointed out that US mayors operated in an entirely different political structure and 'this may not be the correct place to look for detailed lessons'. The German and Italian examples were also different in that city government in these countries had been reconstituted as part of the post-war restoration of democracy. Overall, 'national political cultures and legal systems vary. It is therefore misguided to hope to find ready-made solutions to London's problems abroad'. Perhaps the most important limitation on this kind of crude policy transfer was that the other countries usually considered the mayoralty to be 'part of the local government structure that has direct responsibility for the delivery of public services'. As such, mayors commonly sat at the apex of large administrations. The creation of a Greater London Authority thus required a leap of faith. There was nothing in British political experience that provided a model for it.

The second novelty of the IPPR's proposals was the attempt to think through the problems of institutional design in which 'a capacity for direction, steering and regulation' could be reconciled with a need for diffusion of political power. Such a diffusion was considered appropriate for an agency whose role was not to deliver services but to lead, to facilitate relationships, and to develop the widest possible network of partnerships. In part, this was to be achieved through checks and balances and an elaborate system of constraints to prevent an undue concentration of power in the mayoral office. In the view of the IPPR, the relationship between the Assembly and the Mayor was the key to the success of the new system. Division of power between them was essential to ensure that 'each had something to bargain with and to exercise functions through'. A division of power, however, raised the possibility of deadlock, particularly if the Mayor and the Assembly majority were from different parties. In order to avert the risk of deadlock, the IPPR made a number of proposals including time limits on certain key decisions and a requirement to publish papers 'so that any disagreements between the mayor and assembly are aired in public'.

If the division of responsibility between Mayor and Assembly was the first mechanism by which the diffusion of power was to be achieved, the second involved restricting the role of political parties. Here the IPPR took a stance that was self-consciously at odds with recent political history. Given the party dominance of British local government 'the mayoral system that is built around shared partisan loyalties would clearly go with the grain of our traditions and current institutions as it allows scope for the management of the system through party politics' (IPPR and KPMG 1997: A21). The risk of deadlock between the Mayor and Assembly would not arise if, as was the case elsewhere in local government, the leadership role operated with the support of a politically compliant representative body. On the other hand, it was also important to ensure that political conflict was contained. The IPPR concluded that 'while recognising that it is likely that group voting will take place on the budget and major policy statement, we believe that it is desirable for party discipline to be less prominent than is currently the case at both national and local levels' (IPPR and KPMG 1997: A21). As there could be no prohibition on party candidacy and no obvious way to ensure that party discipline did not intrude, the diffusion of power would have to be sought through a combination of elaborate constitutional arrangements, and an electoral system designed to prevent any party achieving dominance.

Although the very concept of an executive mayor appeared to imply a weak assembly, the IPPR view was that the Assembly would and should have a substantial and positive input into the decision-making process rather than remain a mere forum for harassing and embarrassing the Mayor. Despite these protestations, the IPPR scheme appeared to be designed to sustain a strong mayoral role. The prestige of the Mayor's office and the strength of his mandate could be expected to carry considerable political momentum. Thus, the IPPR proposed that appointments to the Mayor's office should not need for-

mal ratification by the Assembly and that they should be essentially political.
The IPPR also advocated extending this principle to the senior official posts. It
acknowledged that the practice of making political appointments 'politicises
senior officers and undermines the tradition of a neutral, non-partisan civil
and local government service'. But this new body would be different: 'the role
of an executive Mayor implies a new type of relation with senior officers. The
latter will need to have a sharper identification with and responsibility to the
Mayor, supplying policy as well as managerial advice' (IPPR and KPMG 1997:
A25).

Against this considerable accumulation of mayoral power, 'the Assembly
will have a key role to play'. In fact, however, the conception amounted to little more than a scrutiny role, explicitly likened to that of a parliamentary
select committee:

The Assembly should certainly have a capacity to initiate discussion on particular policy matters itself, in addition to debating proposals from the mayor. This will allow it to
do more than simply vote for or against executive proposals. Policy matters could be
referred to the mayor who would then have to address them in the context of his financial and policy plans. (IPPR and KPMG 1997: A26)

Whereas the IPPR section of the joint report dealt with political sensibilities,
the KPMG part focused on executive action. KPMG proposed standing committees on finance, land-use planning, transport, economic development,
police, housing, environment, fire and civil defence, and arts and leisure, with
an additional role for the assembly to consider reports from four scrutiny commissions. Scrutiny of the Mayor, accountable bodies, and other London bodies should be undertaken through these standing committees which would
conduct public hearings and enable assembly members to make formal recommendations to which the Mayor must respond.

The KPMG paper went so far as to put forward a clear organizational structure with the key positions and staff resources required to support the work of
the Mayor and the Assembly. The role of the Mayor's office was envisaged as
supporting him in developing and implementing strategic policies and initiatives, setting and controlling the budget for the GLA, dealing with press and
public enquiries, and undertaking public functions. The private office would
have the overall responsibility of coordinating policy, finance and administration, and more specifically, providing the administrative and secretarial
support and acting as a link between the Mayor and the Assembly. In effect,
these two consultants' proposals called for a new style of managerial, consensual politics. Both suggested that political conflicts and disagreements
between the Mayor and the Assembly were to be resolved within the
Authority. Collaborative working was essential so as to encourage the third
parties—the government, regulatory bodies, and the private sector—to implement a particular course of action.

This, then, was the state of the debate on the governance of London when
the government held its promised referendum of the proposals in May 1998,

a dress rehearsal for the mayoral contest itself. Possible candidates were already staking out their positions, while a dispute over the terms of the referendum question threw into sharp relief the central issue of the reform: the location of the executive and representative functions in London's new government.

Asking Londoners

Since it was a general-election manifesto commitment, the planned GLA arguably did not need separate endorsement in a referendum. On the other hand, a referendum that produced a positive result would have the advantage from the government's point of view of giving the new authority added legitimacy. By the same token, it also gave it a quasi-constitutional status. As one civil servant interviewed pointed out, it was 'an odd thing to do in a way because they had very recently voted for a government that was committed to doing it. But again, it makes it harder to abolish if the administration changes'. The second aspect, of course, could be a mixed benefit.

The London Referendum Bill was published on 29 October 1997. The vote was to be held on 7 May 1998, simultaneously with the London Borough Council elections. Labour Party activists at first responded negatively to the government's plan. Some demanded that the mayor should be drawn from the ranks of the elected assembly members, while others supported the assembly being given tax-raising powers (*ES*, 24 November 1997). Significantly, Ken Livingstone, the single personality most associated in the public mind with the idea of a powerful mayor, and widely assumed to aspire to that post, came out against a directly elected office holder and threw his weight behind a campaign to give London instead a GLC-type elected assembly with tax-raising powers. Claiming that only four of London's 57 Labour MPs and few ordinary Londoners supported the proposal for a directly elected mayor, Livingstone attacked it as 'barmy' (*ES*, 23 October 1997). Concern about the intensity of opposition within the party led the Labour leadership to postpone the London regional conference due in February 1998 until after the referendum. The prospect loomed of delegates voting against the 'integrated' Mayor and Assembly referendum question, so opening the door to a strong assembly with taxing powers and without a separately elected mayor. Constituency parties, including those of key Department of the Environment, Transport and the Regions (DETR) ministers, flooded headquarters with expressions of concern, Hampstead and Highgate expressing 'unease about the quasi-presidential role of the Mayor' (*ES*, 12 December 1997).

Meanwhile, the Conservatives under William Hague had changed their policy and now supported the creation of a directly elected mayor, while opposing a directly-elected assembly. In early 1998 the party's position was that an assembly 'would impose [on London] an unnecessary and confusing layer of government on top of the already existing structures' (Yeo 1998: 9). A few months later, this had been abandoned in favour of the view that the Assembly's members should be drawn directly from the 32 boroughs, thereby building on the existing base of inter-borough joint action (Beresford 1998). Thus Richard Ottaway, the Conservative front-bench spokesman on local government, recast the party line with a declaration that 'while a mayor would be hugely beneficial to London', without a base in the boroughs 'members of the Assembly will have little in common—and little contact—with the London boroughs, there will inevitably be clash and conflict between the new authority and them' (Ottaway 1998: 28). The Tories were not against a mayor and assembly, just against this kind of mayor and assembly; and Lord Bowness, former Leader of Croydon and LBA chairman, led the opposition to the bill in the House of Lords.

There were now three bodies of opinion: that of many Labour—and Liberal Democrat—activists who sought an assembly without a directly-elected mayor; that of the Conservatives who now wanted a directly-elected mayor but without an elected assembly; and the government's own view that both were required. A DETR spokesman commented that 'a Mayor without an Assembly would not work, and neither would an Assembly without a Mayor' (*ES*, 24 November 1997). The government sidestepped the problem by posing a single referendum question that offered a stark choice: 'Are you in favour of the Government's proposals for a Greater London Authority?' With this question, Nick Raynsford claimed, 'Londoners will know what they're voting for. This is the only way we can have a clear mandate to go forward if Londoners vote Yes' (*ES*, 22 December 1997).

The scheme's opponents, within the Labour Party and outside it, naturally disliked the single question. The Conservatives wanted two questions, asking Londoners 'do you want the Mayor?' and 'do you want the Assembly?' 'While London would clearly have said "yes" to the mayor', according to the Tory spokesman later, 'it is far from certain that they would have said "yes" for the assembly. What's more, the government knows it, which is why it did not allow two questions' (Ottaway 1998: 28). Having lost the issue in the Commons, the opponents continued the battle in the Lords, where a majority of peers, persuaded that Londoners were being asked to take a leap in the dark, voted for a postponement of the referendum until such a time as full details had been published. The victory was a temporary one. The government was able to use its majority in the Commons to get the referendum bill back on schedule, offering as its excuse that Londoners would have sufficient opportunity to study the government's proposals, as the White Paper was to be published ahead of the referendum date together with an explanatory leaflet to be issued six weeks before the vote.

A 'Yes' vote campaign was established in January 1998 under Labour auspices, with Trevor Phillips, the London Weekend Television (LWT) presenter, at its head. A number of groups were set up to campaign against the government's proposal. Most important was Communities First, set up by a former Conservative councillor, Simon Fawthrop, campaigning on borough rights, and claiming that the assembly would be an expensive talking shop and the mayoralty 'an ineffective ego trip' (*ES*, 21 April 1998). Londoners, it argued, neither wanted nor needed another layer of bureaucracy, and the proposed Greater London Authority would do little to solve London's problems. The other principal 'No' campaign was established by Simon Randall, a Bromley Conservative who had played a crucial part in the abolition of the GLC. The title Randall chose for his group—'Oh No, Not the New GLC'—was intended to evoke the spectre of the old Council's alleged extremism. Neither group seems to have made more than a negligible impact on the referendum campaign.

Tony Blair launched the Labour manifesto for the referendum on 1 April 1998 under the title *Let's Get London Moving*. The manifesto declared ringingly that

London faces serious problems. We know, for example, that the transport system is creaking at the seams. We know that too many Londoners live in fear of crime, that in many places the city is dirty and run-down and the air quality is poor, and we know that there are still not enough opportunities for work. These are London problems and they demand London solution . . . The government can't do everything and London needs its own voice in shaping the City's future.

The government's slogan 'London Decides When You Decide' was intended to present the referendum as a genuine choice. The main anxiety was not that the proposal would be defeated but that support for it would be embarrassingly *sotto voce*. With London local election turn-out typically below 40 per cent, the fear was of mass abstention. The fear was justified. Although the referendum on 7 May coincided with the London borough elections, only 34 per cent of voters bothered to take part in it. Those who did vote, however, supported the proposal by 72 per cent to 28 per cent. Support was proportionally strongest in working-class boroughs like Hackney, Newham, and Southwark, but turn-out was greater in middle-class areas like Bromley and Kingston, where the 'No' vote was relatively higher.

It was a muted triumph for New Labour. However, it was combined with a growing, in some circles almost poignant, irony. For Blair's success in gaining Londoners' support for his scheme was sharply reduced, if it was not removed altogether, by a dawning realization that the strongest contender for the Labour nomination for the post of mayor was the one person the Prime Minister least wanted to be elected. The emerging nightmare of a Livingstone bid, in the absence of a plausible Labour alternative, was unlikely to go away. However, it was now too late to go back. To a large extent, the drafting of the bill became an exercise in damage limitation.

An Idea into Law

A simple and symbolically powerful idea—an elected mayor for London—involved a major legislative operation. It was a process, recalled a member of

TABLE 5.1. Result and turn-out in the London referendum

Borough	Yes vote (%)	Turn-out (%)
Barking and Dagenham	73.5	25.1
Barnet	69.6	35.7
Bexley	63.3	35.0
Brent	78.4	36.6
Bromley	57.1	40.2
Camden	81.2	33.3
City of London	63.0	30.6
Croydon	64.7	37.6
Ealing	76.5	33.2
Enfield	67.2	33.2
Greenwich	74.8	32.6
Hackney	81.6	34.5
Hammersmith and Fulham	77.9	34.1
Haringey	83.8	30.2
Harrow	68.8	36.6
Havering	60.5	34.2
Hillingdon	63.1	34.8
Hounslow	74.6	32.3
Islington	81.5	35.0
Kensington and Chelsea	70.3	28.2
Kingston upon Thames	68.7	41.3
Lambeth	81.8	32.0
Lewisham	78.4	30.1
Merton	72.2	37.9
Newham	81.4	28.7
Redbridge	70.2	35.6
Richmond upon Thames	70.8	45.0
Southwark	80.7	33.0
Sutton	64.8	35.2
Tower Hamlets	77.5	35.6
Waltham Forest	73.1	34.1
Wandsworth	74.3	39.3
Westminster	71.5	31.9

Source: DETR figures.

the bill team, 'really of turning the one paragraph, or two, in the manifesto, into the largest piece of legislation in human history, or whatever it is—since the Government of India Act, or whenever . . . ' The team was around 30 strong at its peak, with a network across Whitehall of more than 60 officials. Close working relations were required with the Home Office, Cabinet Office, Downing Street, Department for Trade and Industry (DTI), and the DETR. A Cabinet committee on London met to agree papers on each aspect of the plan, particularly during the drafting of the White Paper and later as the legislation took shape. John Prescott chaired the committee; Nick Raynsford, as Minister for London, played a key role, supported by Glenda Jackson as Minister for Transport.

So complex a bill was never likely to be fine-tuned before its introduction. Only around the time of the referendum, the result of which was no surprise, did officials instruct counsel on the bill. One civil servant recalled:

I think the sheer scale of the stuff that was being generated by us and the terrible short-age of parliamentary counsel, meant that it just took a very long time to be drafted. And actually, I think that, probably, in retrospect, the department didn't put enough resources into the legal side as well. So there was lawyerish problems really, in turning thoughts into law . . . But the key constitutional bits were done in good order and in good time . . . [But] we were drafting large slugs of transport while we were in the House of Commons and the House of Lords, so we had to introduce oodles of amendments that annoyed people no end. I think a lot is made of its size and of the number of amend-ments, but I think in terms of the number of amendments per clause it wasn't all that abnormal, but in absolute terms it was a very big bill and there were lots of amendments. It was actually remarkably uncontentious and we had no hostile amendments to it at all in the end.

When the Greater London Bill was published it contained 277 clauses and was clearly set to occupy a considerable amount of parliamentary time. Introducing the second reading, John Prescott claimed the GLA would restore power to the people of London 'stripping away the shadowy committees, the burgeoning bureaucracies and the quangos created by our predecessors'. It proved less simple than that, and the government, as is often the case, was forced to think on its feet through the legislative process, introducing more than 500 additional amendments of its own. Civil servants were pleased that the bill had a smooth passage and gave credit to their ministers for being good at 'selling it'. A large number of representations were made and an official interviewed claimed to have made a point of being 'very good at talking to everybody about it . . . an open door to anyone who wanted to come in'. The aim was to make the legislative process as consensual as possible and that meant reaching agreement with interested groups, and the environmental lobby in particular, before votes were taken in Parliament. In this way, amend-ments sponsored by sympathetic MPs were minimized. As for the opposition parties, one observer recalled that 'basically they came quietly because I think they recognized that the time had come, there had been a referendum, there wasn't much mileage for them in causing trouble'. Almost the only contro-versial proposal made during the passage of the bill was for a power to be given to the Assembly to impeach the Mayor. The government vigorously resisted a Liberal Democrat amendment to that effect, officials privately conceding that the example of New York had made them wary of a provision that could para-lyse decision making.

What Freedom for London?

A key issue, as the bill took shape, was the inclusion of substantial reserve pow-ers whereby the Secretary of State could overrule decisions of the new author-ity. Conservative criticism was muted by their earlier decision not to oppose the creation of the Mayor, and centred instead on Tory concerns about the role of the Assembly. 'We were right to abolish the GLC', claimed Gillian

Sheppard, shadow environment secretary, referring to fears that the assembly would recreate that body, 'and we make no apology for doing so' (*Hansard*, 14 December 1998). Conservative backbenchers similarly claimed the new authority would create opportunities for conflict and a clash of mandates between the Assembly and the boroughs.

None of this prevented them from pointing out, along with the Liberal Democrats, that the powers envisaged for the London Mayor had been massively reduced since they were first set out in Tony Blair's speeches. Instead, the question of whether the GLA was destined to be a powerful body became key, with those who had initially opposed its creation—and done nothing to bring it into being when they were in office—arguing for a set of rules that would render it innocuous. For example, clause 25 of the bill conferred powers on the GLA for the purpose of 'promoting economic and social development in Greater London and the improvement of the environment in Greater London', while clause 27 provided that 'the Secretary of State may by order . . . prevent the authority from doing . . . anything which is specified . . . in the order.' Richard Ottaway, the Opposition's London spokesman, poured scorn on the government's insistence on retaining control. 'In truth', he argued,

the first Mayor of London is going to be John Prescott because he is going to be having more powers than the Mayor. He is the man who is going to make all the decisions and he has got the powers to decide how the budget is spent. There are now grave doubts about whether the Mayor is going to be the man they thought he is going to be and the Assembly has been virtually emasculated. All they have got is a two-thirds veto on the budget. The rest of the time, they'll just be sitting around talking. (*Hansard*, 17 December 1998)

Government spokesmen claimed in their defence that the Secretary of State's powers were simply a reserve, with no expectation that they would be used. At this point, Ken Livingstone entered the frame, putting it slightly differently: the Secretary of State, he suggested, would in practice have political difficulties if he or she sought to overrule the GLA. 'We could get a judicial review of any decision by the Secretary of State that would be unreasonable or damaging to London', he maintained; 'they can't just play silly buggers' (*ES*, 17 December 1998).

There was also the argument that, after so much fuss, the GLA would be *expected* to be powerful, which might cause the government difficulties of a different order. Thus, Simon Hughes, the Liberal Democrat MP for Bermondsey, claimed that the Mayor would be 'attached to John Prescott's apron strings':

The public will assume that the Mayor will be very powerful, the level of expectation will be huge and there will be a great difficulty for the GLA and the Mayor to be able to deliver . . . There will be a demand for the power of the authority to grow and that will lead to more confrontation—not less—with the government. (*ES*, 17 December 1998)

These were perhaps the government's secret fears too. Nevertheless, John Prescott responded vigorously to this claim dismissing the suggestion that 'the

Mayor will be under Whitehall's thumb'. Instead, the London Mayor, elected to represent 5 million London voters, would, he insisted 'be a force to be reckoned with'. The bill provided for 'an enormous devolution of powers' from central government. 'The Mayor, not the government, will run transport in London, to name but one example' declared Prescott, pledging that money raised by congestion charges will be retained by the mayor for ten years (*ES*, 18 December 1998).

In the press, there was a feeling that the Deputy Prime Minister protested too much. Critics were unimpressed. An *Evening Standard* leader pointed out that neither Prescott nor Stephen Byers, the Treasury minister who had supported his claims, was likely to be in office in ten years time:

And all the while, the Treasury will be exerting pressure . . . Beside London, some 95 councils around the country are planning to introduce congestion charges, and a further 40 authorities want to introduce road tolls. The revenue from all these will amount to billions of pounds. How much chance is there, realistically, that the Treasury will not exert its powers to siphon off some of that money—and in London to insist, specifically, that Mayoral revenue be used to help fund such projects as Crossrail and the privatisation of the underground? It may be that Ken Livingstone is right, and that the Mayor with a mandate of five million London voters behind him can raise such an outcry that no Secretary of State will dare seize these tax revenues . . . Meanwhile we have to take it on trust that these Draconian powers given to Ministers and Whitehall are what we are asked to believe they are: prudent, failsafe measures put in place in case London one day gets as Mayor a modern equivalent of Genghis Khan. (*ES*, 23 December 1998)

An Act for London

The general powers of the GLA, as laid down in section 30(1) of the Act, began with a stirring statement of general competence, that 'the authority shall have power to do anything which it considers will further any one or more of its principal purposes'. This broad power was, however, qualified by a balancing power of the Secretary of State, who could issue guidance concerning the exercise of that power and setting out his ability to impose, by order, limits on the expenditure which might be incurred by the authority in pursuit of its general power. The authority was unable to spend money itself on housing, education, social or health services, or where the provision in question was made by a London borough council or other public body, although expenditure on 'co-operating with' these bodies or 'facilitating or co-ordinating their activities' was not ruled out. The aim of these limits was to prevent competition with London boroughs, and significant reserve powers were conferred on the Secretary of State who could, by order, extend the restriction on the GLA activities. A further limit to the GLA powers was that it was not permitted to spend on things that might be done by the functional bodies, that is, Transport for London, the London Development Agency, the Metropolitan Police Authority, and the London Fire and Emergency Planning Authority. Overall, the operation of the GLA powers was heavily circumscribed by a broad duty to consult with London local government, with the voluntary sector, with business, and with bodies representing London's racial, ethnic, national, and religious groups.

These limitations to the general power were explicitly related to the GLA's 'principal purposes'. They were defined as promoting economic development and wealth creation; promoting social development; and promoting the improvement in environment in Greater London. Moreover, in determining whether or how to exercise these general powers the GLA needed to have regard to its effects on the health of the people of Greater London and the achievement of sustainable development in the UK as a whole. It had to exercise them in a way in which it considered best calculated to enhance these two objectives.

The Mayor's specific role was to define policy objectives, to formulate London-wide strategies, and to ensure their implementation. A series of statutory strategies were laid down, but one of them, the Spatial Development Strategy (SDS), had special significance. It dealt with the spatial implications of all the other strategies and was subject to a series of requirements relating to its preparation and adoption in which various specified parties had formal procedural rights. The other strategies, by contrast, were prepared and published informally and the Mayor had simply to keep them under review and revise them in whatever way he considered necessary.

Other than the SDS, the other strategies were for transport, for economic development—prepared under the Regional Development Agencies Act 1998—for biodiversity to conserve and promote wildlife, for municipal waste management, and for air quality, ambient noise, and culture. These strategies had to be consistent with one another and with national policies and international agreements. They needed to pay regard to the availability of resources for their implementation. They also had to relate to the Authority's principal purposes and have regard to the health of Londoners, to sustainable development, and to the desirability of promoting and encouraging the safe use of the river Thames for both passenger transport and freight transportation. Some of these provisos, such as one requiring mutual consistency, seemed obviously necessary, while the need to have regard to the availability of resources indicated that the development of a strategy needed to be tempered by realism. The Mayor had also to set targets and objectives in relation to these strategies, and these needed be no less demanding than any existing national targets and objectives. With the exception of the SDS, where the Secretary of State's reserve powers were extensive, and the transport strategy, where the minister had certain powers of direction with regard to achieving consistency, the Secretary of State stood aside from the development of these strategies, empowered only to intervene if the Mayor was in default.

The requirement that the strategies must have regard to national policy—as well as international agreements—was a potential catch-all. Section 424 (1) of the Greater London Authority Act 1999 defined national policy as any policy statements which were 'available in written form and which . . . have been laid or announced before, or otherwise presented to, either House of Parliament; or . . . published by a Minister of the Crown'. This could cover almost any ministerial statement, and appeared to give carte blanche to central government to set the agenda for London should it choose to do so.

Crucial to the development of London's strategies was the relationship between the Mayor and the Assembly, the pivot on which the new government of London turned. A powerful elected mayor needed to be balanced by an elected forum where other political views or interests could be aired. To this end, the Assembly's primary duty was to secure the accountability of the Mayor on behalf of Londoners. It was responsible for scrutinizing all of the Mayor's activities and the bodies responsible for transport and economic development and could initiate scrutiny of such other issues as it judged to be of importance to London. The Assembly would participate in appointments and was expected to work closely with the Mayor on the budget and strategic priorities, approving or amending them as necessary.

This role allowed the Assembly to question the Mayor and his staff, to hold public hearings on issues of importance to them, and to have access to relevant people, papers, and technical expertise. The Mayor had to report to each meeting of the Assembly in written form, and was obliged to attend each meeting. He had also to provide an annual report on the exercise of his statutory functions, in particular progress on implementing the several strategies that the Act required him to prepare. Finally, he had to report such information as the Assembly might require at the beginning of the year to which his annual report related. Assembly members, for their part, could question the Mayor orally and in writing.

The relationship between the Mayor and the Assembly was seen as unique:

The authority is a new type of government organisation, to which the usual rules regarding collective action and responsibility cannot apply. The Mayor has . . . a degree of autonomy from the Assembly for which there is no parallel in local government generally, nor in central government or in statutory public bodies. Each is a component part of the authority, and neither has any independent existence from it. All action is taken by them on behalf of the authority. But the act then assigns functions between them. Certain actions may be taken on behalf of the authority by the Mayor acting alone or by the Assembly acting alone. Others require their joint action. The default position where no actor is specified is that the power is exercisable by the Mayor alone. (PEMB 2000: 35)

Thus, the principal executive power and authority were vested in the Mayor. In common with conventional local authorities, he or she would be unable to delegate functions to a single elected member of the Assembly, with the exception of the Deputy Mayor, who was part of the executive function of the Authority.

This separation of powers between the Mayor and the Assembly was central to the process of budget setting. The overriding consideration here was to prevent deadlock through an elaborate sequence of stages. First, and in advance of presenting the budget—which included a precept upon the London boroughs—to the Assembly, the Mayor was required to consult representatives of the Assembly about plans for the functional bodies and authorities. At the second stage, the budget and plans were presented in draft form to the Assembly for their consideration. By a simple majority of those voting, the Assembly could endorse the budget or propose amendments to improve or adjust the budget, giving reasons for its amendments. The Assembly was not permitted to reject the budget without amendment, and, if a majority in favour of amendment could not be mustered, the budget would be deemed to have been approved. Following consideration of any amendments and the Assembly's reasons for them, the Mayor presented the final budget to the Assembly. A vote was then taken to approve or amend the budget and the level of precept. Rejection at this stage required a two-thirds majority in favour of an alternative budget. Failure to gain such a majority meant that the Mayor's budgetary proposals would be passed and the budget, and precept, set.

All this added up to a marked asymmetry between the powers of the Mayor and those of the Assembly. Some felt that it rendered the Assembly toothless. One official involved in creating the plan saw it as a blueprint for a rubber-stamping body:

Well, the plan was to have a strong mayor. And so the intention was not to make it too easy for the assembly to block the mayor's proposals because we wanted a mayor to be accountable for his own proposal. We didn't want a situation where the mayor can say 'Oh well, I would have done this, that and the other but the assembly has been blocking it.' So there was an ability for the assembly to block things, but only if they could get a pretty substantial majority in favour, which is why we wrote this two-thirds rather than dictating a majority. So, it tends to be difficult, certainly, to block things. It is a sort of a safety valve, in a sense, because if the mayor goes completely crazy and comes up with things which nobody supports at all and everybody thinks is completely barmy, then there is a way of blocking that, there is a check.

How this arrangement of powers will work out in practice, particularly in times of conflict between Mayor and ministers, remains to be seen. Before the new authority was set up, a simulated 'fantasy authority' exercise designed to role-play the way in which the new system might work out, came up with some interesting pointers. On the 50th floor of Canary Wharf, 50 officials and other key Londoners acted out the Authority's first year with the television presenter, Jon Snow, as the Mayor. Assembly members proved unpredictable and 'conducted a marvellous coup to overthrow the Chair in the course of the morning'. A civil servant from GOL played the role of central government:

I spent the morning absolutely lonely and bored. And I sat at my table and nobody came to me at all. Central government was totally irrelevant! The whole emphasis was the mayor. But I got my own back later in the day when part of the scenario was a big planning development—a sort of Disneyland place in Hackney Marshes. So I called in the Secretary of State's permission, and I won.

The role-play hints at one possible future direction: a highly visible Mayor, a lightning conductor for attention; Assembly members whose ambitions and tactics are hard to guess; and, in the background, the Secretary of State—the key decision-maker in waiting.

6

London in Transition

THE GLA was conceived as an administrative solution to a long-standing political problem. Yet it had no sooner been put together than ancient political conflicts arose to upset its major assumptions. For New Labour, the biggest obstacle to the success of the enterprise was starkly simple: the ambitions of Ken Livingstone and other Blair opponents to restore the former GLC leader to London's top position.

The process of creating the new London authority differed from previous local government reorganizations in that the transition was rapid and carried out under the watchful eye of central government. The elections for Mayor and Assembly were due to take place on 4 May 2000, with the new bodies assuming their responsibilities just eight weeks later on 3 July. The pace of change was unprecedented, as was the mode of preparation. The management of transition in the past had involved early elections to a 'shadow' authority, followed by a transfer of power up to twelve months later. New Labour's determination to get the new GLA in place by mid-term dictated a short transition.

The organizational structures to lay the ground for the GLA were put in place using powers under the Greater London Authority (Referendum) Act 1998 that allowed the government to spend up to £20 million on preparations. Preliminary work was undertaken during the period between the referendum vote in May 1998 and the second reading of the Greater London Authority Bill in the Commons in December, with expenditure possible after that date. This process paid due deference to London and parliamentary opinion but, when coupled with the almost immediate assumption of power in July 2000, left little time to put the new machinery together. Organizational and management structures had to be prepared, along with finance, information technology (IT), and personnel systems. An initial staff group was put together with secondments from central government, local government, the Audit Commission, and the private sector. In addition, accommodation decisions had to be made about the short-term arrangements for the GLA, and work on a long-term solution put in hand. Procurement decisions might need to bypass established procedures.

No previous reorganization had tackled problems of this magnitude in such a compressed timescale. At the same time, the entire transitional period was limited by a difficulty that was political rather than legal or administrative. Creating a new machine and establishing its initial relation-ships was bound to have a constraining effect on those who were eventually elected to manage it. Without a shadow authority there was no way of assuming political direction for the transitional period, and the application of Cabinet Office rules to a civil service transitional operation restricted informal political consultations.

Meanwhile, there were key but as yet unanswerable questions. What effect might the possibility of a Labour Assembly with a non-Labour Mayor have on planning the transition to the new system? How well did the transitional arrangements serve the needs of the new elected authority? And to what extent did the Mayor and Assembly find it necessary to adapt or modify what they inherited? The uncertainties inherent in this rapid transition were accentuated by the disarray of the major parties over their mayoral candidates.

Planning the Transition

The changeover period spanned four distinct phases. The first covered the preparatory work done during the period between the referendum vote in May 1998 and the transition proper, which began in March 1999. The second phase ran from then until the election in May 2000. The period between the election of the Mayor and Assembly and the formal 'go live' date for the GLA in July 2000 marked the third phase of the transition. The fourth and final stage comprised the initial operating period during which temporary structures, staff, and ways of working were to give way to more permanent arrangements confirmed by the Mayor and Assembly.

These four phases provided a structure for planning the transition. Civil servants at GOL planned the phasing in terms of the likely timescale of the parliamentary process, possible local election dates, and financial years. A 1 April start date, the traditional appointed day for local authority reorganization, had an obvious appeal to them, but as one recalled:

We spent quite a lot of time looking at that, but eventually we decided that the right thing to do was not to create the new body before the elections, create it soon after the elections, but not taking over the full responsibilities for a period. We argued about how long that period should be and eventually decided probably two months or so. Full powers came in on 3 July. So that set the parameters that we knew we had . . . It was decided the elections would be the usual time for local government elections, the first Thursday in May, which meant 4 May. We have previously been looking at perhaps having an election in autumn 1999 or early spring, but autumn 1999 looked a bit ambitious, we didn't really think we'd get the bill through in time.

Crucially, the transitional structures and arrangements would have to 'provide the building blocks which the Mayor and Assembly could assemble in different ways as they decide upon more permanent arrangements'. The transition team's own planning was predicated on the assumption that royal assent would be given in July. That the bill was delayed, and completed the legislative process only in November, postponed the making of any permanent appointments and seriously complicated the transitional preparations.

In reality, establishing the core GLA itself was not the only exacting task to arise during the transition period. GOL officials faced a huge task of 'financial engineering' in drawing together what they had learned to call 'the GLA family'. They would be

bringing together bodies that previously had been some local government, some national government. London transport was a nationalized industry, some bits were quangos, some bits were local government joint bodies [and] some bits were private sector . . . So we were trying to bring all these bodies together, each with their own different financial regime, their own different rules . . . It was quite difficult to produce an account on a common basis when you have got things like that . . . That could have been really messy, but I think it's actually gone quite smoothly. I think the fact that it is not in the papers is a good sign.

Robust and adaptable arrangements for managing the relationships with the four functional bodies also required consistency in approach to interfacing effectively with their forerunners, the existing bodies working in transport and regeneration in particular.

Throughout, the main challenge facing the transition team was to strike a balance between two guiding principles: to establish an effective office without at the same time pre-empting decisions that were properly the Mayor's and Assembly's. The tension between pre-emption and inadequate preparation flowed directly from the timescale of change, since the traditional 'overlap' period of shadow and operational authorities had avoided such dilemmas in the past. In particular, when the Greater London Council had been created, its entire organization, staffing, procedures, and initial policies were established during the eleven months that elapsed between the first GLC election in May 1964 and its assumption of power in April 1965. Without the cushion of such a shadow period—indeed, some had pressed for an acceleration of the change process—it was hard to see how the demand to 'hit the ground running' could be met without to some extent pre-empting, perhaps unwittingly, decisions that might have been taken differently under a more prolonged timescale.

Respecting the right of the Mayor and the Assembly to form the structure of the GLA and re-configure their working relations with the other bodies, the transitional team's task was to ensure that the newly elected GLA could move on to make those choices. The key to the success of this approach would be to put in place the necessary infrastructure and build the capacity to support the work of the GLA, putting forward well-considered options for decision immediately following the election. This distinction, though nobody apparently expressed it in these terms at the time, was between 'decision-making'—the transitional officer group's role—and 'decision-taking'—that of the authoritative bodies.

Whatever the terminology, it was a finely gauged difference. In steering a course between the two guiding principles—to establish without pre-empting—officials were mindful of KPMG's advice that there was

in effect, a tension between leaving key decisions to those with the electoral mandate—the Mayor and Assembly—and the practicalities of good governance which require the GLA to be established as an effective operational organisation from the beginning of its life. (KPMG 1999: 5)

As one GOL official later explained, it was a matter of striking a balance:

A basic problem that we had and the basic question we had to ask ourselves all the time was: how much do we put in place, and how much do we leave to the Mayor and the others? And that was pretty difficult because it wasn't a situation where we got a lot of existing bodies where you were just changing the labels. We are talking for the most part about creating totally new structures and the basic principle that ministers adopted was that we would put in place the housekeeping, we would put in place enough that bills were paid, that people were paid, that there were buildings and so on. But we wouldn't pre-empt the key appointments and we wouldn't pre-empt the really key decisions except in a few cases.

One such case was the new building for the GLA. Identifying sites and running a competition absorbed a great deal of time and it was judged better for GOL to do this work than risk having the Mayor and Assembly bogged down with it in their first year.

Thus the timescale within which transition had to be accomplished raised issues of political practicality as much as of administrative feasibility. One of the architects of the scheme recalled that there was no right answer to the dilemmas of change to a mayoral system:

If you take the transition period we had an argument at one stage about whether the mayor should take power on the day of the election or three months later or six months later or a year later. Now the civil servant in me would say a year later would be more sensible. A whole year to sort things out and get the whole thing in place. Now the politician in me . . . it's hopeless, it just wouldn't have worked.

An elected mayor meant that pressure for immediate action would be strong and the shadow period before taking power had to be as short as possible. Another civil servant explained:

I suppose if you have all the time in the world, well you could have a longer transition, longer trial period, which would have enabled a bit more planning to have been done. But I don't think you could have a long time after the Mayor was elected. I think the three months [sic] that we had was about the longest, because really, he is the Mayor, in everyone's eyes he is elected, so you couldn't have him mucking around for a year getting things going, I don't think. I think it was probably about right but it was never going to be easy or neat.

The disadvantage of departing from the traditional 'shadow' mechanisms was that there was no way of giving political direction until the final stage, when the Mayor and Assembly had been elected. Despite the best efforts of officials, some Assembly members were frustrated by the result. The transition team, one complained in an interview, were 'not politicians, and the framework in which they constructed this authority was a kind of technocrat's dream'. The system had 'no political shock absorbers'. In reality, the team had been caught between Nick Raynsford's insistence that the Assembly should have no political support staff and the Assembly members' desire that they should. Eventually, counsel's opinion identified a way out.

Settling the ways in which the new institution would work meant thinking through the implications of the Mayor's powers and duties together with, and in relation to, those of the Assembly. From these could be derived the necessary support structures for the Mayor's office and the Assembly members. Some new Assembly members interviewed protested that the officials planning the transitional process 'need[ed] in some way to engage more than the civil servants, they need to engage the politicians, but they also need to engage other kinds of people'. Engaging with politicians in advance of the election was politically difficult—though it was to some extent accomplished—but considerable effort was put into engaging with others. The transitional period was marked by a stream of apparently open discussions with a wide range of interested parties, statutory, voluntary, and private. It was in many ways a listening exercise.

Consideration had to be given in advance to policy and strategy, and it is here that the difficult of avoiding any suspicion of pre-emption arose. If time was not to be lost—and the example of the ill-starred GLDP was very much in mind—initial work on the spatial development strategy as the GLA's overarching strategic tool would need to begin immediately. This entailed a review of existing policy and research work relating to the entirety of the GLA's responsibility, identifying research capacity and research needs and analysing the manifesto commitments of mayoral candidates for clues as to possible future directions. Similar considerations would carry over into the work of the functional bodies with the implication that policy and strategy would have to be addressed during the transitional period and in advance of any authoritative policy pronouncements.

The GLA would be required to take defensible decisions immediately on assuming power on 3 July 2000. In particular, the Mayor would be faced with possibly contentious planning applications and would need to operate the statutory planning functions of the Authority in advance of declaring a Spatial Development Strategy. During this period, the existing Regional Planning Guidance would remain in force as the authoritative context for development control and Unitary Development Plan (UDP) reviews by the Mayor. It would thus be necessary to establish channels for liaison and consultation with the local planning authorities on strategic planning applications and UDP reviews. Similarly, such channels needed to be established to DETR and GOL if a planning hiatus was to be avoided.

There were other teething troubles. Given that a proportion of the staff would be transferring from absorbed bodies such as the London Ecology Unit

(LEU) and the London Research Centre (LRC), transfer of employment was bound to take precedence over new recruitment. Projected patterns of staff growth showed a steady build-up of transferred staff reaching their peak in April 2000 and declining as a result of rationalization after July. In parallel, the numbers of new staff would take off sharply after April and by the end of 2000 they would be the predominant element in the GLA staff structure of around 400 core people. Many of the GLA staff were already employed in the absorbed bodies and their functions could be expected to continue with little change until such time as the Mayor and Assembly determined the future shape and working of the new authority. Their training needs would be quite different from those appointed to new functions, but all would require training in GLA procedures to ensure that systems were operational no later than April 2000. The entire organization would need a well-developed IT infrastructure on the appointed day, raising foreseeable issues about the compatibility of systems in the absorbed bodies. Meeting routines and committee procedures would need to be established and the board memberships of the functional bodies would need to be identified and preliminary work done on the nomination of candidates.

Finance was another of the key matters to be addressed during the planning period. The immediate tasks were to establish the financial structures and processes, including setting up the core finance function, the recruitment and selection of staff, embedding finance into the wider administrative processes of the GLA, and ensuring the acquisition and installation of appropriate technology. An accounting system had to be designed, and provision made for debt and credit management. Financial reporting arrangements with the functional bodies would also need to be constructed. As well as establishing the finance function in this way, those responsible for the transition would need to do preliminary work for 2001, develop a financial strategy for the GLA to cover both revenue and capital planning, open channels for grant negotiation, and deal with the liabilities of the bodies due to be merged into the GLA. Above all, the new body would have to handle financial transactions—in particular payroll—from the moment it came into being.

Uncertainties remained. In particular, it was difficult to identify in advance the point when the new organization would move from transitional to operational status. In a purely legal sense this was obvious enough. However, the key issue was political, not legal. While the Mayor and Assembly, once elected, sought to flex their muscles by appointing and directing staff of their own choosing during the run-up to their assumption of power in July, they were crucially limited by the fact that the GLA's first annual budget was set in Whitehall.

Managing the Transition

How was the challenge of the transition handled in practice? KPMG (1999) recommended that a single transition team be formed to handle the identified work programme, create the infrastructure of the core GLA, and forge links with the forerunners of the functional bodies. The initial transition team would be small and come into being as early as April 1999, reach its peak in September 1999, and contract in April 2000, gradually being replaced by the core GLA staff. For example, the initial finance strength was estimated at three staff, rising to nine at the peak, and declining again to six as the appointed day approached. The numbers of policy staff and those concerned with operating the procedures would, on the other hand, build steadily.

In August 1999, the GOL published the transition team's proposals for the initial organization of the GLA in a consultation paper titled *The Shape of Things to Come* (Transition Team 1999). A number of organizations responded to the consultation exercise, including London boroughs, potential functional bodies of the GLA, government agencies, professional, public, and private groups, trade unions, and political parties. The problem identified by KPMG was how best to strike the right balance, between the need to maintain a viable organization and the need to keep options open for the Mayor and the Assembly. The GOL paper acknowledged this dilemma and was anxious to respect the boundaries. Responses to the consultation showed how difficult it would be to achieve that balance to everyone's satisfaction. Thus, the consultation document stressed the need for continuity and called for recruitment of core staff to enable the organization to function effectively during and beyond the transition. No posts should be filled over the £40,000 salary level, and appointments should be restricted to the personnel, capital finance, and IT functions, with no policy staff to be recruited at this stage. The opposing view, argued by some who responded to the consultation, was that all posts should be on a temporary basis so as to ensure flexibility, limiting even senior appointments to a maximum of one year.

There were other staffing issues—notably staff structure and deployment—that related directly to the Mayor and Assembly members' freedom of manoeuvre. For example, the IPPR had recommended a common press and public communications staff for the GLA, to serve both Assembly members and the Mayor's office. The *Shape of Things to Come* extended this principle, and proposed a flexible pool of staff as preferable to a rigid division between those working for the Mayor and those working for the Assembly (Transition Team 1999). In proposing 'single structures' as preferable to 'parallel structures' the GOL staff were respecting the 'no-pre-emption' requirement. Their calculation was that it would be easier for the mayor and assembly to divide a single pool of staff between them than to re-combine two different teams, should this be the course they chose. But it was also apparent that the transition team envisaged an idealized relationship 'based on trust and negotiation, rather than conflict'. Was this realistic? A number of the respondents argued that a single structure would not be sustainable, given the separate and potentially conflicting roles of Mayor and Assembly. Indeed, although the majority of respondents favoured this consensual approach, it was far from clear that the proposed protocols would work where staff were required to deliver confidential policy advice to the Mayor, and at the same time scrutinize his policies on behalf of the Assembly. Another issue concerned the organization of staff, which GOL considered should be around 'competencies' rather than technical specialisms (Transition Team 1999). Such a model threatened the future of the specialist staff who would be inherited from the LEU, London Planning Advisory Committee (LPAC), LRC.

The dedicated transition team recommended by KPMG took over the planning process in April 1999. Dr Bob Chilton, a former local authority chief executive who had headed up the Local Government Commission, was seconded from the Audit Commission to be head of the team. Chilton was to have three principal responsibilities. The first was to provide leadership and project management for the transition process, with a need to ensure that sufficient resources were secured, timescales adhered to, and the crucial linkages made between parts of the project. Crucially, he was accountable for delivering to the new Mayor and Assembly a fully operational core GLA. Second, the transition team would be expected to secure the involvement and engagement of the wider stakeholder community including, in particular, the bodies which were to be absorbed into the GLA, the forerunners of the functional bodies and the London boroughs. Voluntary organizations and business interests were also to be involved to the extent that they would be affected by the transition process. Third, in leading the process, the team had to be capable of making the necessary imaginative leap that ensured that the transition was driven by the needs of the future authority rather than those of the existing governmental bodies. In the words of the KPMG report, this would require the head of transition to

provide a degree of 'GLA pull' rather than simply Government Office for London (GOL) 'push' to the process. The orientation of the post holder must be such that they are capable of thinking always about the needs that the core GLA will have, on day one and immediately afterwards. They must advance that perspective in the transition process and in contributing to wider GOL discussions about new London governance. (KPMG 1999: 27)

It was also expected that the head of transition, while operating as in effect the chief administrative officer of the embryonic authority, would essentially be a short-term appointment rather than a chief executive designate. The post would not be a long-term career opportunity and an appointment from spring 1999 to autumn 2000 was envisaged. The focus was entirely upon the delivery of a working organization within strict limits. It was thought appropriate for the head of transition to be formally endorsed by the Assembly as its acting head of administration immediately after its election in order to ensure continuity and the provision of advice from someone who had been centrally involved in the creation of the organization.

Whether there should be a chief executive post at all was by no means universally agreed. Chilton never thought so, pointing to the special status of the Mayor as a directly elected chief executive; the corollary of the mayoral role was one of general manager. The bill had been prescriptive on the need to appoint an official to a conventional chief-executive role. Chilton succeeded in persuading GOL to amend the bill to return this power to the GLA. In the event, the Assembly, once elected, decided that it did want an appointed chief executive.

There were symbolic issues as well as practical ones. A new home would be required for a new London government, and this was bound to raise spectres. Many who had campaigned since the abolition of the GLC for the restoration of a London-wide government argued that London's County Hall, on the South Bank across the river from Westminster, was its natural home. Built for the LCC, the building was famously used after 1981 as the base for its successor's opposition to the Conservative government. The London Residuary Body set up to dispose of GLC assets had managed the building up to the point of sale, before selling it to a Japanese company, Shirayama Shokusan. This transition was seen by critics as the hasty disposal of a potent political symbol. During the planning enquiry that accompanied the sale of the building, objectors raised this point, demanding that its future should be safeguarded as the home of a future council or authority.

The opponents included supporters of the former GLC, who sought to breathe new life into the symbolism, arguing that the debating chamber at the former LCC/GLC county hall would provide a suitably dignified focus for conducting London's affairs. Returning this historic site to the use for which it was designed would not only offer historical continuity, it would also once again place the site of the capital's government across the river from, and directly opposite, the Palace of Westminster, so conferring upon it appropriate gravitas.

The Japanese owners, anxious not to appear as a corporate obstacle to London democracy, indicated that they would be cooperative. Within weeks of the May 1997 election they had offered 200,000 square feet of vacant office space, together with the council chamber, to the new government. However, the Prime Minister was believed to have ruled out County Hall as the home for the new Mayor and Assembly on the ground that it was too large. Few doubted the real reason. The new body was to be no 'son of GLC'; instead, explained a spokesman, 'We are determined that the new Assembly is seen as a new start for London, something that will break the mould. There is no room for ghosts from the past' (*ES*, 26 February 1998).

Partly for this reason the GOL chose not to pass the question of the GLA's home on to the transition team—and by extension to the new Authority itself—to settle. Instead, a competition was held under GOL management to produce a new building. The competition was won by Sir Norman Foster, with a scheme for a circular glass building to be built further along the South Bank near Tower Bridge. The idea was for a structure erected by private developers with a 25-year lease to the GLA, reverting to the developers at the end of the period. The competition was so arranged that the government was choosing among packages of site, architect, and design submitted by rival developers. This allowed little discussion of the actual function of the building or its most appropriate form. In the event, Foster's winning entry had to be extensively redesigned to meet the points raised. The result still came under fire as having 'something about it of a master criminal's lair' and, more particularly, for costing £150 million, unrecoverable because of the lease-back arrangements (*ES*, 16 November 1999).

Electing the Mayor and the Assembly

Meanwhile, preparations for the first new-style London elections were under way, alongside the administrative work of the transition team. The electoral areas for the GLA were finalized in August 1998 when the Local Government Commission's proposals for 14 new constituencies were accepted by the government. The Commission's chairman, Malcolm Grant, explained that

in reaching our proposals we have borne in mind the need to achieve reasonable electoral quality, so that a vote cast in one electoral area carries the same weight as a vote cast in another electoral area. We decided there was a case for combining similar boroughs in the new areas so that differing perspectives on strategic issues can find a voice in the new Assembly. (*ES*, 25 August 1998).

This grouping reflected a new sophistication in the composition of electoral areas, extending beyond mere equality of representation to considerations of how the new Assembly might work. As such, it appeared to run counter to the DETR's vision of what kind of body the Assembly should be. However, the sheer size of the constituencies was seen as a bulwark against local vested interests gaining too powerful a voice in the Assembly.

At the same time, the most significant novelty was not the constituency basis but the electoral system itself, which introduced full-scale proportional representation for an English poll for the first time. Instead of the simple first-past-the-post system, the 25-member assembly was to be elected by the German-style additional member system (AMS). Under this system, each elector has two votes: one for a constituency member, the other for a party list. This gives the opportunity to an elector to split his or her vote at will. Constituency members are elected under the first-past-the-post system, with votes for the party list allocated for the election of additional members, so as to secure a degree of proportionality. Whereas in Germany—and, indeed, in New Zealand—the two types of member are equal in number, the AMS system adopted by the Scottish Parliament and the Welsh Assembly—and, subsequently, for the GLA—prescribes fewer list than constituency members. It was not a system that had commanded much support historically within the Labour Party. In particular, the creation of two classes of representatives—one with constituency roots, the other without—was thought a source of weakness (Bogdanor 2001: 221–7).

For the GLA, 14 of the 25 members were directly elected from constituencies with around 350,000 voters each. The remaining eleven were allocated to party nominees in proportion to their share of the popular vote London-wide. This provision was intended to overcome one of the characteristic effects of any constituency-based system whereby a party with a reasonable level of support could fail to win any representation if that support were dispersed rather than concentrated geographically.

Under the GLA rules, the ballot paper provided for the Assembly constituency members to be elected on the first-past-the-post basis, but also for the expression of choice of a London-wide party. 'London-wide' votes were then to be allocated between the parties on the basis of the so-called d'Hondt formula, a continental system that worked in a series of stages. First, the total number of votes for each party would be calculated. The total was then to be divided by the number of constituency seats the party won plus one—one was added to avoid dividing by zero when no seat was won. The result of this calculation would known as the party's 'London figure'. Any independent candidate would be given a London figure equal to his or her vote. The first of the London-wide seats was allocated to the party with the highest London figure. For that party the London figure was then to be recalculated on the basis of the new total number of seats—again, plus one—the next seat allocated on the basis of the highest London figure, and the winning party's London figure again recalculated until all the London-wide seats had been allocated. There was also a threshold for election: no party or candidate could win any of the London-wide seats without polling at last 5 per cent of the total number of London votes. The aim of the scheme was twofold: to ensure that the Assembly should not be dominated by the major party blocs and, through the London-wide seats, to balance any tendency towards 'parish-pump localism'.

The mayoral system was different, involving the 'supplementary vote', a version of the alternative vote that had been advocated for UK parliamentary elections by the Labour Party's Committee on Electoral Reform chaired by Lord Plant in the early 1990s. Voters were asked to indicate their first and second choices on the ballot paper where three or more candidates contested. If any candidate gained more than half the first preference votes, he or she won outright on the first ballot. However, if no candidate won an overall majority then second preference votes were to be counted. The two candidates with the most first preference votes went forward while the others dropped out. Second preference votes for the eliminated candidates were then to be redistributed between the two leading candidates and added to their own second preference votes. The candidate who had the largest total votes, of whatever kind, would be returned as mayor. One aim of this supplementary vote system was to reduce the scope for a maverick non-party candidate—an aim which it spectacularly failed to achieve. The expected composition of the Assembly was intended to provide appropriate checks and balances, as it was felt unlikely that any one party would have a majority and hence there was little prospect of a directly elected mayor being backed by a majority of members.

There were further novelties. The first was electronic scanning of ballot papers, which had to be printed in a machine-readable form. It was estimated that, given the complex electoral system, a manual count of the vote would take three days, while electronic scanning would give a result within hours. Another innovation was the introduction of a scheme to allow electors to vote in the week before polling day. This new concept of 'early voting' was part of the government's wider plan to increase electoral participation by making voting easier. To a large extent, this also failed.

Choosing the Candidates for Mayor

'The only explanation for the present panic', wrote Simon Jenkins in July,

is that Labour has lost faith in the whole reform. It is obsessed with keeping control . . . Yet, there is absolutely no point in having as Mayor of London a Cabinet clone. To set up an independent political entity in the capital, to let London elect its own spokesman and then to manipulate the choice for a cabinet placeman, is the height of cynicism . . . Those enthusiasts who watched the Mayoralty evolve over the past four years have done so with mounting dismay. The London government bill has been diluted and doctored at every turn to ensure continuing control from the Treasury and the Whitehall. London is to have the only elected Mayor in the world without a single proper tax to his or her name (New York has six). Yet, even neutering this wimp of a civic functionary, Downing Street cannot leave him alone. It must have its own man in the job. (*ES*, 5 July 1999)

Indeed, press attention rapidly ceased to focus on the powers of the Authority, and concentrated instead on the dawning realization among politicians that, in contrast to the expectations of virtually every British contest, the running would not be made by the major parties. Fantasy candidates for Mayor whose names had been mentioned in the early days of planning for the new London dropped out of the picture. In particular, Richard Branson who had allowed speculation about his possible candidacy at the beginning, indicated that he would not stand. More worrying for the government and the Opposition, however, was a marked reluctance among orthodox politicians of the front rank to allow themselves to be considered. Suddenly there was a realization that the monster that had been created was out of control. As the selection process approached, two well-known public figures stood out, each almost equally unpalatable to his leader, though for different reasons: Ken Livingstone and Lord Archer.

New Labour's instinct was to look for a reliable placeman. Unfortunately, the more desperate the leadership became to find one, the more reluctant particular individuals became to take what, in the face of Livingstone's challenge, increasingly looked like a poisoned chalice. The problem was to find somebody who simultaneously had a strong 'Labour' record, a high profile, popular appeal, and a willingness to take a major risk. One name, widely canvassed, was that of the black broadcaster, Trevor Phillips, who was considered acceptable to the Labour Party as well as attractive to the wider public. Phillips showed initial interest. He lacked political experience, however, and polls indicated that he had little support. From within the political arena, another early possibility was Nick Raynsford, Minister for London, MP for Fulham, and widely respected for his grasp of policy issues facing the capital. However, Raynsford was a junior minister, and for the Prime Minister to have picked him as Labour standard-bearer would indicate that he regarded the Mayor's post as a relatively lowly one or, alternatively, that he could not find anyone more senior to take it. Instead, Blair chose Frank Dobson, Secretary of State for Health and former leader of Camden council. It was in some ways an ironic choice. Although the nominal author of Labour's pre-election plan for London, Dobson had made clear his reservations to the Prime Minister and more widely about the need for, and workability of, the 'modernization' of London government.

In retrospect, it was not merely ironic: a less suitable candidate could scarcely have been found. Dobson was popular within the Labour Party, and had made a good impression on the public in his short period as a minister. However, he was unable to shrug off an initial impression that he was the Prime Minister's poodle, that he was a reluctant runner, and that he was standing only as an alternative to early demotion from the Cabinet.

Dobson's bid had to be tested first in a rapidly concocted and, it was widely felt, singularly undemocratic selection process. At the beginning, there was one important issue: would the party managers succeed in blocking the choice of Ken Livingstone as Labour Party candidate? Later, a second emerged: if they did not block him, would he embrace expulsion from the party and run as an independent? Few doubted that he was the overwhelming choice of the rank and file. Few doubted, either, that the leadership would seek to do everything in its power to obstruct this choice. This meant either refusing to accept his nomination in the first place or allowing the nomination to go forward, but with a selection system under which he could not win. It tried both.

What added to the embarrassment to the party leadership was the growing realization that Livingstone was the choice not just of the party but of ordinary voters as well. Opinion polls consistently showed him to be the most favoured candidate. Evidence was growing, moreover, that even if he were to run as an independent, with Dobson on the Labour ticket, he would win comfortably, pushing Dobson into third place. The party drew comfort from the prediction that, if Livingstone were not on the ballot paper, Dobson would win by a respectable margin. Close analysis indicated, however, that Livingstone had a unique capacity to draw votes from the supporters of all parties: as many as a quarter of Conservatives and more than half of Liberal Democrat supporters would turn out for him.

Downing Street and Millbank faced a dilemma. They needed to win the mayoralty but they also needed to keep the Labour politician with the best chance of a convincing victory from gaining office. The objection to Livingstone was part political, part psychological. 'New Labour' had consistently taken it as its mission to oppose and resist members of the 1980s 'hard' left on the grounds that it damaged the party's image and threatened to make it unelectable. At the same time, New Labour had accepted and forgiven former left-wingers who accepted the error of their past ways. Livingstone was not only the single best-known figure, apart from Tony Benn, still in politics who was most closely identified with the hard left. He also made it clear that he was unrepentant, and was prepared to attack the Blairite administration at any opportunity. For New Labour, crushing him became a sacred duty—the more so as Blair and his lieutenants made public their antipathy.

Anticipating a long guerrilla war, the Labour leadership began by looking for ways of preventing him running at all. A panel convened under the Parliamentary Labour Party chairman Clive Soley to vet the prospective candidates, subjected Livingstone to a prolonged inquisition. Some members seemed determined to dispose of the issue once and for all by refusing to short-list him, and there was excited speculation that the panel would find reasons for regarding him as unsuitable. Livingstone, confident of his position, was uncompromising, and refused to give the panel the assurances it sought about the manifesto position. The panel agonized—and then agreed that his name should be included among those going forward to the electoral college set up to determine who should run as official Labour candidate. As well as Livingstone, the shortlist included Dobson and the Hampstead MP and actress, Glenda Jackson.

The leadership, however, failed to foresee that the electoral college itself might lack moral authority. The system adopted was complex. Votes were to be divided in groups among London MPs, Members of the European Parliament, and Assembly candidates; affiliated organizations, trade unions, and cooperative societies; and individual members of the party. Under this system, the vote of an individual MP would be worth many times that of an individual party member. While party members and MPs would cast their votes individually, the trade unions could cast a block vote reflecting their total affiliated membership. Unions handled the process in various ways. As they were not required to ballot their members before casting their votes—as had happened in the election for the leader of the Labour Party in 1994—it was open to them, if they chose, instead to cast their entire vote according to the preference of the executive. This was the course chosen by the Amalgamated Engineering Union (AEU), whose general secretary, Sir Ken Jackson, was later accused of having 'stolen the election' for Millbank.

For a time, the outcome seemed to hang in the balance. The result, after redistribution of second preference votes, was a narrow win for Dobson by a margin of just over 3 per cent. Livingstone had dominated the individual membership section of the ballot with almost 55 per cent of the first preferences, and 60 per cent after redistribution, on a very heavy turn-out of 73 per cent of the London members. The result was settled in the other two sections of the college. Livingstone had significantly little support from MPs. He won just nine votes to Dobson's 64, picking up the single second preference vote originally cast for Glenda Jackson. Union votes were divided, but nevertheless gave the victory to Dobson. Livingstone won in those unions who balloted their members; but the greater part of the block vote was cast against him (D'Arcy and Maclean 2000).

However, for Frank Dobson and Blair, victory soon turned out to be pyrrhic. Although Dobson emerged as Labour candidate in the selection, the outcome did nothing to boost his popularity among Londoners. There was an atmosphere of anti-climax and guilt. Rebellion was in the air. The sense that the outcome was a fix by the party machine increased support for Livingstone, who, so far from accepting defeat, produced a catalogue of complaints: unions and cooperative societies that did not ballot their members, alleged leadership pressure on Labour MPs, and the secret passing of the party membership list to the Dobson campaign. Clive Soley declared that 'this has been a bruising contest' (D'Arcy and MacLean 2000: 149). Would Ken stand anyway? Amidst media speculation, Livingstone announced that he would take his time to review his position. At a meeting with John Prescott and party secretary, Margaret McDonagh, on 28 February, he was warned not to run as an independent, and of the consequences of doing so. His own constituency Labour Party in Brent East urged him to 'fight his corner inside the party' and not run separately (D'Arcy and MacLean 2000: 189).

If he needed any encouragement from Londoners, another ICM poll provided it, showing a huge majority in favour of Livingstone standing as an independent and predicting that he would beat the other candidates by a large margin. He hesitated: wanting to be Mayor, but knowing that if he were expelled, and then lost, there would be no second chance. Over the next week he kept up the war of words, urging Dobson to make way for him as candidate and repudiate the 'tainted' electoral process. Then, on 6 March, he announced his decision. He would run. He recognized the anger that this would cause in some quarters but he was characteristically bullish about his decision: 'I offer no weasel words of equivocation', he said. He apologized for breaking his promise to abide by the selection process, knowing that to run against an official Labour candidate meant automatic expulsion from the party. However, he did not intend 'to take any lectures from those who set new standards in ballot rigging' (D'Arcy and MacLean 2000: 201).

Meanwhile, Labour was not the only party with candidate difficulties. The race for the Conservative candidature attracted just as much attention in its early stages. Under William Hague, the party had undergone a process of organizational reform designed to produce a transparent and accountable form of leadership; and the system chosen to find a candidate for London Mayor reflected the new approach. The system involved a screening committee that would vet would-be mayoral candidates, before submitting their names to an electoral college which would draw up a short list of those who would then speak at the hustings meetings of party members. The vote taken at the meeting would determine the top two candidates, whose names would then be put to a ballot of the party's 39,000 London members. Jeffrey Archer, Steven Norris, and a couple of lesser-known Conservatives survived the first stage of the short-listing process and four of them went through to the electoral college, which narrowed the field to two. The London party membership then had to choose between Archer and Norris. It chose Archer by a majority of two to one, reflecting not only the novelist's high profile and popularity but also a feeling that he was the candidate best placed to beat a strong Labour candidate. Archer's campaign turned out to be brief. Its most memorable moment was provided by Hague's presentation of him to Conservative party conference as a 'man of integrity and probity'. Eight weeks later, he was forced to step down when a former friend, Ted Francis, who had provided an alibi to protect him in an earlier libel trial, admitted to doing so at Archer's request. As a result of Archer's withdrawal, the contest was re-run. Norris was at first barred from the short list but was then readmitted and triumphed over a little-known councillor in the final run-off.

Dobson and Norris were both well-known national politicians. The Liberal Democrats, by contrast, fielded a candidate with no previous political experience outside London: Susan Kramer, an investment banker, who had easily beaten her rivals within the party's primary. The Green Party candidate was Darren Johnson, a recent politics graduate from Goldsmiths College in South London.

A Mayor and an Assembly are Elected

The elections for the Mayor and Assembly took place on 4 May 2000. Ken Livingstone, running as an independent, secured a convincing victory on a turnout of 33.65 per cent, with a total first-preference vote that nearly equalled the Conservative and Labour votes put together. Dobson was beaten into a humiliating third place, only marginally above the Liberal Democrats. Following the distribution of second-preference votes, Livingstone increased his poll by some 19 per cent, Norris by 15 per cent. In a political culture that nearly always delivered votes to party standard-bearers and looked askance at independents, it was an astonishing result. It was a reverse for Blair, who had done everything in his power to prevent it happening. Yet in a way it was also a vindication of the philosophy around the mayoralty idea, showing that the idea of a well-known individual as the capital's leader appealed to the voters and indicating that Londoners took the powers seriously enough to decide for themselves.

The additional member system produced a markedly different outcome for the Assembly from the one that might have resulted from first-past-the-post. The Conservatives won the most votes and seats in the constituency section, followed closely by Labour. None of the other parties won a seat in this section. In the party list vote Labour led the Conservatives, giving both nine seats overall in combination. Here, the distribution of the party list votes also brought Liberal Democrats and Greens into the Assembly.

Some saw the Assembly result as perverse, or at any rate the predictable effect of a perverse system, others as a demonstration of its fairness. The out-

TABLE 6.1. Voting in the mayoral election 2000

Candidate	Votes	%
First count		
Ken Livingstone (Independent)	667,877	38.96
Steven Norris (Conservative Party)	464,434	27.09
Frank Dobson (Labour Party)	223,884	13.06
Susan Kramer (Liberal Democrat Party)	203,452	11.87
Ram Gidoomal (Christian Democrat Party)	42,060	2.45
Darren Johnson (Green Party)	38,121	2.22
Michael Newland (British National Party)	33,569	1.96
Damian Hockney (UK Independence Party)	16,324	0.95
Geoffrey Ben-Nathan (Pro-motor)	9,956	0.58
Ashwinkumar Tanna (Independent)	9,015	0.53
Geoffrey Clements (Natural Law Party)	5,470	0.32
Second count		
Ken Livingstone (Independent)	776,427	57.92
Steven Norris (Conservative Party)	564,137	42.08

TABLE 6.2. Final result of the Assembly elections, 2000

Constituency			Party list			Overall Seats
Party	Votes(%)	Seats	Party	Votes(%)	Seats	
Conservative	33.2	8	Conservative	29.0	1	9
Labour	31.6	6	Labour	30.3	3	9
Lib. Dem.	18.9	0	Lib. Dem.	14.8	4	4
Green	10.2	0	Green	11.1	3	3
Other	6.1	0	Other	14.8	0	0

come was a distribution of seats that expressed popular choice, but did not provide a governing majority. As such, it seemed to fulfil the aim of encouraging consensus and coalition building in an Assembly which was intended to scrutinize and check the Mayor rather than either control or be dominated by him.

The scene was now set for the next four years. Livingstone had been a paradoxical candidate for Mayor, not least because of his vociferous opposition to the New Labour scheme and in favour of a powerful GLC-type assembly. His view of Tony Blair's advocacy of a Mayor for London was both acid and accurate:

He took up this idea of having a mayor like they do in the United States—somebody with a close relationship with big businesses in the area, somebody who was not bound by a party caucus system. He thought the job would attract the best and brightest from the world of business—people who would give up great corporate jobs to work for the community. Of course the problem is that people who run big business have real power and they are not going to come in here and flog their way through all the procedures of consultation and listening to Londoners . . . it was a move towards a more American-style of politics that is about individuals rather than parties with ideologies and history . . . My proposal would have been that the leader of the largest party in the Assembly become the mayor. That was Chirac's position in Paris: he was never going to be directly elected. My worry is that it's going to be too easy under the government's scheme for any half-way cynical, manipulative mayor to keep the assembly sweet. (Carvel 1999: 272–3)

What kind of Mayor, then, would he prove to be?

The Mayor Appoints his Team

Ken Livingstone's initial strategy was to seek to counter political isolation by drawing in opponents and neutralizing their opposition. The Mayor had promised a broad-based advisory cabinet onto which he invited some prominent members of the Assembly from all parties. Some members were sceptical, rightly seeing 'cabinet' as a misnomer. Despite its official title of 'executive board', the body had no executive power; members were not be bound by collective responsibility and could in no way bind the Mayor's hands. Meanwhile, Livingstone recruited advisers from outside the Assembly: Lee Jasper and Kumar Murshid as advisers on race and immigration, and John McDonnell MP, a former close associate from GLC days, as adviser on local government.

Balancing these controversial figures, the new Mayor recruited a Conservative, Judith Mayhew, chairman of the City Corporation's Policy and Resources Committee, as his adviser on City affairs. Glenda Jackson became his adviser on homelessness, Diane Abbott adviser on women's issues, Yasmin Anwar, head of multicultural programming on Channel Four, adviser on cultural strategy. Richard Stone was appointed to advise on community relations and Caroline Gooding on disability rights. Sean Bain was brought in from the London Voluntary Services Council. From among the Assembly members the Mayor appointed the Green Party mayoral candidate, Darren Johnson, as his environment adviser, and the Liberal Democrat peer, Lord Tope, as adviser on equality and human rights. Other members of the team included Toby Harris and Valerie Shawcross. The architect Richard Rogers was later brought in to advise on urban renewal.

In making appointments to functional bodies, the Mayor was obliged to ensure that nominations from the Assembly members were proportionate to their respective party strengths. Twelve were nominated to the MPA, nine to LFEPA, as well as 15 to the board of the LDA, including two from ranks of the Assembly, some from his advisory cabinet, and others from business and other backgrounds. Appointments to the board of TfL, which he himself would chair, were made following open advertisement and review by independent assessors. More remarkably, Livingstone's election opponents Steven Norris and Susan Kramer were among those appointed to the several boards to serve alongside him. George Barlow, Chairman of the London Development Partnership and former chief executive of the Peabody Trust, was appointed

TABLE 6.3. The Mayor's Advisory Cabinet and portfolios

Member	Portfolio
Assembly members	
Nicky Gavron (Labour)	Deputy Mayor; SDS
Toby Harris (Labour)	Police; Chair, MPA
Valerie Shawcross (Labour)	Chair, LFEPA
Graham Tope (Liberal Democrat)	Human rights and equalities
Darren Johnson (Green)	Environment
Lynne Featherstone (Liberal Democrat)	Transport
Others	
Glenda Jackson	Homelessness
Judith Mayhew	City and business
George Barlow	Chair, LDA
Kumar Murshid	Regeneration
Lee Jasper	Race relations
Diane Abbott	Women and equality
Richard Stone	Community partnerships
Sean Baine	London Voluntary Services Council
Caroline Gooding	Disability rights
Yasmin Anwar	Chair, cultural strategy group
Richard Rogers	Urban strategy
Sue Atkinson	Health issues
Rod Robertson	Trade union issues
Angela Mason	Lesbian and gay issues

chair of the London Development Agency. Barlow had authored the key document on *Building London's Economy* on which the LDA was expected to base its initial policies.

The Assembly Conservatives, on the other hand, were frozen out, the principle of 'inclusiveness' notwithstanding. Conservative members accused Labour of being co-opted into the Livingstone project, claiming

we don't know who is in charge of London's Labour Party—Tony Blair or Ken Livingstone. The other Parties are all accepting goodies from Ken and have effectively become part of his administration . . . The whole idea was that the mayor should have the power and the assembly would hold him to account. But they have taken the mayor's shilling and so the whole idea is being subverted from the start. (*ES*, 12 June 2000)

To the Conservatives, the Mayor's inclusiveness was in any case disingenuous. Having originally announced his intention to make the post of Deputy Mayor rotate between the parties, towards the end of his first year he withdrew his offer to the Conservatives and invited Nicky Gavron to continue in post. At the same time, and with some justice, he accused the Conservatives of being 'oppositional' and of attempting to obstruct his mandate for improving transport and police in London. A Conservative deputy, he claimed, would 'seek to roll back my policy agenda' (GLA news release, 20 February 2001).

The Conservatives' exclusion from key posts ensured that they would operate from then on as an official opposition. The other parties had been drawn into the Mayor's web, neutralizing or at least moderating their opposition. To Labour, it looked rather different, and together Labour and Liberal Democrat spokesmen rejected the criticisms, arguing that the GLA was a new type of institution and should be free from inter-party wrangling. For example, while Valerie Shawcross had been appointed chair of the LFEPA, she accepted only on the condition that she should consider herself bound by Labour's policies and not the Mayor's. A similar arrangement was made to enable Nicky Gavron to take up the post of Deputy Mayor. In particular, it was agreed that the Mayor would have to drop all threats of launching a judicial review of the government's commitment to introduce a Public-Private Partnership to modernize the Underground. Meanwhile, Labour eschewed any acceptance of responsibility for the Mayor's policies, emphasizing that the cabinet was no more than an advisory body with no powers of its own. From where the party stood, the Mayor and his kitchen cabinet of personal advisors appeared to be the real administration.

Taking Power

The Mayor and Assembly assumed their powers on 3 July 2000. On taking the chair for the first time, Trevor Phillips used the opportunity to define the relationship between the two:

We know that the Mayor is not above taking a risk or two. The Assembly's formal role is that of scrutineer. It is our job to ensure that the mayor and his team act in the interests of Londoners and not against them. I can assure you, Ken, that is genuinely meant. Our scrutiny role will not just be critical, we also want to be constructive . . . We want to influence your policy and we want to work with you and, should you be successful, we will carry you in triumph through the streets. That does not, however, mean we are servants of the mayor. We remain servants of the people of London. This is a democracy—not a Kenocracy. If you decide to use your position to advance policies that are not in the interests of Londoners, or if you choose to use the platform for other political ends, we will, I promise, kick your ass. (*ES*, 3 July 2000)

The Mayor, though reportedly irritated, and aware of the animosity between the two of them, was nonetheless dismissive. 'Things will settle down' he declared, 'Trevor is entitled to say what he said and I defend his right to do so' (*ES*, 3 July 2000).

An awesome raft of pressing matters had by now been stockpiled for the new Assembly, awaiting decision. Foremost among them were the structures and working arrangements of the Assembly itself, and the chief and other officer posts that would support its work. Decisions made during the transition period could have had the effect of pre-empting choices that would be better made by the GLA. This danger was largely avoided. The transition team had successfully steered a course between over-determination and under-determination of the structures and processes the Mayor and Assembly would need from the outset. From an administrative point of view, it was a well-executed operation. Ordinary members, however, felt that more could have been settled in advance and less left to them. When they arrived at Romney House, the GLA's temporary headquarters, they were presented with extensive briefing packs describing what had already been done and what remained to be decided, together with a survey of the issues they would need to consider. For some of the incoming members, the immediacy of the demands was bewildering. Despite their notionally full-time role, many members had extensive commitments elsewhere, and some of those interviewed complained about the officers' expectations that they would arrive 'with empty diaries and empty heads' to take the decisions presented to them by the transition team.

An immediate task for the Assembly was to consider the form of the standing orders under which it would operate. Interim standing orders had been prepared by the transition team and adopted at the first meeting of the Assembly to enable it to function. Putting matters on a more permanent basis turned out to be a significant test for the new members. A desire for the familiar once again revealed itself in relation to these ground rules. The transition team had urged that the Assembly, as an entirely new type of body without executive functions, would need to operate in a far more flexible fashion than local authorities, with their electorate procedures and standing orders. The more senior among the new members, however, had extensive experience at the borough level, and instinctively rejected the advice given to them while they searched among sets of borough standing orders for a suitable model to adopt.

It was hard to throw off the legacy of old-fashioned local authority politics. One Assembly member complained in an interview that

In the first instance bringing the habits and the background of local authorities here is a mistake. What we really needed was a critical mass of lawyers and journalists, whose business is interrogation, that's what we really ought to do . . . to interrogate what's wrong, what are the possible solutions, who can do it, and force evaluation . . . we have got a culture which was brought from local authorities which is really about managing things, and that's not what we do . . . we spend an awful lot of time already on [management] but in fact we ought to be spending a lot more on our scrutiny function, and that I think would demand a different sort of person . . . I would myself promote the interests of lawyers, journalists, some of the campaigning voluntary organizations' people, because they are really who we need.

In practice, the operation of the Assembly meetings has been more open and informal than might have been expected from this, partly because of the lead taken to the chair, Trevor Phillips. Phillips, having no local government background, set a style that some found more appropriate to the Authority's function.

Under the arrangements confirmed in the summer of 2000, the GLA conducted its business through fortnightly Assembly meetings and committees. Statutory meetings of the Assembly questioned the Mayor and received his reports. Plenary meetings of the Assembly, which alternated with them, held discussions on areas not covered by the committee structure, including regular sessions on the police, fire, and health services. They also considered crosscutting issues in relation to the Mayor's several strategies and the Assembly's committees. The Assembly could launch short-life investigations of any matters relating to London. Four principal committees—transport policy and spatial planning, transport operation scrutiny, environment and sustainability, and economic development—were set up to handle the main business of the Assembly, appointments to which were subject to the political proportionality requirements of the Local Government and Housing Act 1989. In addition, an appointments committee, an interim budget committee, an audit committee, a standards committee, and a standing orders committee were set up, some of them time-limited.

These committees had to look both inward at the Mayor's strategies and outward to the functional bodies through which they were in large measure expressed. The transport policy and spatial planning, and the environment and sustainability, committees focused on the relevant strategies and monitored their implementation. The transport operation scrutiny committee monitored the performance of TfL as well as the implementation of the Mayor's transport policy. The economic development committee, in addition to reviewing the implementation of the Mayor's strategies in so far as they related to economic development and regeneration, monitored the LDA and was charged with ensuring that the GLA was consistent in its promotion of the London economy, nationally and internationally, and promoting and encouraging training and employment initiatives across London. Additionally, an informal 'bureau' of leaders was established to coordinate Assembly business across the parties. During the transitional period, the four party leaders met with the transition team weekly to plan and structure the new organization, and were joined on a monthly basis by the Mayor.

The membership structure was naturally something on which the Assembly members had opinions based on their prior experience—and on which they were concerned to influence the outcome. It was less easy for them to do so in respect of the officer structure. Neither the organizational structure of a local authority nor the established role of chief executive easily adapted to the GLA. Although an officer needed to be designated as head of the paid service, and Chilton occupied that post on a temporary basis, his team had questioned whether the role of the Mayor as elected chief executive made it appropriate to confer the same title on an officer. However, Assembly members felt more comfortable with traditional roles and labels, and were conscious that the GLA would need a clearly identifiable 'face' to represent the Authority at officer level, meeting government officials eye to eye. The team's advice was set aside, and in October 2000 Anthony Mayer, a career civil servant who made his reputation at the Housing Corporation, was appointed as chief executive at a salary of £130,000.

At its first meeting the Assembly had considered the proposals for staff structures put forward by the transition team, which sought to 'create the maximum flexibility for the Assembly to remodel'. The traditional approach to local authority organization dictated the setting up of professionally based departments which were focused on key roles in the cabinet or the Assembly. The problem with importing such a structure into the new Authority was highlighted by Chilton, who pointed to the difficulties of supporting a large number of dedicated units, and argued that a partitioned structure was likely to shield inefficiency and impeded cross-cutting working (GLA 2000*b*).

Instead, the GLA was advised to adopt the principle of continuous flexibility on the grounds that it was more suited to the Assembly's 'mobile agenda, small headquarters body and substantial resources both within the functional bodies and in other London bodies'. Chilton proposed a nodal structure around the Mayor's key strategic responsibilities. These nodes would comprise staff in 'competence reservoirs' to undertake projects. Such an arrangement, he argued, would 'maximise the contribution of the limited staff available, deliver support to priority areas, avoid the inefficiency of a heavily partitioned organisation and facilitate a joined up approach to London problems'.

Above all, the way in which the GLA organized itself for strategic purposes should, according to Chilton, 'flow from the unique responsibility of the GLA to take a panoramic perspective of London's possibilities and to impart that view through strategic and operational objectives' (GLA 2000*b*: para 18). Here too arose the dilemma which Chilton's earlier transition team had focused on: that of striking a balance between providing maximum choice and flexibility on the one hand and getting the GLA off to a rapid start on the other. A good deal of preliminary strategic thinking had already been done by the various 'enthusiastic bodies', preparing papers with a view to the GLA 'hitting the ground running', but, he warned, they risked 'topic strategies developing without reference to each other, or to the Mayor's view of London'. The team's proposed strategy directorate would be 'at the confluence of ideas, not only from strategic thinkers outside the GLA, but also within the functional bodies'. Its role would be to develop a coordinated approach to strategy across the range of functional bodies. The process would not be one of developing extensive and detailed strategy documents but rather a 'mean and lean' approach, centred on short, succinct statements.

Yet the transition team had avoided making any permanent appointments to the proposed strategy directorate. Their hesitation reflected more than the general need to provide an adequate range of choice. The team wanted to avoid taking on staff from the merged bodies for these key roles; were the GLA to have recruited in the market place 'it might not have employed the current professional profile of staff'. Many of the core staff of the Authority were to be filled by the existing staff of the LRC, the LEU, and the LPAC. If the GLA had not been required to absorb these bodies, it could have started from scratch with the professional staff profile it required for its functions. This might require a small intelligence function and would certainly require developing nodes of specialists, while a commissioning rather than direct provider role would have kept numbers small.

Instead, in Chilton's view, while the 20 staff of LPAC had the right skills for the strategic GLA planning role, the skills of the LEU staff 'do not immediately align to issues of air quality, waste management and noise'. This was not too great a handicap; they were few in number. On the other hand, while the staff of the LRC had built up around the research and intelligence role of the former GLC, 'they have less experience of policy development and strategy work'. Given this, Chilton proposed the reconstitution of the larger part of the LRC as an arms-length consultancy, undertaking external work and reliant upon income earned in the marketplace. For, while consuming budget and space, these specialists did not 'map on to the GLA strategic role'. It was a damning judgement, and one that brought a hostile press. The Assembly, however, had no taste for this kind of radicalism.

Skill mismatches apart, absorbing existing staff groups risked carrying established cultures into the new organization. This danger may have been apparent in relation to the LRC group, many of whom had served the former GLC and remained in post through the 14 years of joint borough control. It would be natural for them to view the appointed day as a return to 'business as usual'. In practice, however, continuity of culture and the associated problem of 'capture' of the new organization arose more acutely in relation to the GOL which, as the parent organization, instinctively sought to shape the values and outlook of the new authority. A civil servant reflected:

If you think about the small group of people in July 1997, some of the people who were there at the beginning were writing the Green Paper. They were the mothers of the child, if you like. When the transition team was set up, when Bob [Chilton] began to get his team, they became the foster parents, and the baby was handed over. Inevitably here, people could have had particular ideas . . . even I had ideas, had my own visions and they saw somebody with a different vision. That caused us some difficulties.

It is a moot point which of these several parties—Mayor and his office, the Assemblymen and women, the transition team and their civil service sponsors—had the clearest and most fitting vision of the task facing the new Authority. And despite these closely considered decisions on structure, some perceptive Assembly members were uneasy about whether it was fit for the purpose of scrutiny. One reflected:

I think the idea of committee is a problem, I think we really haven't found a dynamic alternative to trailing these issues through the machine properly. Now one thing we have begun to do is to use the idea of the special inquiry, the formal/informal inquiry, potentially more creatively. If I've got a model in my mind, it's rather as Congress uses its committee system, to pick an issue and whack it, call the executive to account and then finish it, go on to something else . . . The standing committees of the Assembly should really be rather kind of low-key affairs, which just keep tabs on things because we're not managing anything, but what we should do is have a series of rather flexible task forces and working groups that are there to answer a particular question.

It was among such doubts that the GLA became operative in July 2000. The new system, with its absolute distinction between executive action and the scrutiny of that action, had everything to prove.

7

London On the Move?

IT is through relationships between the GLA and other London-wide bodies that much of the Mayor's strategic influence will be exerted. Roads and public transport were the dominant political issues during the life of the GLC, from the ill-fated motorway box to the short-lived Fare's Fair policy. Now, under the 1999 Act, Transport for London (TfL), a new body, has absorbed the functions of a range of agencies, including some of those of the Government Office for London. Responsibility for London Regional Transport, the operator, passes to TfL once agreement has been reached on financing the modernization of the underground. This takes place outside the Mayor's transport strategy, which addresses a wide range of issues and is directed to public transport improvements and restriction of the motor car.

The Act requires the Mayor to consult with the boroughs and the City on the preparation and revision of transport strategies where they affect local interests. As a high-profile political figure, he needs to ensure that TfL and these other bodies deliver on his objectives, as Londoners apparently care more about public transport than about any other single issue. Despite the choice of an executive agency for this function, this will be no arms-length relationship, for Livingstone has exercised his right to chair the TfL board.

Throughout the Mayor's first year, the battle with the government over the terms of Tube financing, dominated London politics to the eclipse of all other issues. None of the devices adopted by the government to resolve this dispute—including the appointment and subsequent dismissal of the Transport Commissioner, Bob Kiley, as chairman of London Transport—had a major impact and, in July 2001, the two sides at last met in the High Court.

The Gathering Crisis

Thus, within a year of the inauguration of the Authority it was already becoming clear how uneasy relations with central government were going to be. There were a number of areas of initial, and potential, conflict. In particular, London's transport and traffic problems were long-standing. The London Planning Advisory Committee cited the conclusion of the Transport Select Committee of the House of Commons in 1982 that the state of transport system in the capital was 'a scandal of international and national significance'.

Despite improvements in later years in the organization and financing of London's transport, problems remained on the roads, rail, and underground:

The congestion of morning and evening peak 'rush hours' is now encroaching into the off-peak periods particularly in Central and Inner London. Despite a limited number of new roads, rail and underground lines, bridges and tunnels over the last 15 years, London becomes ever more congested and overcrowded and its parking and other problems ever more intractable. Those in Central London, town centres and a wide range of suburban locations near railway or underground stations are now particularly intense. (LPAC 1988: para 2.41)

On the railways themselves the problems of overcrowding, discomfort, access, and security were worsening. Reliability had scarcely improved, while levels of service and indicators of public satisfaction were measurably declining. The number of customer complaints was rising steadily and, in the case of British Rail's Network South East, 64 per cent more complaints were made in 1988 than in 1981 (LPAC 1988: para 2.41). Meanwhile, safety on the underground system had become a concern, particularly after the Kings Cross fire of 1987.

LPAC argued that the scale of London's transport problems was having an adverse effect on economic and employment growth in the region:

It is already clear that transportation problems have cost jobs in the capital itself, by making the city a less hospitable and efficient place in which to hold a job. They are directly damaging the tourism and entertainment industries, and poor transportation could be affecting the level of international business undertaken in London. Inefficient transportation systems are adding to the costs of goods and services, reducing the operating efficiency of many businesses through access and parking problems and reducing labour mobility. (LPAC 1988: para 2.46)

For all these reasons, transport continued to be the dominant issue in discussion of London's problems, and it became inseparable from arguments about the need for an overall transportation authority for the metropolis. Before the abolition of the GLC, the London Regional Transport Act 1984 had removed control of London Transport from the GLC, reversing the decision taken by the Labour government in 1969. The Act established London Regional Transport (LRT) on 29 June 1984 as a statutory corporation which, in 1990, reverted to trading as London Transport. It also set up the London Regional Passenger Committee to represent users. LRT's statutory duties were to provide, or secure the provision of, public passenger transport services for Greater London, having regard to transport needs and to the efficiency, economy and safety of operations. Responsible for the coordination of fares, services, and charges, it was obliged to consult and cooperate with British Railways.

The LRT board had twelve members appointed by the Secretary of State for Transport. In addition to the chairman, three were full-time executive appointments with specific responsibility for buses, underground, and finance. LRT was financed by a combination of fare revenues and central government grants made up partly from a precept on London ratepayers, determined by the Secretary of State, and not exceeding two-thirds of LRT's capital and revenue grants. The Secretary of State also set financial targets for LRT, the most important of which was to reduce the level of revenue support from ratepayers and taxpayers from £192 million in 1984–5 to £95 million in 1997–8. Four specific tasks were also given to LRT in its foundation year: to improve bus and underground services within the resources available, to reduce costs and secure better value for money, to promote better management through smaller operating units, and to involve the private sector wherever that was deemed to be more efficient.

On the roads

Bus privatization was at the heart of the Conservative government's policy of seeking to expand transport choices through the creation of a liberal and deregulated transport market. Following the creation of LRT under the 1984 Act, London Buses Limited (LBL) was set up to run bus services in preparation for competitive tendering. In 1994 this was hived off and split into a number of bus operating companies which were then sold to the private sector. A new company, LT Buses, was established at that point to coordinate bus-related functions within London Transport, responsible for route planning, service contract tendering, and performance monitoring, while the privately owned companies were responsible for services and for setting their own fares. The intention was that a profitable bus service would operate without subsidy on a commercial basis, with LRT ensuring the provision of additional socially necessary services on contracts secured through competitive tendering (LRT 1988). LRT sought to manage the transition to deregulation in such a manner as to gain maximum benefits, while it continued as the tendering authority for the provision of unprofitable but socially necessary routes. The terms of bus deregulation differed in London from those applied across the country and, in the course of time, generally seem to have been more successful, leading to cost savings of around 16 per cent (Mackie, Preston, and Nash 1995; Kennedy 1995).

London's bus services continued to face problems of movement and reliability. In large part, they flowed from the increasing congestion on London's roads. The answer to road congestion in urban areas had in the past been to increase capacity. From the 1970s, when the London motorway box was abandoned, opinion swung away from provision towards restraint. Transport policy professionals came to recognize that building more motorways would neither eliminate peak-period traffic congestion nor improve rush-hour travel:

In large and dense urban areas, there is a huge level of 'suppressed demand', a large pool of public transport users ready to switch to driving when more road space becomes available. So after road space is added, congestion returns to the roads as new drivers clog up the new roads. (LRC 1998: 194)

Road pricing—or, in urban areas, congestion charging—was favoured for some years as the solution to overcrowded city streets. The technical possibilities had gradually clarified, although a government-commissioned study published in 1995 concluded that electronic road pricing would not be available before 2010. The principal objection remained one of public acceptability. The political difficulty in road pricing was bound to be the resistance of the driving public. For most people who have access to a car, it had long been the mode of choice for almost all journeys except where the inconvenience and cost of congestion and of parking make public transport preferable.

This was the hurdle that policy had to overcome, and London Transport made much of the running in pushing the debate forward. LT's director of planning argued that in the long term the only solution to road congestion lay in road pricing, a view that was consistently supported within the organization (Bayliss 1992; Goldstein 1989). In 1990 LPAC produced a study recommending the introduction of road pricing throughout London, with rates falling with distance from the centre. A survey of 500 Londoners, sponsored by the National Economic Development Office (NEDO) in 1991, confirmed the importance they attached to relieving congestion, but concluded that the provision of high-quality public transport was a prerequisite for the introduction of congestion charging (Harris Research Centre *et al.* 1991). Conversely, other research showed that measures to improve bus services in urban areas would have a negligible effect unless supported by measures to reduce road use by private cars by pricing fuel, parking, or road space itself (delle Site and Filippi 1995).

Whether traffic restraint should precede or follow public transport improvements, it was coming to be regarded as inevitable following the passage of the Road Traffic Reduction Act 1997:

The alternative is not no restraint but restraint by congestion, which is accepted as extremely inefficient, increasing delays and unreliability, possibly deterring local economic activity, increasing pollution for a given level of traffic, and wasting resources, estimated at many billions of pounds each year. (Murray 1997: 13)

By the late 1990s it appeared that congestion charges were becoming more attractive to politicians but were still a long way from being sufficiently acceptable to support their introduction (Moran 1999).

In November 1998, London First launched a study of road pricing, to be carried out by consultants Halcrow Fox. The aim of the study was to determine the technical and political feasibility of congestion charging and to identify the kinds of trips that could be deterred. The consultants were asked to examine both low-cost paper pass schemes and electronic measures to curtail unauthorized use of roads as well as to delineate the possible boundaries to impose charges. London First claimed that the aim of the study was to improve London's competitiveness and the quality of life for Londoners. In response, the RAC attacked the unfairness of charging people to drive on routes where there was no suitable public transport alternative and where some people could not afford the extra charge to use their car (*ES*, 18 November 1998).

What brought congestion charging finally onto London's political agenda was the movement toward an 'integrated' transport policy. In 1996, LPAC put forward what it described as an 'objective led approach' to the production of 'a single all inclusive transport programme' funded by a single transport budget for London (LPAC 1996). Following this study and the publication of the London Pride Partnership's *London's Action Programme for Transport 1995–2010*, the GOL and the Department of Transport jointly published a *Transport Strategy for London*. This document was to form the basis of the transport policy environment that the GLA inherited. Its key features were the promotion of walking, cycling, and public transport as alternatives to car use. Measures for car restraint were to be coupled with major investment in the public transport infrastructure and in the region's strategic road network, along with comprehensive traffic management and limited new road construction. The planning system was to be used to reduce the overall need to travel and an air quality strategy would be developed under the Environment Act 1995. Though welcomed by many in the business community, the government's paper was criticized for being in large measure aspirational and for making no firm commitment on investment beyond the first two tranches, and in particular for the seemingly perpetual postponement of Crossrail. The joint chairman of London Pride Partnership commented that 'there is now virtually no disagreement across London about what should be done: the only issue is how soon' (LT 1996: para 2.2).

Modernizing the Tube

Following the establishment of the LRT, the programme of station modernization, started in 1981, with an initial capital investment programme of £107 million, was extended to track, train controls, and ticketing, although only per cent was devoted to rolling stock. By the end of the decade it had become clear that considerable further investment was required. In the 1991 autumn statement, the Conservative government announced increased levels of investment in the underground, ostensibly in response to an adverse report from the Monopolies and Mergers Commission (MMC 1991). Twelve months later, however, with a general election behind them, the re-elected administration withdrew the increased funding, with cuts on the projected expenditure of between 25 per cent and 35 per cent falling in each of the next three years. In their evidence to the House of Commons Transport Committee, London Transport demonstrated just how drastic these reductions would be for station modernization in particular, although train modernization and infrastructure improvement would also be hard hit. Investment was to run at around £500m annually, or a little over half the level required to achieve LT's objective of a 'Decently Modern Metro' with ten years, and at around two-thirds of the level deemed 'essential' (LT 1993). During this same period, other major cities, notably Paris, were investing heavily in their metro systems.

Although new trains were the most potent symbol of underground investment, LT continued to prioritize station modernization as the key to increasing capacity on the underground:

Almost all the underground lines have sections where the trains are overcrowded, particularly inwards from the mainline termini, but also on longer stretches of the Central,
Northern, Victoria and Piccadilly lines. In some places the overcrowding is severe and
many of the busier stations have areas where passenger flows exceed station design
guidelines. In addition, many journeys involve inconvenient interchange, and many
stations have cramped and awkward layouts. In places the existing system cannot cope
with a significant increase in use at peak periods. (LT 1996: para 5.5, 5.6)

Even with planned improvements, overcrowding on lines through central
London was expected to increase by 2001. Modernization of both underground trains and stations was thus seen as imperative if rising demand were
to be met, even at the existing levels of overcrowding.

However, further improvements threatened to be self-defeating: by attract-
ing further traffic, they would lead to further overcrowding. According to
London Transport, the salvation of the underground lay not in increasing its
capacity as such but in developing projected overground rail links across
London as 'regional metros'. Under this plan, Thameslink improvement
would relieve the Northern, Victoria, and Piccadilly lines. The projected
Crossrail would relieve 'the most intractable congestion', notably on the
Central line and also the Jubilee, Bakerloo, Metropolitan, Hammersmith and
City lines and the western reaches of the Piccadilly lines. The planned Chelsea-
Hackney line would relieve overcrowding and accommodate further growth in
demand through the central area. Investing in this way in the regional metros
'could increase the capacity of rail network across the central area by at least a
third—equivalent to building six dual three-lane motorways'. Ultimately,
some 500 million passengers could use the three lines each year, while pressure on the underground would be greatly diminished by reducing the need
to interchange at some of the busiest stations in the network (LT 1996: para
5.7–5.8). The scale of these problems prompted London Transport to make a
vigorous bid for massive new investment. In a 1996 report LT provided a rigorous analysis intended to demonstrate that heavy investment in transport
infrastructure was critical if the government's aims for London as a competitive world city were to be realised (LT 1996).

Although the new Labour ministers had emphatically rejected the
Conservatives' private finance initiative (PFI) in the run-up to the election,
they had not been explicit about how private finance might be attracted to
major investment projects. 'Wholesale privatization' of London Underground
(LU) had been specifically ruled out in the election manifesto, and Glenda
Jackson, as shadow transport minister, undertook that with an election held
on Thursday 'privatisation would be scrapped on the Friday'. At the same time,
Conservative ministers recognized that the scale of public investment necessary to modernize the Tube was greatly in excess of anything their expenditure

plans would permit, while the need to push public borrowing below the Maastricht limit of 3 per cent of GDP constrained them still further. In order to escape Treasury limits on borrowing by public enterprises, the underground network would have to be at least 50 per cent privately owned. There was a problem: if that was seen as 'privatization', then the government was likely to come under attack from its own supporters. Hence, the delicate use of the term 'wholesale' in the manifesto promises. The solution was to use a modified form of the PFI.

Labour's favoured term—public-private partnership (PPP)—had been much bandied about but less often explained. As it happened, explanation was required far sooner than the government expected. After being interviewed on BBC 1's Panorama programme in June 1997, John Prescott accidentally left behind in the studio documents that outlined the government's thinking on financing Tube modernization. These documents included a draft letter from the Deputy Prime Minister to the Paymaster-General, Geoffrey Robinson, telling him that financial advisers were about to be appointed to consider the options 'for public-private partnerships for London underground', under which private companies would take a majority shareholding in the Tube. A major row erupted, with Prescott accusing the BBC of theft and insisting that his plans did not amount to 'privatization by the back door'.

In reality, the government's view of the Tube issue was undoubtedly shaped in part by a conviction that private management would prove more efficient than public. Thus, ministers were constrained by the arguments that while bonds could be floated at a lower interest rate than that at which the private sector would need to borrow, private investors would need to borrow less in the first place: £12.5 billion as against £15.5 billion for the bond issue. The difference was accounted for by efficiency savings which private management could be expected to deliver through manpower reductions and the use of more experienced management. The private sector consortia were specialists in project management and infrastructure provision, while LU's expertise lay in passenger movement.

For ministers, the timing of the bidding process and the subsequent hand-over needed to ensure that the issue should be settled before the successful mayoral candidate took office. The urgency with which the government moved forward took transport groups and the City by surprise, but a number of prospective investors emerged to express their interest. Bids for the contracts for the modernization of LU—valued at that stage at up to £7 billion—were invited in July 1999 for the first pre-qualification stage. Known as 'infracos', the bidders were specially formed consortia, including French and Japanese construction and finance groups as well as the major civil engineering undertakings in the UK: Balfour Beatty, Taylor Woodrow, McAlpine. The first two contracts would be for 'deep-tube' franchises: the BCV—Bakerloo, Central, Waterloo, and City and Victoria—lines and JNP—Jubilee, Northern, and Piccadilly—lines. The third contract, for the older sub-surface lines—the Circle, District, Hammersmith and City, and East London—was to be negotiated exclusively with Railtrack, which was barred from bidding for the other two. The scheme to involve the much-criticized Railtrack was based on the expectation that ways could be found to integrate the underground and main-line railway track operations, with main-line trains running on the northern section of the Circle line taking them from Paddington to Kings Cross and the City. When John Prescott announced that this last proposal was to be withdrawn as integrated use of the track had been found not feasible—indeed, Tube managers had ridiculed it—it was widely seen as a humiliating climb-down.

As a prospective mayoral candidate, Lord Archer had strongly opposed PPP as unworkable and advocated instead full privatization of the system (Archer 1999: 8–9). The biggest threat to the PPP, however, was the prospect of a Livingstone candidacy. Ken Livingstone had been quick to claim credit for the collapse of the Railtrack deal. 'If this is what I can achieve in two weeks as a candidate', he observed triumphantly, 'think of what I can do for London if I am Mayor'. In the campaign, he set out his stall arguing that a policy of incentives to use public transport through fare reductions was more likely to succeed than one based on making car use more difficult (Livingstone 1999: 20, 22). As the bids went in, Livingstone predicted that if the government went ahead with the PPP then the mayoral election would be 'transformed into a referendum on the future of London'. He argued that the majority of Labour Party members supported him in his opposition to Tube privatization. His claim was given credibility by reports that the Prime Minister had written to every Labour Party member in London to persuade him or her of the merits of the PPP. Thus, the party leadership itself had made Tube privatization the pivotal issue in its candidate selection process, yet had failed to convince its own followers. Seizing on this advantage, Livingstone called upon the government to 'abandon the attempt to trample on Londoners by imposing on them a potentially unsafe transport system'. Despite ministers' best attempts to create the opposite impression, Livingstone's victory in the May 2000 election was widely read as a vote against the PPP.

The way the transport debate developed between the establishment of LRT in 1985 and the mayoral election 15 years later prepared the ground for the London Mayor to take the lead role. True, the Mayor would not be able to shape the immediate pattern of initial investment in the underground: central government had reserved this role to itself. It was also true that he would have only the most limited influence on overground rail provision, although liaison with the new Strategic Rail Authority was intended to achieve a greater degree of coherence in rail services. But the issues had been fully aired, and the essentials of a strategy for transport in London were already in place by the time the Greater London Authority came into being.

New directions for London's transport

The GLA Act 1999 gave the Mayor wide-ranging powers over transport in London. He was charged with developing and implementing policies for the promotion and encouragement of safe, integrated, efficient and economic transport facilities and services to, from, and within Greater London. He was made responsible for developing a coherent strategy for London and for appointing the board of TfL. When the Mayor took office, he exercised his right to chair the board of TfL, appointing as his vice-chair Dave Wetzel, the former GLC transport chairman. The Act also gave the Mayor power to introduce road user charges and a levy on workplace parking. While the London boroughs continued as local transport authorities, they now had to draw up local implementation plans (LIPs) within the context of the Mayor's transport strategies, for which they would be accountable to him. If the Mayor considered that a borough's LIP did not adequately reflect his own transport strategy, he could refer it back for rewriting or rewrite the LIP himself.

The Act brought about a streamlining of the organization of transport in London (see Fig. 7.1). TfL absorbed the role of the Traffic Director for London, the Public Carriage Office, the Traffic Control Systems Unit, Docklands Light

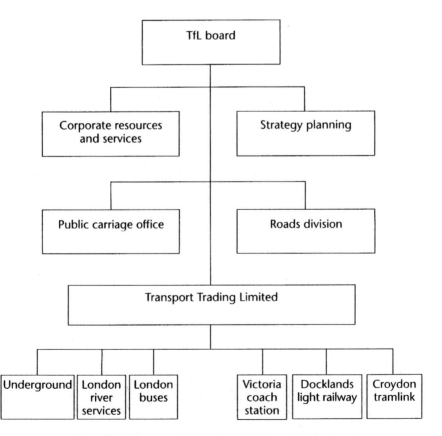

Figure 7.1: Transport for London: the intended structure

Railway, London Regional Transport, and part of the Highways Agency. Regulation of the bus companies also passed to TfL, with licences granted to private operating companies. It was left to TfL to define the London Bus Network and procure services for these routes. The Mayor acquired responsibility for fares, and could enforce decisions providing they did not prejudice the financial or other interests of London Transport. Additionally, TfL took over responsibility for the black cabs and for the regulation of minicab operations. LU kept a separate existence until completion of the PPP arrangements, at which point it would be absorbed into the TfL structure. Once the PPP was in place—the original target date was April 2001—TfL would become responsible for operating underground services through a new London Underground operating company, responsible for services, ticketing and fares, drivers, network and station staff, safety, and signalling. The new London Underground would manage the contracts with the private companies that were awarded the tenders to maintain and modernize the infrastructure, stations, and rolling stock. When their contracts expired, the assets would revert to the public sector.

Congestion Charges

John Prescott's Transport White Paper, published in July 1998, promised a 'new dawn' for all forms of transport (DETR 1998b). Local authorities would be required to produce five-year transport plans after consulting local residents and businesses, and powers would be given to enable them to levy charges on workplace parking, although earlier proposals to levy a parking-place charge on supermarket and leisure centres were dropped. Councils would also be given powers to levy 'anti-congestion' charges to reduce congestion and exhaust emissions. The money raised thereby would be used exclusively for transport improvements. The proposal to recycle congestion charging revenues into transport improvements represented a victory over the Treasury's antipathy towards hypothecated taxes. The government had originally intended to give all local authorities the power to set and collect the charges but was nervous of the possible electoral backlash. Ministers were fearful of the public reaction and of giving the Opposition an opportunity to capitalize on dissent by presenting themselves as the 'party of the motorist'. The transport bill accordingly provided for no more than localized pilots and experiments other than in London, where the GLA could be expected to pursue congestion charging as it would be its sole source of revenue.

A congestion charge could raise £400 million a year in London and a tax on workplace car parking a further £100 million, sums which could be invested in public transport while discouraging car use and thus freeing up the roads. The revenue from the GLA charges was to be hypothecated for a ten-year period. Thereafter, the Treasury was expected to make a bid to seize it. Although congestion charging was the sole tax-raising power bestowed upon the Mayor, the responses of would-be candidates for the mayoralty varied widely. Broadly, the left was supportive, the right opposed it. Frank Dobson was provisionally in favour, while Glenda Jackson indicated that she thought congestion charging was potentially a valuable tool. By contrast, both Jeffrey Archer and Steven Norris promised not to levy a charge, with Norris defending the right of free car use together with the possibly incompatible pledge to 'get London moving'. Ken Livingstone thought such a scheme necessary and the charges reasonable, and had little fear of a motorists' backlash.

In the middle of the campaign, the congestion charging issue moved into the foreground with the publication of the Halcrow Fox report for London First, assessing the options for charging. The favoured scheme involved the cordoning of a large central area bounded by Marylebone to the north, Old Street and Tower Bridge to the East, Elephant and Castle and Kennington to the South, and Victoria and Marble Arch to the West, from 7 a.m. to 7 p.m. on weekdays. Free access would be allowed only for emergency services and scheduled bus and coach services. Other vehicles attempting to enter central London during these hours would need to display a paper token costing £5–£10 a day on their windscreen. Their second, admittedly 'controversial', option involved a system of licensing whereby drivers wishing to enter the central area would log their registration numbers on to a central database, with roadside sensors scanning number plates and matching them to the permits. With as few as 100 surveillance cameras backed by a substantial police presence, there would be an 80 per cent chance of catching evaders. The scheme would, however, cost some £50 million to install, with an annual operating, enforcement, and administrative cost of a further £50 million. A third possibility put forward by the consultants was a workplace parking scheme to levy a £3,000 annual charge on employers, providing parking for their staff and business visitors over a much larger area covering parts of Camden, Islington, Tower Hamlets, Southwark, Lambeth, and all of Hammersmith and Fulham.

The congestion charging lobby gained momentum when, in May 1999, a survey by London First of 300 of their business members found overwhelming support for a £5 charge on private motorists and van drivers, with medium-sized trucks and heavy goods vehicles paying £10 and £15 respectively. London First claimed that while the charging scheme would impose a cost on firms of £55 million a year, almost all of the firms surveyed would be willing to meet the costs, providing the revenue was applied to transport improvements. In contrast, when the parking tax was first mooted the Association of British Chambers of Commerce warned that it would cost business £2 million a year.

Making it work

Leaving aside the consequences for business and residents of such an exclusion zone and the levels of congestion along the avoidance routes, enforcement was clearly going to be both costly and difficult. On the consultants' estimates a substantial force of inspectors would be required, with at least 400 officers and police support needed to achieve a one-in-five chance of catching a driver attempting to evade the charge. Further congestion would follow from cars being stopped for checks, causing serious delays on the very roads the congestion charge was intended to free up. Local authorities would have to provide at least 150 stopping bays for these checks. Such a level of detection and all the attendant possibilities of tactical avoidance would make it a difficult scheme to implement. A report to the Metropolitan Police Authority from the Metropolitan Police Service highlighted the potential problems of enforcing the congestion charging scheme (MPA 2000). Policing non-compliance with enforcement cameras at the boundary of the area and dealing with the likely increase in spontaneous congestion on the inner ring road and linking roads would have substantial resource implications.

Although environmental groups had made the running in the debate about traffic in London, the publication of detailed proposals elicited a raft of objections and potential problems, many of them put forward by the motoring organizations. Seeking to widen the debate, the RAC called for a London-wide strategic review of traffic calming measures, arguing that local councils had been panicked by the Road Traffic Reduction Act into 'hindering traffic' rather than considering their effect on the overall traffic flow patterns. The RAC argued that speed reductions were achieved at a high cost in terms of pollution and damage to cars and inconvenience to emergency services. 'Some councils do little more than throw lumps of concrete at the road', said an RAC spokesman. 'We are increasingly seeing councils install large schemes which significantly alter traffic flow where it is undesirable' (*ES*, 16 November 1998).

Would the scheme work? Revenue raising was one thing, cutting down on traffic another. On the face of it, the charging proposals did not look like a particularly effective means of reducing congestion. It was estimated that the reduction in central London during the morning peak would be no more than 10 per cent. Thousands of essential car users would be excluded along with black-cab drivers unless granted exemptions, thereby abating the benefits of the scheme. Motorcyclists could be expected to protest, as would residents within the zone who would pay a substantial charge for use of their cars. A new campaigning group, Road Charging Options for London, attacked the scheme as an inadequate solution, warning of heavy congestion on the periphery of the zone and of widespread evasion with any windscreen permit-based scheme.

The boroughs most affected by the proposed charging zone—Westminster, Wandsworth, Kensington and Chelsea—joined together to campaign against the congestion charge, representing it as an additional tax on residence and business, adding to congestion with drivers using peripheral roads and parking on the edge of the zone. Wandsworth's transport committee chairman warned that

the ordinary Londoners will suffer most. They will be the ones to pay out of their own pocket. White van man will find ways around the charge while corporate fat cats will get their firms to pay. With this charge the government and the Mayor for London will between them have added up to £1,800 a year to the road tax bill for anyone whose livelihood depends on taking their car into the centre of the city. All charging will achieve is to make the roads slightly less congested for the benefit of those who can most afford to pay. (*ES*, 1 August 2000)

Kensington and Chelsea's deputy leader warned that the charges would 'result in utter chaos' while Westminster's Transport and Highways Committee chairman predicted businesses would be driven out of central London (*ES*, 24 July 2000). The London Chambers of Commerce agreed, arguing that a paper-based charge was unlikely to work and, in getting the wrong scheme, the Mayor risked public embarrassment and harming the London economy. The Conservative Party had opposed congestion charging from the outset and Angie Bray, the Conservatives' transport spokesman on the Assembly, predicted that

[t]his charging cordon will throw up a 'Berlin wall' through London communities. It will make the school run prohibitively expensive and turn the outer periphery of the cordon into a giant car park. Families who have routinely driven around their own neighbourhoods or go to school will suddenly have to pay for the privilege or be unable to do so. Many drivers will end up cruising the boundary, worsening congestion in the areas not covered by the charge. And in the evening as they drive to theatres and restaurants, we could see thousands stopping at the side of the road outside the cordon, engines on, waiting for the magic hour when restrictions end at 7 pm. (*ES*, 1 August 2000)

It was obvious that the Mayor's own proposals, when they came, would get a rough reception.

The Mayor's proposals

Ken Livingstone had urged congestion charging during his election campaign. The Labour manifesto for the Assembly, while not opposed to charges in principle, had promised they would not be brought in until there were proper public transport alternatives in place, along with a workable electronic checking scheme. This gave a boost to the scheme's opponents. In the House of Commons on 10 May, William Hague seized the opportunity to extract an undertaking from the Prime Minister that the GLA Labour group would support the Conservative Assembly members in blocking the introduction of congestion charging, a promise that Blair, to the discomfort of some, readily gave. When the Assembly met the following day, the Conservatives tabled a motion deploring congestion charging as a 'damaging measure', noting 'the opposition of the majority of Londoners to congestion taxes', that of the Labour members' manifesto, and the Blair promise in the House of Commons. Livingstone's response was uncompromising, warning that the party leaders should not 'block the will of Londoners' by instructing their Assembly members. 'We have two years to build a consensus', he argued. 'Originally, the white paper didn't give the Mayor a congestion charge and I wrote asking for them to give the Mayor that power, so it seems strange that they should oppose it now' (*ES*, 11 May 2000).

Launching Transport for London, Livingstone declared: 'There is no point in being Mayor unless you have the courage to institute congestion charges. I will stake my political career on that . . .' (*ES*, 14 July 2000). Privately, he was confident of being able to proceed, given the limited power of Assembly members to block his budget and the tacit support of a number of supposed opponents. Darren Johnson, Livingstone's environment adviser and Green Party spokesman, gave encouragement, reporting the Mayor to be 'absolutely committed to seeing it go through. Both the Liberal Democrats and the Greens would like a congestion charge in the first term and a number of Labour members are sympathetic' (GLA press release, 11 May 2000).

In the event, the Assembly position proved harder to predict. The Assembly established a congestion charge scrutiny panel under a Liberal member, Lynn Featherstone, to examine the plans in detail, noting that 'the implementation of the Mayor's proposals for congestion charging will bring the biggest civil change to London since the second World War' (GLA 2000*a*). The report, described by Ms Featherstone as 'sensational', was dismissive of the Mayor's proposed timetable, which envisaged the introduction of the scheme by the end of 2002 and called for sufficient time to be allowed for consultation and for full consideration of representations. The timetable was 'extremely optimistic' and 'it would be better to introduce congestion charging later than December 2002 than to attempt to do so too soon with the consequent risk of failure':

It is important that if congestion charging is to be implemented, it must be done in a way which secures the confidence of all those affected by it, in whatever way. We are convinced that this is such a critical policy that, if it is to be introduced, it is better to introduce it later than currently planned (i.e. beyond the Mayor's starting point) but with a very high probability of a fully successful implementation, than to keep to the published timetable and the risk either that the system and/or the necessary associated and complementary measures are not ready, or that the system proves unreliable. (GLA 2000*a*: 3.11.12)

The scrutiny panel was also sceptical about the impact of the proposed charge on the level of congestion in central London, and called for the effects to be more fully investigated. The fact that no work had been done by the Mayor's team on the implications of the scheme for businesses of different types, and particularly small businesses in different parts of the capital, was condemned as 'unacceptable'. They doubted that the Mayor's staff had the necessary technical skill to develop the scheme. Finally, the panel took seriously the promise to link congestion charging to public transport improvements and insisted that charging 'must not be introduced until and unless' these improvements have been made. Further, it argued that the Assembly should require the Mayor to set specific targets for bus and train improvements that would have to be met before any steps to implement charging were taken. Taken forward initially on a cross-party basis, the scrutiny report lost the support of the Greens, caught between unconditional support for congestion charging and the force of the logic of the panel's criticisms.

The transport policy committee, to which the congestion panel reported, took up the issue of the Mayor's failure to provide the panel with a budget and a project plan. TfL officials thereupon stonewalled, claiming that the scheme contained commercially confidential information, the disclosure of which would prejudice their plans to purchase property at the boundary of the zone. The Assembly, however, was unconvinced and threatened to use its powers under section 62 of the GLA Act 1999 to serve a notice requiring the information to be produced. Lynn Featherstone complained that, with the Assembly's concerns about congestion charging well documented, 'it's incomprehensible that TfL is still unable or unwilling to provide the Assembly with a full budget and project plan' (GLA news release, 6 March 2001).

Demonstrating the feasibility of the scheme would prove an uphill struggle, but the stakes for the Mayor's administration could not have been higher. Only the Liberal Democrats and Greens wholeheartedly supported congestion charging, while Labour members were ambivalent and the Tories opposed. The scrutiny had weakened the overall level of support by highlighting the practical problems. It was a further blow when a technical report from the government's Transport Research Laboratory demonstrated that registration records were so out of date that enforcement would be impracticable unless the record system was overhauled before the introduction of charging, a process which itself could take several years. Livingstone, meanwhile, ignored his own officers' predictions that the timescale would slip and remained confident that improved bus services would be in place by the end of 2002 with road improvement schemes, more conductors, and flat fares.

Opinion in the Assembly was gradually hardening against the scheme. Labour began increasingly to detach itself from the Mayor and to define a distinct position. It proposed specific modifications—such as an amnesty period following introduction—and a direct linkage between the charges and improvements in air quality. It also sought assurances that the scheme would be delayed if the consultation revealed major problems. Labour members insisted that improvements in public transport would have to be introduced before the charge came into effect, and demanded explicit reassurance that the scheme would not add to congestion in areas surrounding the zone. When studies appeared to show that air pollution from traffic could rise in areas just outside the restricted zone, John Biggs, Labour's transport spokesman, accused the Mayor of focusing more on revenue raising than on actually reducing congestion and pollution (*ES*, 20 April 2001). In July 2001 the Labour members of the Assembly moved against Livingstone to force an admission that congestion charging might be delayed until summer 2003. Biggs then accused the Mayor of consistently ignoring calls to amend the scheme to make it fairer and more workable. He hinted darkly that the Mayor's real motive 'appears to be to delay implementation until after the next Mayoral election' (London Labour Party news release, 19 July 2001).

Digging Deep for PPP

Congestion charging was potentially the most important political issue facing the Authority. However, it had not been so in the public perception before the GLA was set up. After the election, Ken Livingstone identified the future of LU to have been the prime issue in the campaign. He claimed that an overwhelming majority of those who voted did so for candidates opposed to privatization of the Tube. On this basis, he called upon the government to 'respect the views of Londoners' and retain the underground in the public sector:

I want to say frankly that it is fifteen years of under-investment in the capital's transport system by the former government, not those who work our tubes and buses, or the unions of which they are members, that are the cause of the appalling problems we face in these areas. I look forward to lobbying with all sections of the City—business, unions, and most of all ordinary Londoners—to get the resources that are required to stop the strain on commuters nerves, and the waste of billions of pounds on lost London's business, caused by the City's transport gridlock. (*ES*, 5 May 2000)

Downing Street was unimpressed. The Prime Minister's spokesman replied bluntly that 'the policy on the Tube was settled. It was in our last general election manifesto' (*ES*, 8 May 2000). This was true. However, Livingstone's victory showed that the matter was far from resolved.

Tactics

The Mayor's ability to confront the government over the PPP was constrained by his need to take the Assembly with him. On 9 May the Labour group on the Assembly, with clear support from Downing Street, issued a statement that Nicky Gavron, to whom Livingstone had offered the post of deputy mayor, would accept the post only if the Mayor dropped his threat of legal action to block the government's plans. The group insisted that 'as part of any agreement to fill the Deputy Mayor's position, we expect the Mayor to step back from the threatened confrontation on the issue of the underground PPP' (*ES*, 9 May 2000). The deal had to be accepted, and part of the price was to accept an independent study of the viability of the two options. However, a number of academics and other independent experts were reported to have turned down the invitation, recognizing that the government would not provide the information needed to make such a study creditable. Unabashed, the Mayor commissioned Will Hutton, Director of the Industrial Society, to undertake the study. In the event, the Mayor was able to turn the Hutton Report to his own political advantage by launching it during the Labour Party conference at which he was a key fringe speaker. Hutton concluded that

The PPP should go forward only if it meets much more rigorous safety and value for money criteria and if it is substantially amended to protect against the risk that contracts are incomplete and over-generous. If it fails to meet these criteria then the bidding companies should instead bid for turnkey projects funded and financed by London Underground within the public sector. (*The Times*, 25 September 2000)

It seemed to be another public relations triumph for Livingstone: the fierce protests of Labour Assembly members, incensed by his tactical skill, could scarcely make the headlines.

The Mayor's strategy had been consistent: to hold fast to his opposition to the PPP even when critics suggested at an earlier stage that he was willing to trade off his commitment to financing by bond issue in return for acceptance back into the Labour Party. At the same time, he was adamant that any disagreement with government proposals for partial privatization remained unchanged. Nevertheless, he was exposed by the apparent absence of a 'Plan B', and his Labour critics pressed him on how he would respond if the government insisted on pressing ahead. 'You're a one-club golfer', accused John Biggs; 'it may deliver the hole in one, but it may also end up broken and tattered. You'll have the PPP, and Londoners will expect you to run with it, not to spend years fighting it' (GLA minutes, 18 October 2000).

The expenditure settlement announced in July was presented by ministers as massively generous to London with £3.2 billion allocated over three years for transport. Despite their confidence that the settlement would be regarded as favourable, the Mayor responded with a sharp attack on the Chancellor of the Exchequer. He had learned that the settlement had factored into it the £104 million bill for cost overruns on the Jubilee line. The row caused considerable bitterness, with John Prescott's office hitting back angrily that the Mayor had been given more funding even than he had asked for, while a photo call for the Mayor and the relevant junior minister, Keith Hill, was abruptly cancelled. 'I am going to have to go back and negotiate a better settlement with more of the money up front', commented the Mayor (*ES*, 20 July 2000). The larger point made was that the bulk of the extra funding would flow in the later years, leaving London starved in 2001–2. Complaining of a 'stitch up', the Mayor openly criticized the public expenditure strategies of the Prime Minister and the Chancellor.

The lack of a role in the consideration of the bids for the Tube contracts did not deter the Mayor from making public his own judgement about the bidding firms. Livingstone had deployed GLA officers and firms of private investigators on researching the consortia, the member companies, and their subsidiaries. On this basis, he listed the charges made against the companies— including environmental violations, arms manufacture, and commercial operation in a number of countries with 'oppressive regimes'. They were 'the worst scum of modern British capitalism', he told a rally of transport union workers. The chief executive of the Construction Industry Council retorted that 'Livingstone is hardly going to endear himself to Londoners that work in the industry' (*ES*, 28 July 2000).

The Mayor's tactics were to exploit every opportunity to present the PPP in the worst possible light. Generally, events favoured him and the government's plan suffered the first of a series of blows in August 2000 when the chief railway inspector privately voiced his concern about potential safety hazards in the scheme. He insisted that the division of responsibility for passenger safety, which had attracted fierce criticisms following railway privatization, was likely to be reproduced under the Tube plan. The inspector's letter was leaked and his comment that the PPP arrangements were incapable of providing proof that systems were working was a gift to Livingstone. John Prescott ordered an immediate meeting between LU and the Health and Safety Executive, but the political damage had been done and the Mayor gained as a result.

The Mayor received two further welcome boosts in December 2000. First, the Conservative group in the Assembly decided to support the Mayor in his opposition to the PPP against the Labour members who were bound by the Labour government's manifesto. Second, the PPP was criticized in a report by Price Waterhouse Coopers as more of a matter of faith than science (*ES*, 12 December 2000). The Mayor had not abandoned his plan to mount a legal challenge should the government not withdraw in the face of this barrage of unwelcome messages. Whatever the likely outcome of judicial review, the threat of a legal challenge on the supply of documentation had the effect of unsettling the private bidders, as did the promise of stringent intervention under the review clauses once the PPP was in place and the Tube under their control. The effect of these subtle threats was that the four final bidders raised their prices to cover the greater political risk, thus making the finances of the scheme even less attractive.

Another tactic used by the Mayor was to align himself with the transport unions in the industrial dispute that was to ensue in January 2001. In their campaign, the Tube unions promoted the safety issue in an attempt to get support from travellers, arguing that the PPP would put safety at risk. This position enabled Livingstone to align himself with the unions against the management, promising them his support at a union rally. Risking accusations of disingenuousness, Livingstone 'saluted' those who were prepared to strike, 'not to increase their pay, not to improve their conditions but to improve the safety of Londoners'. He would, he promised, join them on the picket line. In the event he did not and, unrepentant, refused to condemn the second strike in March or the third in April, despite warnings that it strengthened the government's hand in the fight against the Tube (*ES*, 25 April 2001).

Most observers saw the series of planned one-day strikes as an attempt to protect jobs in advance of the PPP coming into force, with the safety issue no more than a tactic to win public support. The unions demanded that there should be no compulsory redundancies without their agreement, a condition that was scarcely likely ever to be achieved. Accordingly, commentators interpreted union intransigence as an attempt to raise the stakes and make the PPP contracts less attractive to bidders. If the private sector could be frightened off by the high potential cost of industrial conflict, then the PPP might collapse and LU continue with a unified structure. The flaw in this strategy, if it was one, was the proviso that LU would not be handed over until the PPP contracts were in place. Livingstone therefore risked overplaying the card that his alliance with the unions had given him.

The Kiley impact

This was the background to an appointment of critical importance to the new mayoralty: that of Robert Kiley, an American troubleshooter as Transport Commissioner for London. A former CIA officer, Kiley had gained a reputation for effectiveness running New York's metropolitan transport authority. His union-breaking 'modernization' of the New York subway made him an unusual choice for a supposedly left-wing Mayor, but an arguably shrewd one for a politician intent on taking on Whitehall.

The Kiley appointment strengthened Livingstone's confidence that ministers would be forced to abandon the PPP scheme. 'When Mr Kiley arrives in January', he warned, 'he will say to the government that it will have to make very substantive changes. Ministers will have to accept them. I don't believe they can press ahead against Mr Kiley's advice' (*ES*, 27 November 2000). His calculation was that the government would not risk confrontation with a general election imminent; and the need for a peaceful solution which would please Londoners, among whom 'privatization' was a bugbear, could be counted upon to swing the decision in Livingstone's direction. In the event, ministers declined to meet Kiley or to deal with him except through officials. In November another row erupted over the provision of information over the PPP contracting process to Kiley, with Livingstone and Keith Hill clashing in the House of Commons over the government's unwillingness to cooperate. At the same time, Kiley, still only commissioner-designate, was beginning to make his own voice heard as a critic of the basic principle of the PPP, namely, the separation of train operation from track maintenance.

Livingstone kept up the pressure on LU's management. He had initially announced that 'dozens' of jobs would be axed among the 'dead wood' of senior management when TfL took over. In November he was professing to have 'a hit list as long as your arm'. He was able to cite Kiley's support for his attacks on the Tube managers, claiming that over 100 senior managers 'have lost the will to govern . . . the key top layer of management has given up. They know they are on their way out' (*ES*, 8 January 2001). The LU Managing Director, Derek Smith, responded accusing him of having 'a disruptive and unsettling effect on morale in the company'. In April Livingstone called the LU management 'dullards and knuckleheads' (*The Times*, 6 April 2001).

Safety was a major concern, perhaps *the* major concern of the travelling public, with the post-privatization main-line rail disasters stoking up opposition to the PPP. Kiley's and Livingstone's frequent statements about the risks of privatization monopolized the headlines, but LU was determined that its side of the argument should not go unheard. Its case against Kiley—that the PPP would amount to neither privatization nor 'part privatization'—made little impression. On safety, its case was that Kiley was peddling 'throwaway alarmist statements' that had no evidence to support them. The existing safety regime had been reviewed and enhanced in preparation for the PPP. The biggest policy disagreements, however, related to investment priorities. Kiley had repeatedly dismissed LU's plans for station improvement as essentially cosmetic, no more than 'a lick of paint' (LU 2001). The LU case, in contrast, was based on the long-standing appraisal of station design as one of the main constraints on capacity. Finally, Kiley's headline-catching promise to renew 85 per cent of the train fleet within the first seven and a half years attracted an easy riposte. LU pointed out that more than 40 per cent of the fleet was less than eight years old. The replacement of the remaining trains was provided for in the programme. Hence, 'given that the life of a tube train is approximately thirty-five years, this undertaking for complete renewal of trains less than 15 years old is a strange priority' (London Underground press release, 31 July 2001).

Within days of Kiley taking up his post, the press was being briefed on a continuing 'deadlock' over the PPP. No further meetings with John Prescott had been arranged when, on 11 January, Livingstone launched the draft transport strategy for London. The urgent need to reach some kind of solution underpinned a continuing set of negotiations, which culminated in early February in a joint statement by Kiley and Prescott. Up to that point the government's line had been that the Mayor and his commissioner would have no influence over the terms of the PPP but would merely administer it once responsibility was transferred. In a joint statement that was widely portrayed as a ministerial defeat, John Prescott conceded that Kiley would play a lead role in modifying the scheme and hinted that the government might accept the Mayor's demand for a unified management control by LU over the entire system.

Both sides put their own interpretations on what seemed to be a breakthrough. For Livingstone, it was a victory. He paid tribute to the Deputy Prime Minister. Both sides now acknowledged that while the private sector could make a positive contribution, TfL's strong management capability justified amending the PPP structure to provide it with a greater role. The Mayor was able to regard the concordat as an important step in reassuring Londoners and tube workers that safety was not going to be compromised. Ministers countered by emphasizing that Kiley had in fact agreed to work within the framework of PPP. It seemed that resolution of the conflict over the PPP was at hand, with the unions sounding conciliatory and looking to Kiley to broker a deal between themselves and LU.

In fact, allowing Kiley a role in re-framing the PPP terms had changed the nature of the process. It now required the preparation and submission of new tenders to meet new conditions. Yet Kiley's key condition of overall public sector management control seemed likely to be unacceptable to the private sector. His intention was to keep the private sector contractors under his control as commissioner, possibly with a majority stakeholding. In fact, the four consortia bidding for the contracts let it be known that they were not minded to accept such a condition. Minor changes could be met by re-submission within weeks but a fundamental change could delay the process for years. 'We are talking about investing billions of pounds', protested the spokesman of one of the consortia. 'If we do that as a commercial concern we do not want somebody else having a controlling interest, it would be a madness even to contemplate such a thing'. Kiley's conditions were quite unacceptable to the bidders. 'Had we known what was in store we would not have become involved in the first place', said the spokesman of another (*ES*, 20 February 2001).

A particular difficulty was that private investors expected a rate of return on their investment that appeared to make the PPP unacceptably expensive. The Treasury calculation, however, was that this higher cost would be offset by the economies achievable by private sector management. The public management of private investment would dissipate these supposed advantages, as well as limiting the scope for a reasonable return on investment. Under other circumstances it might have been expected that the contractors would walk away. However, the rules of the tendering process were such that if the goalposts were significantly moved the bidders could claim compensation for the additional work done, sums that were estimated at £15–£30 million each. Were they to withdraw, they would forfeit the right to this compensation. They—indeed all parties—were locked in.

By late February deadlock was once again looming. Livingstone began a campaign to drive a wedge between Downing Street and Treasury, claiming that Treasury officials had been obstructing a deal with their implacable commitment to the PPP. Sir Stephen Robson, the Treasury official responsible for the PPP, had been adamant in his support for it, and his retirement at the end of January was read as signalling the chance of a breakthrough. But this had by no mean been achieved. The official who took over the brief was no more inclined to compromise the basis of the scheme. Livingstone accused Treasury officials of briefing the press against him, and alleged Treasury obstruction soon displaced 'safety' as the most newsworthy aspect of the dispute.

In late February, the Prime Minister called Prescott and Brown together in an attempt to resolve what was coming to look like a direct confrontation between his two most senior ministers. Unwilling to be pushed into any compromise, Treasury officials made a point of ridiculing a report from Kiley on the grounds that it lacked any coherent framework for action:

We have seen the seventeen-page document from Kiley. Only one page of that sets out his proposals. You need more than one piece of paper to set out a plan to manage a fifteen billion pound project. You need more than a couple of bullet points. (*ES*, 26 February 2001).

If the situation had not reached an impasse before Kiley was allowed to play a part, it certainly reached one afterwards. Kiley himself attacked the government proposals publicly, portraying the PPP as an

impenetrable system of complex and confidential arrangements that would put the day-to-day management of the Underground into a state of suspended animation . . . The more TfL has seen on the PPP, the more it appears fatally flawed. Even after adjustments to the scheme proposed by the Government on February 28, the public is left owning the system, but without the power to control it. (*Daily Telegraph*, 5 March 2001)

Central to Prescott's response were proposals to give the commissioner the power to nominate members to the boards of the successful bidders, to sack their chief executives, and to redirect their work programmes. He would have the specific veto over the adoption of business plans and budgets; transactions with shareholders or affiliates; the acquisition and disposal of assets; the raising of new debt other than working capital; and the payment of dividends other than as permitted under the revised contracts. Despite these exceptional provisions, the basic structure of the PPP remained, with no concession of a single management structure. Kiley and TfL, with the tacit support of Livingstone, rejected Prescott's letter and declared their intention to test the PPP in the courts.

The dispute, however, involved not just two parties, but three. The private contractors reacted to these concessions with disbelief. Reportedly 'furious at concessions to Kiley', a spokesman for TubeRail, bidders for the Jubilee, Northern, and Piccadilly lines, commented that the government's new position was 'impractical and would create difficulties for the investors and lenders'. His opposite number at the competitor Tubelines agreed that it would 'make the business unworkable and unfinanceable'. Another elaborated: 'No bidder is going to be idiotic enough to sign up to this. They'd never get finance.' All four consortia agreed they could live with minor alterations to the original PPP, but were stunned by the proposal that Kiley should take a controlling interest in the companies. As one explained, 'We are talking about investing billions of pounds. If we do that as a commercial concern we do not want somebody else having a controlling interest, it would be madness even to contemplate such a thing' (*ES*, 20 February 2001).

With the government now committed to £57 million in compensation payments to the bidders if it scrapped the PPP, it was now in a dilemma. The compromise proposal appeared to kill the prospects for any private-sector involvement without going far enough to persuade Livingstone to call off his opposition (*Daily Telegraph*, 2 March 2001). On 1 March 2001 the Mayor authorized Kiley, with the unanimous support of the TfL board, to start proceedings against the Environment Secretary. Accused of brinkmanship, Kiley replied that this was no more than the way governments deal with one another. There was still time to talk even after the application for judicial review had been lodged: 'the door is always open'.

To the High Court

In an unexpected turn of events the Prime Minister intervened in the PPP row, in effect by overruling Gordon Brown and John Prescott—appointing Bob Kiley to replace Sir Malcolm Bates as Chairman of London Regional Transport with immediate effect. This put Kiley in the position of negotiating the private sector contracts of which he had been a vigorous critic, while the legal proceedings against the government continued. One unnamed government source took an uncharitable view of the intervention: 'this is Number 10 overruling the Treasury and the DETR. No 10 has the heebie-jeebies over the political position and wants to sort it before the election', adding 'no-one knows where PPP is headed with Kiley in charge' (*Daily Telegraph*, 5 May 2001).

The accusation that Kiley's appointment to the chair of the LRT board was no more than pre-election window-dressing, boomeranged when, in July, he was summarily removed from the same post. Kiley seems to have been appointed chairman for the specific purpose of bringing to a conclusion the negotiation with the bidders on terms that met his concerns as Commissioner. Deciding that these conditions could not be met, he instructed the LRT staff to suspend negotiations without clearing this with the board. The majority of the board's membership wrote to the Secretary of the State, now Stephen Byers, to tell him that they could no longer work with Kiley. Byers then terminated his appointment and reappointed Sir Malcolm Bates.

The imminence of the judicial review may well have shaped these events. The High Court ruling was in favour of the government's having the last word, although the drafting of the act was criticized as having 'side-stepped' the question of ultimate responsibility by not making clear that there was no obligation to reconcile the PPP scheme with the Mayor's transport strategy. London Transport staff were delighted. Derek Smith hailed the judgement as 'a great result for London' and called upon the Mayor and Kiley to 'put the arguments on one side now. Work with us to make sure we get the best possible deal for the underground and its passengers' (London Transport news release, 30 July 2001). The Secretary of State, Stephen Byers, meanwhile, called on all sides to work together and put passenger interests first. 'There has been a disagreement about the way forward', he declared, 'and that was dealt with, hopefully, in the court case.' He pledged that the Health and Safety Executive would review the safety aspects of the PPP and undertook to revise the government's plans, if the proposals were found to be in any way unsafe (*ES*, 1 August 2001). The Mayor's Transport Strategy, published immediately before the court case, was effectively nullified.

8

London's Crimewatch

CRIME was second only to transport as an issue facing the new Authority. Indeed, if US city government was the model for London, reports of crime reduction were a major reason. Thus, two major features of the Greater London Authority Act were the creation of a Metropolitan Police Authority to establish 'a strong and effective partnership between the police, local authorities and local communities', and the transfer of power to it from the Home Secretary. According to the Act, the Mayor appoints Assembly members to twelve of the 23 seats on the MPA, and through this means may influence police policy and practice. The long history of attempts to place the Metropolitan Police under the control of a Greater London Authority, however, suggested that this could become a problematic relationship, while policing remained the public service least comfortable with accountability through local government structures. The Mayor was to be concerned with crime reduction, a prominent electoral issue. At the same time, police-community relations, racial discrimination, and sensitivity to London's multi-ethnic composition, already headline issues in the wake of the MacPherson Report on the murder of black teenager, Stephen Lawrence, were given a new political priority (MacPherson 1999).

The White Paper *A Mayor and Assembly for London* (DETR 1998a) set out the government's proposals for a new police authority. The MPA was to be an independently constituted authority comprising elected and non-elected members, able to decide in consultation with the Commissioner its own strategy and policing priorities. The Mayor and Assembly were to have a close connection with the MPA in order to facilitate a London-wide approach. The White Paper ruled out a geographical basis for representation on the MPA, although local views were to be heard and taken into account. The MPA was required to publish an annual policing plan, setting out objectives and how its resources were to be used to meet them, and this plan had to be reconciled with local community safety plans, which focused on the protection of ethnic and other minorities.

Controlling London's Police

Like other aspects of British local government, the history of policing has combined incremental growth and occasional douche-like reforms. Structurally, changes have been in the direction of consolidating police forces and increasing the controlling power of the Home Office. London stands apart in the relative stability of its arrangements since the foundation of the Metropolitan Police. For 170 years the police authority for London was the Home Secretary, advised in recent years by an appointed Metropolitan Police Committee (MPC). Operational matters were left to the Commissioner of Police appointed by the Home Secretary, who did not, himself, normally interfere. Founded in 1829, the Metropolitan Police District (MPD) acquired an extensive boundary stretching far beyond the built-up area of London—even Greater London—well into the Home Counties. The City Corporation retained its status as a separate police authority throughout the subsequent period. Repeated attempts to combine the two forces and bring one of the City's most important functions under the control of a London—and later Greater London—Authority came to nothing. Successive governments had been adamant that the policing of London was a matter of national concern, affecting the safety of the Crown, government, and Parliament. The most serious threat to the Home Secretary's control of London's policing came with the London government bill introduced in the House of Commons during Gladstone's Liberal administration in 1883. The bill had been drafted by J. F. B. Firth, a keen advocate of a powerful authority for London who believed 'that the control of the police force ought . . . to be in the hands of those responsible for the peace of the town' (Young and Garside 1982: 46).

This was also the view of the Prime Minister, who saw no reason to exempt London from the principle that the control of the police was the most important of all municipal functions. However, the Home Secretary, Sir William Harcourt, blocked the bill in Cabinet, arguing that to transfer the control of the Metropolitan Police to a London authority was 'a thing that is neither wise nor safe, and it is one which I think the government ought not to make to Parliament' (Young and Garside 1982: 46). The reformers feared that this stalemate over the police would jeopardize the prospects for creating an elected council for London, and Gladstone was persuaded to compromise by agreeing to an interim period before handing over the police to the new municipality. But time had already been lost and the bill slipped in the legislative timetable. The unemployment riots of 1886 effectively put an end to the hopes that London's police would be taken under democratic control. The split in the Liberal Party that same year ensured that the settlement of the London issue would be a matter for a Conservative-dominated government (Young and Garside 1982: 46–7).

However, the dominance of the early LCC by the (Liberal) Progressive Party ensured that the issue would remain on the agenda. In 1889, the Council, which had the unique privilege of bringing before Parliament an annual general powers bill, used it without success to bid for control of the police. The bid failed, but a satirical pamphlet published in 1892 sketched an imaginary future in which the Metropolitan Police, now under the control of the LCC, refused to protect the House of Lords, which was resisting the passage of a bill to abolish the City of London Corporation. The Lords' revolt defeated the government of 'Lord Tulipstalk', the army took control, Parliament abolished the LCC, and police powers returned to the Home Secretary (Young and Garside 1982: 66–7).

However, despite the Home Secretary's control, the functions of the Metropolitan Police developed in a similar fashion to those of police forces elsewhere in England and Wales. Meanwhile, the capital's police force gained additional responsibilities for the protection of royalty and foreign diplomats. Thus, a Special Branch was established with responsibilities for national security, together with the special services of the National Identification Bureau and the Forensic Science Laboratory, which were made available to provincial police forces. Provincial police contributed to its databases and in turn made use of them. Over time, the past practice of provincial forces 'calling in the Yard' declined as reorganization in the 1960s created larger, stronger provincial forces.

Within London, the Metropolitan Police gained major responsibilities in traffic control. In 1968 the police and the GLC created a joint traffic executive for Greater London. Technical officers from the two parent organizations worked together to agree priorities for joint action in highway and traffic matters. It was their job to ensure that traffic regulations and orders were capable of economic enforcement, to speed up decision-making and, generally, 'to promote good order and efficiency in the use of the roads of Greater London' (Commissioner of Police 1969: 15–17).

In 1986 the Metropolitan Police force was reorganized into eight areas and 75 divisions. The realignment of the structure produced a closer relationship with the London boroughs. Despite this limited modernization, 'the Met' continued to retain traditional features. Policing strategy continued to be determined by the Commissioner with the support of a policy committee including his deputy, four assistant commissioners, the receiver, and a deputy receiver. These last two officers were appointed by the Crown to manage the finances of the force. The receiver, charged with negotiating the force budget with the Home Office, was a more powerful official than the treasurer of any provincial police authority. More than half of the Metropolitan Police Service (MPS) funding was, and continues to be, provided in the form of a direct grant from the government and the remainder is raised by precept upon the local authorities.

Although the Labour Party in London was committed throughout its existence to gaining control over the Metropolitan Police, its ambitions in this regard were tempered by the very limited accountability that provincial police forces were required to give to their police committees. Local police committees had a substantial representation of magistrates whose influence tended to limit that of the councillor nominees. At the same time, while police committees appointed, with the concurrence of the Home Secretary, the chief constable and his deputies, they had no control over the operations of the police force or over discipline and promotion, and merely received reports from the chief constable. Police authorities rarely took an active role, discouraged by the vagueness of their powers and by chief constables who often refused to discuss 'operational' matters.

These limitations helped to keep alive, and to fuel the demand for, 'democratization'. Having lain dormant for many years, the proposal was revived by the Livingstone GLC in the wake of the 1981 election. In the same year the GLC established a committee to consider the policing of Greater London, law enforcement and public order, and links with other relevant bodies. One of the committee's first tasks was to hold a consultation to discover whether there was public support for a new, locally accountable police authority to replace the Home Secretary, using the violent disorders in Brixton that summer as a platform. In March 1983, the GLC police committee published a further paper on *Democratic Control of the Police in London*, and its recommendations on the subject of a new police authority became GLC policy. A further consultation was held as one of the last acts of the GLC before its abolition in 1986, on the basis that 'the post abolition arrangements will be undemocratic, expensive and cumbersome', impelling a future government to reintroduce a strategic authority, thus creating an opportunity to take control of the police (GLC 1986).

The Labour GLC's position went beyond seeking to substitute elected councillors for Home Secretary, for 'simply changing the structure will have little effect on policing at street level where the daily practice of abuse has become a fact of life' (GLC 1986: 129). For the police committee, the principal argument was one of policing policy and powers:

Making the Met accountable to Londoners does not simply involve creating new structures. It also requires a thorough reappraisal of the powers which we give to the police in order that they may carry out the role we expect of them. At present, particularly in the light of the 1984 Police and Criminal Evidence Act, the police possess discretionary coercive powers which are so extensive that any new police authority, no matter how democratically constituted it may be, will find it impossible to exercise proper control and effective supervision of the actions of the police officers. (GLC 1986: 208)

In this, the most polarized period of post-war British political life, it did not seem outlandish to call for the repeal of legislation on the prevention of terrorism, on criminal evidence, and on public order:

With no outside supervision the force has slid into crisis. It is unable to achieve the confidence and co-operation of large sections of the community particularly of the black community. Reports of corruption, police abuse of their powers and disregard of instruction indicate that the force is out of control . . . The activities of the [Special Patrol Group] and the local district support units have further alienated people who see no place or need for British police in riot gear. (GLC 1986: 210)

On the basis of this document, the GLC congratulated itself on having made a 'significant and valuable contribution to the argument in favour of a new police authority'. It had moved the debate on from whether there should be such a reform to the shape it should take and the powers it should possess. Specifically, boundaries should be realigned on both the metropolitan fringe and within Greater London; the City police should be merged with the Met; and national policing functions should be separated from the policing of London. Within very few years, these last points were to enter the mainstream.

An internal Scotland Yard document on the GLC's police committee support unit, obtained and published after abolition, reportedly commented that 'Labour is determined to shake off its anti-police reputation . . .The GLC's policies must be seen as the extreme . . . moderate socialist opinion favours similar policies but presentation is different' (LSPU 1987: 18). For its part, the GLC leadership insisted that it was not 'anti-police' in the sense of not recognizing the necessity for a police force, while declaring that major reforms and in 'some areas fundamental changes' in policy were required (GLC 1986). Despite the worst fears of their critics, the Labour GLC would have confined its reforms to structural and policy issues, leaving operational matters in the hands of local commanders or other senior officers and 'would have [had] no power to intervene in the decision to arrest and charge any individual person(s)'.

The abolition of the GLC closed the issue for the time being. However, the repeated calls from London Labour councillors after abolition persuaded successive commissioners that they could not insulate the MPS from local political pressures indefinitely. Clearly, the MPS required sweeping change if it were to satisfy London Labour opinion and there was a need for something much more than the provincial model of restricted accountability to a mix of elected and appointed committee members. Sir Peter Imbert, the Commissioner, could foresee that a Labour government, whose election might be imminent, would restore some form of London-wide local government. Thus, he was the first commissioner publicly to claim, in 1991, that he could live happily with an elected police authority for London. It seemed that the days of Metropolitan Police's special and protective relationship with the Home Secretary might be numbered. The chairman of the Police Federation himself recognized that creating a London authority would revive demands to put the control of the Met on a more politically acceptable footing:

The Commissioners of the past may have found their good fortune in not having, like provincial chief officers, to battle with local politicians and compete for cash with housing, roads, and education committees. Now, with more power than ever concentrated in the centre, there appears to be less of a financial advantage for the Metropolitan Police in their constitutional position. This may be one of the reasons why the present Commissioner is the first to have endorsed the idea of a locally elected police authority for London. When we recall the hysterical behaviour of Labour-controlled police authorities at the outset of the '80s, it is quite astonishing to hear Sir Peter calmly announcing that he could live happily with a local police authority in London.

[However] I think that such a body might emerge as part of a major reform of local government in the Capital, with an elected Mayor exercising the kind of powers we see in the United States. (Eastwood 1991: 276)

It turned out to be a remarkably accurate prediction. But it was public concern with crime and with police performance rather than dogma that prompted New Labour to adopt an old policy.

The Problem of Policing London

Would shifting the locus of direct power over London's police materially affect the maintenance of law and order? All major cities face major problems of policing and social control, for obvious reasons. The opportunities to profit from crime are much greater in big cities and the possibilities of detection so much the less. At the same time, major cities harbour areas of deprivation with high rates of neglect, family breakdown, and domestic violence. There is also a danger of public disturbance and affray. The creation of the Metropolitan Police in the nineteenth century was a response to just such problems, which did not, however, go away. Social change in post-war Britain produced a rising tide of crime in which London was the centre for criminal activity. In the mid-1950s the number of indictable offences recorded in the Metropolitan Police area approached 100,000 annually. By 1961, this figure had doubled and five years later it had increased to nearly 300,000. It continued to rise rapidly, reaching more than 800,000 by 1993. The number of robberies exceeded 1,000 for the first time in 1962 and doubled in the next five years.

An obviously important variable in the ability to cope with crime is the manpower strength of the force. In 1945, the Metropolitan Police had an authorized strength—or establishment—of 19,600 officers, with just over 14,000 actually in post. Although the authorized strength was steadily increased to almost 22,000 by the end of the 1960s, the force remained at that date more than 20 per cent under strength. In 1965 the Home Office launched an intensive recruitment campaign to ensure that London had enough police officers to meet the rising demand. Throughout the last half century, however, police numbers rose by less than 50 per cent while recorded crime increased ninefold. Recruitment continued to pose great difficulties. In mid-2000 the

TABLE 8.1. Crime trends in the Metropolitan Police District

1969	1973	1977	1981	1985	1989	1993	1997
316,012	349,812	554,417	601,923	708,647	713,945	865,000	1,052,047

Note: Notifiable offences known to police pre-1977; thereafter indictable offences to 1993; thereafter recorded crime.
Sources: Home Office Criminal Statistics; Home Office Statistical Bulletin.

number of officers actually employed reached a 20-year low. The numbers leaving exceeded the numbers of new recruits, and the ageing force seemed likely to shrink still further as the older officers retired.

With the Metropolitan Police struggling to fill posts, the Metropolitan Police Commissioner, Sir John Stevens, initiated a restructuring of the force with the intention of transferring manpower from management to operational roles. With help from a special Home Office crime-fighting fund, 445 posts were allocated to the districts, most of them in the boroughs hardest hit by increases in street crime and burglary: Brent, Camden, Ealing, Hackney, Haringey, Islington, and Lambeth. The Commissioner undertook to hold the line on police numbers at 26,500 and to increase them from that base. Meanwhile, a detailed analysis of police recruitment and retention identified a number of problems. During 1999–2000 only 15 per cent of all persons who enquired about joining the MPS actually applied, compared with a figure of 43 per cent in 1995–6. The average age of recruits had also declined—from 27 to 23—and continued to show a downward trend. London house prices, difficulties of commuting, and inadequate pay were some of the key factors contributing to the difficulties of attracting people into the service. Premature resignations and transfers to other forces in recent years had led to an increase in the turnover of police officers from about 1,250 a year in 1995–6 to over 1,600 during 1999–2000. On average, officers resigned with five years service and transferred at nine years, against a target length of service of 30 years. Apart from the problems of recruitment and retention, the overall approved levels were increasingly called into question. Comparisons were inescapable: the policing problems of Paris were dealt with by as many as 50,000 officers and those of New York by 40,000.

Some of the special problems of policing London—public order, fraud, terrorism—drew the City and the Metropolitan Police forces into close engagement, highlighting the apparently anomalous status of the smaller partner. The demonstration against global capitalism in the City of London in June 1999 highlighted the inability of the City force to handle such incidents. Following a review, it was agreed that in future, major public order episodes would be overseen from Scotland Yard, with senior metropolitan officers ready to take control if the occasion demanded. For its part, the City force had developed a key specialism in dealing with white-collar crime, essential to maintaining the integrity of London as a world financial centre. The anti-terrorist argument, on the other hand, cut both ways. A detailed surveillance regime established in the wake of Bishopsgate bomb in April 1992, with which the IRA caused £350 million of damage, established an unparalleled safety zone. Yet the City could not match the anti-terrorist intelligence capabilities of Scotland Yard.

The long-standing issue of the continuation of the City police was bound to surface again with the creation of a Metropolitan Police Authority. The City police, with its budget of £68 million, served a resident population of just 5,500 but with more than a quarter of a million workers coming in during the business day. The Association of London Government pointed to the creation of the Mayor and the new police authority as the right occasion for the rationalization of London's policing. With 778 officers for the square mile, the City was well policed and a tempting target for any empire builder at new Scotland Yard. A senior Metropolitan Police officer, however, made a realistic assessment:

if you gave the problem to Ernst and Young, they would say 'this is ridiculous, absorb the two immediately'. But that is not what it is about. You would have a battle on your hands with the burghers of the City and they would fight tooth and nail against it. There are very powerful and influential forces at work here. (*ES*, 23 August 1999)

Apart from the special circumstances of policing London, maintaining public confidence and good police-community relations had been a preoccupation since the early 1980s. In the last years of its life under the Home Secretary's overall control, the MPS was able to boast of a reduction of 18 per cent in the total number of public complaint allegations recorded. During April–November 2000 a total of 3,844 public complaints were made against the MPS in which the largest proportion—1,683 allegations, 43 per cent—related to oppressive behaviour. Even in this category there had been a significant fall since 1997 when the comparable figure was 3,712. Similarly, the number of allegations of assault declined from 2,050 in 1997–8 to 1,509 in 1999–2000 and the number of complaints concerning breaches of stop-and-search procedures from 287 to 102 during the same period. The MPS informally resolved 34 per cent of all allegations in 1998–9 and 31 per cent in 1999–2000. The six major metropolitan forces—Greater Manchester, Merseyside, West Midlands, West Yorkshire, South Yorkshire, and Northumbria—with which the Met was commonly compared achieved no better than a 13 per cent reduction during the same period. On the evidence of these figures, senior officers in the MPS were able to claim that they were already sensitive to the demand for public accountability and for measures to improve confidence.

A New Police Authority for London

The appointment of Sir John Stevens as Police Commissioner in August 1999 virtually coincided with the creation of new arrangements for London. Every previous Commissioner had been accountable only to the Home Secretary, and had used this distinctive status to keep the Metropolitan Police at a distance from London's politics. To be placed under the control of an elected London-wide body was the traditional nightmare for the senior officers at Scotland Yard. The Greater London Authority Act 1999, however, was far from being the realization of this historic nightmare. Instead, it provided a complex and highly ambiguous set of accountabilities that fell far short of popular control. First, the Commissioner himself was to be appointed by the Queen upon the advice of the Home Secretary who, 'before recommending to Her Majesty that she appoint a person as Commissioner of Police of the metropolis . . . shall have regard to any *recommendations* made to him by the MPA, and any *repre-sentations* made to him by the Mayor of London' (emphases added). With Commissioner Stevens taking up his five-year appointment on 1 January 2000, there would be no possibility of the first Mayor and MPA, and perhaps even the second, influencing the choice of the commissioner.

The composition of the MPA, however, did not give much scope for influence on the part of the Mayor and the Assembly. Of the 23 members, twelve were appointed from among the Assembly members and one by the Home Secretary. Four were magistrates. The remaining six 'independent' members were chosen from Londoners who responded to an advertising cam-paign run by the government. The Home Office appointed a panel of three community leaders to consider the applications. This list was passed to the Home Secretary for consideration, and the 'cleared' short list was then passed to the GLA members on the MPA who selected the final six names. Some Labour boroughs objected to their exclusion from any influence over the new police authority membership and considered calling upon the Assembly to set up a committee to scrutinize the MPA itself. Given the size and diversity of the Metropolitan Police district, concern was also expressed about the capacity of a 23-strong police authority—smaller by far than a provincial police commit-tee—to cope with the work. In contrast to police authorities elsewhere, resources were devoted to supporting the MPA members in their work, in acknowledgement of their more important policy role, for which they would be given support and training .

The Conservatives, having long fought to insulate the Metropolitan Police from local accountability, were eventually reconciled to the change. Sir John Wheeler MP, a powerful voice on home affairs on the Tory backbenches, gave a guarded welcome to 'the extension of the democratic process over policing in London' and to the opportunity it gave to bring the management of the Met into closer touch with public expectations. 'The time has certainly come', he conceded, 'to democratise the administration of policing in London.' At the same time he expressed his 'unease'. He acknowledged that the Mayor would neither be able to give orders to the Commissioner nor 'to say who will be arrested or not as the case may be' nor 'directly interfere on operational mat-ters'. Nevertheless:

It will be the practice of this theory that raises most concern. The police in this country are fortunately independent of politicians . . . in today's world of intensive media pres-sure, there will be a great temptation on the part of the executive Mayor to respond to London's perceived crises and dramas by telling us via our television screens what he will be doing and what he will be saying to the Commissioner, all in the style of New York . . . Although the Commissioner can be sent for by his present boss, the police authority for London—who is the Home Secretary—a private discussion in the Home Office will be quiet different from the relationship with the hands-on Mayor with a view to re-election. (Wheeler 1999: 16–17)

Thus, by the time Labour had introduced the Greater London Authority bill, the argument for making the Metropolitan Police responsible to a new, partly elected police authority had been won, and fears of a radical take-over dissipated. The candidacy of Livingstone, however, complicated matters. Although generally careful to please business interests and reassure the more nervous voters, his apparent support for anti-capitalist demonstrators in 1999 attracted fierce criticism. His equivocation in failing to condemn unreservedly the desecration of the Cenotaph and other Westminster monuments the following year were thought to have damaged his chances of becoming Mayor. At the same time, they also raised the question in some people's minds of the possible consequences if control of London's policing fell into irresponsible hands. Meanwhile, the debate on the control of the police moved on. Livingstone's Conservative opponent, Steven Norris, called for the Mayor to have the power to appoint the Commissioner, balancing this proposal with a preparedness to concede the national policing functions of the MPS—the anti-terrorist squad and the Royalty and Diplomatic Protection Group—to the Home Secretary. Unwittingly, no doubt, Norris was echoing key proposals of the old GLC police committee.

Livingstone's victory in May 2000 immediately focused attention on the nominations he would make to the MPA. He had identified a number of individuals as possible members of his cabinet, four of whom, controversially, had previously been vetoed as potential Labour candidates for the Assembly. Among them was Lee Jasper, a leading figure in the National Assembly Against Racism, a pro-Livingstone splinter group that had broken away from the Anti-Racist Alliance. Described as 'the most powerful black man in London' (*ES*, 2 October 2000), Jasper was appointed as the Mayor's adviser on race, policing, and immigration. Within days of the election result he had attacked the government's handling of asylum seekers and was accusing the Conservatives of encouraging the growth of the far right. Jasper had been approved by the Home Office advisers for the inclusion of possible appointees on the MPA, although it seemed increasingly likely that Jack Straw would veto him. In the event, the Home Secretary allowed Jasper's name to go forward, but in June, when the GLA members of the Police Authority met to decide on the independent members, he was not selected. One factor appeared to be his close relationship with the Mayor, something that might have constituted a conflict of interest, although the MPA Chair, Toby (now Lord) Harris, dismissed claims that the vote against Jasper was 'Millbank's revenge' (*ES*, 7 June 2000).

The initial skirmishes between the Mayor and the MPA turned on the issue of who had effective power over the Metropolitan Police: the Mayor or the MPA itself? The Authority members had chosen Lord Harris, one of Livingstone's nominees from the Assembly, to lead them. Harris was seen as a safe pair of hands, a government supporter who would protect the MPS from operational interference on the part of the Mayor and his advisers. He would be expected to act as a buffer between the Met and the Mayor. He proved quick to take up cudgels on behalf of the new Authority. The MPA's first meeting was the occasion of a humiliating rebuke to the Mayor. Livingstone had publicly expressed the view that the Met should immediately settle the compensation claims lodged by the parents of the murdered teenager Stephen Lawrence. Whatever their views on the merits of this step, MPA members regarded his intervention as a clear breach of protocol. Lord Harris demanded that the Mayor should acknowledge that his comments on the Lawrence affair 'breach his undertaking not to intervene in matters concerning the Met without prior discussion with myself or the Metropolitan Police Commissioner.' He reminded Livingstone, who was there to observe the meeting, that

The chair of this authority is elected by its members not appointed by the Mayor, the Home Secretary or anyone else . . . we are independent of the Mayor and he needs to remember that. He must also remember that responsibility for policing matters is vested with us and not with him. (*ES*, 30 June 2000)

The Mayor was reported to be discomfited by this attack, commenting that he was 'elected by the people of London to tell these people to get their act together and that's what I'll do' (*ES*, 30 June 2000).

The Labour government's Crime and Disorder Act 1998 had placed considerable emphasis on close cooperation between the police and local authorities. The Greater London Authority Act provided an opportunity to facilitate this cooperation by redrawing the boundary of the metropolitan district to bring it into line with Greater London. The new Metropolitan Police Authority would then correspond exactly with the area covered by the 32 London boroughs. This lack of coterminous boundaries had bedevilled police-local authority relations since the creation of the GLC in 1964. The MPD covered a more extensive area than Greater London, and the realignment meant ceding considerable slices of it to London's surrounding counties. Surrey gained the largest area, taking in Banstead and Reigate as well as the remaining part of Elmbridge, Epsom and Ewell, and Spelthorne. Hertfordshire gained Cheshunt, Waltham Cross, and Hoddesdon, making a Broxbourne division and creating a new Hertsmere division. Essex acquired a small area including Waltham Abbey and Loughton as well as the remaining half of Epping.

A number of officers chose to transfer out of the Metropolitan Police service to the several counties. The effect was to reduce the Metropolitan Police establishment by 750 officers and other civilian staff. Officers in the transferred divisions were given the option of voluntarily joining the county force, and thus losing their London allowance, or staying with the Met and accepting redeployment. The possibility of a secondment for a transitional two-year period was also offered as an inducement when it was realized that very few officers were likely to chose to transfer employment. By the end of March 2001 some 367 officers were on secondment out of the MPS.

The impact of the new regime on existing financial disciplines and procedures of the MPS was profound. Detailing his plans, the Chairman of MPA, Lord Harris commented that

The Met has never been subjected to the same rigorous financial regimes as most other parts of the public service. This will now change. The MPA has a legal duty to secure 'best value' over the next five years. There are enormous potential savings to be had by cutting back on bureaucracy and red tape, by simplifying processes and by using modern technology. The authority must make sure that those savings are achieved and are ploughed back into the frontline policing. (*ES*, 26 June 2000)

In September 2000 the Mayor launched a review of the scope for rationalization of police administration, declaring that savings of £200 million over three years could be found. Duplication between the MPA and Metropolitan Police administrative offices could be eliminated, and more rigorous financial control of the MPS introduced.

The first budget under the new system for 2000–1 included a £37.5 million increase agreed by ministers and formerly covered by the grant from the Home Office. Under the new system, however, the bulk of the increase was to be funded from the GLA precept upon the boroughs. This caused some consternation and a number of boroughs protested to the Home Secretary about the effect on their council tax levels, which were locally limited to an increase of 4.6 per cent, while the increase in precept was 17 per cent. Lord Harris complained that 'London boroughs have acted responsibly. An average increase of below five per cent for borough taxes demonstrates that councils are considering ordinary Londoners. The stereotype of the high-spending, inefficient London council is a thing of the past. It is a shame the government did not match the boroughs' prudence while setting the Metropolitan Police element of council taxes' (*ES*, 30 March 2000). The police element of the precept was the only element to survive the protest, apparent testimony to the breadth of support for the Mayor and MPA's policy of 'more police in the streets'.

A further consequence of the creation of the MPA was to bring about the integration of the Metropolitan Police into the national framework of representation, and thus put it on a similar footing to the police elsewhere in Britain. The Association of Police Authorities (APA) represented all police authorities in England, Wales, and Northern Ireland, provided central support services to assist police authorities, including guidance, advice, and training, and had an established national role in negotiating with the central government on key policy matters. The Association worked closely with the Home Office ministers and representatives from Her Majesty's Inspectorate of Constabulary (HMIC), Association of Chief Police Officers (ACPO), and the Audit Commission. During the transitional period, and in anticipation of the creation of the MPA, three seats on the APA had been allocated to the Home Secretary's advisory Metropolitan Police Committee, and three to the Association of London Government. In recognition of its new status, the MPA attained direct representation on the APA in order to gain more influence over policing matters, nationally and regionally as well as locally.

The development of the MPA was carried forward through a committee structure that emphasized planning, consultation, and evaluation, reflecting the fact that responsibility for operational matters continued to rest with the

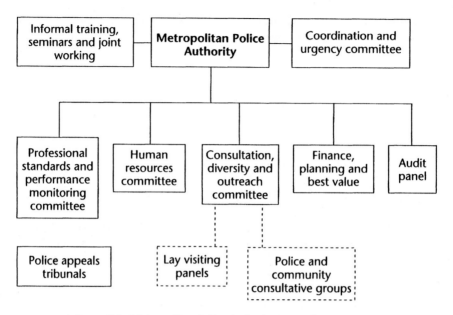

Figure 8.1: Metropolitan Police Authority: committee structure

Commissioner. The coordination and urgency committee considered matters affecting the whole authority, and took decisions on those issues that could not wait. The finance, planning, and best value committee took the lead on strategic planning. Independent appraisal of the MPS's achievement in terms of regularity, probity, and value for money was carried out by the audit panel that advised the authority and approved its internal and external audit arrangements, while the professional standards and performance monitoring committee investigated and reviewed the authority's complaints matters. The MPA's determination to modernize the MPS focused attention on human resource management. The human resources committee considered matters relating to the appointment and terms of conditions, while the consultation, diversity, and outreach committee led on issues of equal opportunities. The police appeals tribunals were not part of the authority's formal structures but were independent bodies set up to hear appeals from police officers who had been dismissed or demoted. Similarly, Police and Community Consultative Groups (PCCGs) and Lay Visiting Panels did not constitute formal committee structures of the MPA; decisions on their future were taken upon the completion of the MPA-MPS Best Value review of consultation.

A London for All Londoners

Changing the structure, of itself, did not change practice or enhance effectiveness. What it was bound to do, however, in a climate of increasing nervousness, was to raise expectations. This, more than the reorganization, affected the priorities both of the MPA and the Met.

Some priorities remained the same—set, for all forces, by the Home Secretary. These included an emphasis on tackling crime and disorder though partnership with other agencies and the public, and on increasing trust and confidence among minority ethnic communities. At the same time, the MPA's consultation with Londoners added a number of acute problems that the MPS would be expected to concentrate on. Foremost among these were street crime, drug dealing, burglaries, and vehicle crime. The MPA's approach to addressing its priorities was to distinguish between *external* priorities—those concerned with services to the public—and *internal* priorities—those concerned with improving the MPS as an organization. Alongside these was a commitment to the development of performance information for monitoring purposes, and the MPA professional standards and performance monitoring committee introduced 'best value' performance indicators for their service priorities.

The MPA defined four specific overarching external priorities. The first—making London's streets safer—entailed focusing on street crime. Street crime had been rising rapidly with a 36 per cent increase in 1999–2000 and a further 18 per cent in 2000–1 against the MPS target of zero growth. Tackling this growth and achieving a modest reduction would involve the MPS working closely with local boroughs to implement their plans, especially in high-crime areas. Partnership with the boroughs also featured in pursuing the objectives of reducing anti-social behaviour. Londoners were particularly concerned about violent crime and especially crime involving weapons, and about tackling the culture of knife possession among young boys. Diverting young people from crime was a broader anxiety, centring on the work of youth offending teams, the rapid processing of offenders, and containing truancy. The second major priority was to reduce burglary rates, a concern also reflected in most borough crime and disorder strategies. Burglary had been falling and in 2000–1 dropped more than 20 per cent to its lowest level for 25 years. Offences, however, still totalled around 110,000 annually, prompting the MPS to target known prolific burglars. A third priority was to reduce damage to London's communities caused by drug dealing. The MPS objective was to reduce the supply of drugs, in particular crack, heroine, and cocaine, the so-called Class A drugs. The focus here was on judicial disposals, that is, charges, summonses, cautions, or previously recorded offences being taken into consideration.

Although these first three priorities were defined by the MPA, the continuity with pre-existing police priorities was striking. There seemed little scope for the MPA to set new directions, particularly when recent Commissioners had anticipated emerging priorities and adapted to them in advance. This was also the case, though to a lesser extent, in relation to the fourth priority: protecting Londoners from 'hate crimes'. Tackling race crime was an aim that the MPA members shared with their counterparts in the London boroughs.

The creation of the MPA and the identification of hate crime as a priority ensured that the debates about the Metropolitan Police in the aftermath of MacPherson became more intense. The MacPherson inquiry (MacPherson 1999) identified the existence of 'institutional racism' within the Metropolitan Police and other bodies and put forward a number of recommendations. Following the MacPherson report, an internal code setting out the principles to govern 'stop and search' was prepared by Scotland Yard. Home Office data for 1999 showed that, within London, Asian people were twice, and black people four times, more likely than white people to be stopped and searched. Despite this statistic, stop and search continued to be a widely used power and was regarded by the Metropolitan Police as a highly effective technique in the detection and prevention of crime. However, once again, the senior officers showed themselves adept at anticipating the concerns of the MPA members to whom they were now accountable, with the Commissioner himself acknowledging the extent of racism in the force. Meanwhile, Lord Harris kept the issues in the public eye by organizing a seminar in late March 2001 to debate MacPherson's recommendations on stop and search.

In order to address the internal priorities—those relating to MPS as an organization—the MPA had established a structure designed to focus the attention of Authority members on the internal working of the MPS. Their priorities were to communicate and consult more effectively with Londoners and with each other, and improve the attractiveness and satisfaction of working for the Metropolitan Police. To this end, the MPS set itself new diversity targets to be monitored by the diversity strategy executive board, chaired by the deputy commissioner. A diversity strategy coordination forum, presided over by the director of the racial and violent crime task force, drew upon much wider representation including senior and middle management practitioners, staff associations, and other representatives. Underpinning this structure was the diversity directorate comprising a newly enlarged violent-crime task force that brought together the Stephen Lawrence review team and relevant sections of the MPS community and partnership branch. Recruitment and retention initiatives specifically targeting minority ethnic communities were the focus of the MPS minority ethnic (recruitment and advancement) working group, comprising lay involvement from the Commission for Racial Equality, PCCGs, the Police Complaints Authority, and private firms.

Here was an area where MPA members could make their weight felt, and the Authority asked Scotland Yard to focus more on issues of discrimination involving gender, disability, race, age, and gender reassignment. The new members argued that the MPS had the potential to influence the promotion of equality of opportunity in employment, in the use of services, or in the supply of goods and services to the MPS. Indeed, there was a statutory basis for this assumption. Section 404 of the 1999 Act required the MPA to have regard to eliminating unlawful discrimination and to promoting equality of opportunity to all irrespective of their age, sex, religion, or sexual orientation. This duty was specific to the MPA and the GLA and there was no equivalent provision for other police authorities. But it was easier to declare such aims than to achieve them. For the financial year 2000–1, the MPS recruitment target of 1,355 was to include 300 from the ethnic minorities: in July 2000 a mere 17 from ethnic minorities were recruited. The January 2000 HMIC report *Policing London: Winning Consent* suggested a target of additional 4,000 ethnic minority officers by 2010; this compared with the July 2000 figure of only 1,049 officers, or 4 per cent, from this group. Concerned about under-representation, the MPS simplified the application procedure, leading Livingstone to complain that the process was still far too complex, comparing it unfavourably with the nomination form for candidates for the mayoralty. It was, indeed, not a well-received comment: the chairman of the Metropolitan Police Federation reported that 'anyone can perhaps become Mayor but there are probably more impediments to becoming a police officer'(*ES*, 3 November 2000).

One key to success in achieving the MPA's goals was effective local working. Community Safety Units (CSUs) had been established in all Met divisions to address racial and violent crime and improve clear-up rates. Local crime audits were reviewed and a range of preventive options for racial and violent crime were to be provided in association with the ALG. However, restructuring the network of local consultation proved controversial. Since the 1980s the Metropolitan Police District had been covered by a network of PCCGs. Set up in the wake of the Scarman enquiry in 1982, the PCCGs brought representatives of local organizations—religious, cultural, or residential—together with their police commander. When the MPA was established it moved swiftly against the PCCGs, reviewing the existing pattern of police committee consultation in London. MPA members judged PCCGs to be unrepresentative of the community, poorly managed and lacking London-wide coordination of their activities. They also found PCCG members were untrained and few had the support of experienced professional consultation personnel. The report recommended that the MPA should take direct responsibility for the PCCGs which had hitherto been independent of local authority control, and that the organizations should be 'rebranded and reformed'. A new model constitution, in which the MPA would have the power to veto the appointment of PCCG chairs, was adopted, with the MPA appointing professional community consultation officers with support staff to work with each borough. Unsurprisingly, local PCCGs protested volubly, accusing the MPA of not understanding the voluntary ethos and destroying all that was good in the present framework. It was in areas such as these, rather than operational policy, that the results of creating the MPA and handing down powers from the Home Secretary could most clearly be seen.

9

Renewing London

L ONDON was the first 'world city'. In the mid-nineteenth century it had no rivals for the size of its population, the vigour of its economy, or the international importance of its commerce. Yet its ability to attract people and investment was not without cost. The British capital became a byword for the strains of urban development, giving rise to apocalyptic visions of 'The Infernal Wen' (Sheppard 1971). For much of the twentieth century, policy-makers sought to contain and constrain its expansion. Celebrating London as an engine of growth fell out of fashion and, in the period immediately after the Second World War, the priority became to move people and jobs out of London to new towns and assisted areas. The radical policies of one era, however, became the discarded conservatism of the next: population decanting, an enthusiasm that began with 1940s reconstruction, lasted only a generation. Decentralization policy was sharply reversed in the late 1970s, partly in response to the 1971 census, which showed a dramatic turnaround in London's population and employment growth. Attempts to limit London by exporting people and industry were abandoned. At the same time, the 'inner-city problem' came into focus.

The inner-city problem was a dominating concern of the GLC in the 1980s as urban unemployment mounted. Under Ken Livingstone, the GLC had developed an economic strategy that was seen as a prototype for a future Westminster government of the left. Central to this 'alternative' approach was the Greater London Enterprise Board, set up to channel investment, together with a new commitment to involve local communities in regeneration. During the interregnum that followed GLC abolition, private business groups and the City Corporation moved to fill the strategic vacuum and, together with the boroughs' joint organization, the LPAC, formulated a broad approach to keeping London an internationally competitive city. With the creation of the Greater London Authority, regeneration strategy was intended to build upon these foundations. It would be for the Mayor to develop the content of the strategy for regenerating London, through the steer he would give to the London Development Agency. By now, however, a key concern was with the image of London as a global city whose standing needed to be protected in the face of international competition.

The Evolving Problem of London

During the inter-war period, London's pattern of growth had been shaped by a combination of population movement from elsewhere in the country, attracted by housing and employment opportunities, and from the urban core to the periphery. The changes in the distribution of the population reflected the dynamics of the economy of south-east Britain. Migration to London and the south-east provided the labour that the new industries were seeking, while the development of the outer London suburbs provided new housing opportunities which satisfied the demands of the lower-middle class.

The need for a master plan to interrelate housing and industrial development, transport, and main drainage was recognized in the early 1920s with the reports of the Unhealthy Areas Committee and the Ullswater Commission. The absence of a Greater London authority meant that reliance had to be placed on the voluntary joint action of the local authorities. This was rarely forthcoming. The Greater London Regional Planning Committee of 1927 and its successor, the Standing Conference on London Regional Planning of 1937, attempted with little success to coordinate action. Moreover, as the international situation worsened, the massing of population in Greater London was seen not just as a problem of public health and movement, but as a source of vulnerability to aerial bombardment.

The Barlow Commission on the Distribution of the Industrial Population was appointed in 1937, but war had already broken out by the time it reported. Sir Montague Barlow's answer was the redevelopment of congested urban areas and the decentralization and dispersal of both industry and its workers so as to balance and diversify industrial development. Barlow became the basis for early post-war regional planning. It was followed by three major master plans: for the County of London, for Greater London, and for the City of London. Abercrombie's Greater London plan—the key to post-war London planning—proposed to restrict further population growth within the region and bar new industrial development in London and the Home Counties. A million people would be moved out from inner London and a ring of new towns built to provide self-contained nodes of industrial growth.

The Attlee government legislated to create a statutory framework for planning with its Town and Country Planning Act 1947. This was intended to remove one of the major impediments to regional planning by vesting new and substantial powers only in the counties and county boroughs. The six counties and three county boroughs of Greater London were given responsibility by the Minister of Town and Country Planning for preparing development plans, in conformity with Abercrombie's prescriptions. Abercrombie divided the London region into four rings: the inner urban, the suburban, the green belt, and the 'outer country ring' lying beyond Greater London as it is understood today. The Minister's policy guidance stressed the need for decentralization, with new industrial development concentrated instead in the new towns, where housing provision would be coordinated with it in order to produce 'balanced' communities. Offices would be dispersed to other parts of the country at the behest of a new Location of Offices Bureau.

The subsequent decade revealed the limits of such planning. Abercrombie assumed that the post-war population would fall: in fact, the trend towards younger marriage and earlier child bearing produced a British baby boom. This, combined with migration towards the increasingly prosperous south-east, pushed the population of the metropolitan region towards 12 million by the end of the century. Already by 1955, when most of the development plans had been approved by the government, it was clear that both the suburban and the outermost parts of the region were growing faster than expected. Strong pressures for growth in the towns and villages of Hertfordshire and in the green-belt ring itself led the Town Planning Institute to warn that the basic planning policy for the London region was in jeopardy (SCLSERP 1974).

Whereas between the wars decentralization had been sustained by the growth of public transport, after 1945 it was driven by mass car ownership, producing a settlement pattern less closely tied to the railway. The number of private cars registered in the London Transport Area doubled between 1952 and 1958, and journeys to work by car increased by 60 per cent. Meanwhile, demand for labour was rippling outwards from London to the outer metropolitan area encouraging further decentralization, first of homes and later of employment.

Such dramatic changes produced new calls for containment. The continued economic expansion of south-east England as a whole had to be taken into account in any future planning, but opinion was divided on methods. Expansion was taking place in ways that obliterated the distinction between London and its surrounding region. At the beginning of the 1960s, the Ministry of Housing and Local Government attempted to take on board the new demographic reality. In 1961, it embarked on a major strategic exercise, the *South East Study*, with a view to promoting the redevelopment and modernization of the region to sustain population growth and continue its role as the national 'engine of economic growth'. When the *South East Study* was published, it was accompanied by a government White Paper proposing the extension of the Metropolitan Green Belt to much of the outer metropolitan area in order to channel growth to planned towns or preferred locations well beyond Abercrombie's London at Ashford, Northampton, Swindon, Peterborough, and Ipswich.

Planning Under the GLC—and After

The *South East Study* provided the backcloth, in planning terms, to the emergent Greater London Council, which took over from the LCC and surrounding authorities in 1965. The Herbert Commission's recommendation that a council should be established for something less than the continuous built-up area raised the problematic issue of the relationship between the 'inner urban mass' of London itself and the larger region in which it was situated. The Commission accepted that 'the problems of Greater London are inextricably concerned with the problems of South East England as a whole', yet thought it the business of central government, not that of the proposed metropolitan authority, to 'hold the balance between Greater London and the rest of South East England' (Herbert 1960: para 720). This meant that many of the larger questions of London's development would still have to be handled by ministers. At the same time, creating a metropolitan authority enabled the internal problems of Greater London at last to be tackled. Accordingly, the powers of the GLC were focused on a new kind of planning role: reshaping and modernizing the metropolitan structure to give administrative effect to the Abercrombie Plan within, broadly, the green belt.

Behind the creation of the GLC lay a long-standing commitment to bring the urban motorway proposals of Abercrombie's plan to fruition. The London Government Act 1963 required the GLC to produce a development plan—the Greater London Development Plan (GLDP)—in the form of a written statement accompanied by two maps, one setting out the proposed urban structure in schematic form and the other the road proposals to be embodied in the plan. These were no more than Abercrombie's so called A, B, and C ring roads, appearing here as 'ringways' 1, 2, and 3, the D ring—the 'ringway 4'—eventually being built by central government as the M25 (Hart 1976). Published with a fanfare and with the support of a cross-party consensus, the roads plan seemed to vindicate the GLC's creation. Very quickly, however, the scheme came under heavy criticism, and the so-called 'motorway box' was eventually abandoned. Of the 23,000 objections eventually lodged against the GLDP, no fewer than 18,000 related to the roads proposals. By the mid-1970s neither party at the GLC dared propose the demolition of 35,000 houses and the incurring of hundreds of millions of pounds of expenditure to set Abercrombie's map in asphalt. A gulf developed between County Hall and Whitehall, where ministers and officials continued to seek major roads improvements either through the agency of the GLC or, as seemed increasingly likely, without it. With the highways proposals drastically watered down, the GLDP was finally approved by the Secretary of State, after years of preparation and inquiry, in 1976. Meanwhile, a simplified planning system had been introduced under which the boroughs would produce unitary development plans for ministerial—not GLC—approval.

By then, the formal planning system had come increasingly to be seen as irrelevant to the urgent policy problems facing London. Foremost among the latter was the newly discovered 'inner-city problem'. Decentralization had been assisted by promotional policies to disperse activity and people from inner London in accordance with the Abercrombie plan, but these policies reinforced, rather than restrained, market forces. While population in the region as a whole soared, it fell sharply in the inner-urban area, and employment fell even faster. At the same time, a process of social decline occurred as younger, more mobile, and more skilled workers followed the jobs. Thus, the

Labour government of 1974–9 channelled funds back to sustain regeneration in Lambeth, Islington, and Hackney, while the Location of Offices Bureau went into reverse, seeking now to promote office employment in inner-urban areas. New-town growth at Milton Keynes, Northampton, Peterborough, Harlow, Stevenage, and Bracknell was constrained as 'saving' London became a prime political concern.

When Ken Livingstone's Labour group took control at County Hall after the 1981 election, an industry and employment committee was set up and an economic policy group established. The GLC's new strategy was to be implemented through two bodies: the Greater London Enterprise Board (GLEB), an arms-length company set up to implement the policies defined in the London Industrial Strategy, and the Greater London Training Board (GLTB), a regular committee of the GLC. The GLEB was founded to provide financial support for new and existing firms, and, importantly, for new forms of municipal enterprise including cooperatives. The importance given to the economic strategy reflected the conviction that the GLC could somehow show the way for a future Labour government by developing an interventionist programme in support of socialist objectives, paralleling the 'alternative economic strategy' espoused by a number of left-wing economists. In 1983–4 GLEB spent £31 million in support of job creation, expenditure which central government opposed as positively harmful, serving only to divert resources to uneconomic activities in failing industries.

The GLC's response to criticism was that its long-term intention was to secure rather than 'create' jobs, both by averting closures with appropriate packages of property and financial assistance for firms with market potential but temporary difficulties, and by promoting industrial democracy and common ownership. The point of difference between the GLC and the government was that the GLC had moved away from a traditional local authority approach on small-area problems, to a sectoral analysis that enabled it to take a strategic view of the prospects of particular industries. This sectoral approach, published in the *London Industrial Strategy*, contrasted with

other strategies adopted by industrial development agencies—some concentrating on small firms, others on property-led programmes, others easing the way for 'sunrise' industries, or reacting passively to new proposals assessing each case on its merits. The sectoral approach involves an active restructuring perspective. It is not limited to the formal sectoral categories of the statistician, but geared rather to the way in which industry itself is organised. The French refer to it as *filière*, the thread of industrial organisation, a thread which may run across traditional categories, in cases such as tourism or films, and which reflects material economies of co-ordination, joint sales, strategic knowledge and so on. But in following that seam, the sectoral production approach aims to consider strategic alternatives, ones which recognise broader social interests than those favoured by the market, around which an active policy of intervention can be built. (GLC 1985: para 1.122)

The GLC's radical approach to planning was reflected in a thoroughgoing revision of the GLDP, explicitly rejecting the past approaches to allocating land in London. It was a direct challenge to the Conservative government. Heading off that challenge, the Local Government (Interim Provisions) Act 1984 relieved the Secretary of State of the statutory responsibility to consider proposals submitted to him for the alteration of the GLDP. Despite this, the Livingstone GLC pressed ahead to rewrite the GLDP in the way that was consonant with their overall socialist vision, submitting 'proposed alterations' as permitted under the London Government Act 1963. Titled *Planning for the Future of London*, the rewrite condemned the existing plan on the grounds that it took account of neither subsequent population trends nor economic and employment change; that it overlooked public concern with environmental and ecological matters and ignored changes in energy prices and the effects of the new technology; and, finally, that it failed to respond to the new emphasis on community needs or the recognized need to tackle discrimination and disadvantage experienced by ethnic minorities, women, and people with disabilities. In sum, *Planning for the Future of London* was a comprehensive agenda for dissenters. The new document's own solution proposed maintaining and regenerating London's economy by creating employment opportunities and improving the skills of the workforce through direct intervention. The result, its authors claimed, would be to reduce social deprivation, improve the environment and upgrade public transport while meeting the needs of pedestrians and cyclists (GLC 1984). Unsurprisingly, the Secretary of State, Patrick Jenkin, declined to consider the GLC's proposals.

As London's collaborative arrangements settled down following the abolition of the GLC, the London boroughs, through the LPAC, began to make an increasing contribution to London's planning (Travers 2001). In 1988 LPAC submitted advice on London strategic planning which shaped the regional planning guidance issued in 1989 by the DoE. In 1992 the LPAC reviewed both its 1989 review and its subsequent guidance and, after wide consultation, published further advice in May 1994. This advice in turn was incorporated in the Government Office for London's 1996 strategic guidance for London planning authorities, the revised RPG3. LPAC's concern was that the planning framework should address the long-term imbalances that characterized London's development, in particular the contrasts between East and West London. It stressed the opportunities for regeneration in the Isle of Dogs, the Greenwich Peninsula, the Royal Docks, and Stratford. The emphasis on a spatially sensitive and targeted strategy was becoming the common currency of the London planning debate and characterized the ALG's London study (1996).

Among the major planning issues that had exercised central government for decades was the special place of central London. The significance of the inner core of the capital had arguably been overlooked in the drawing up of the new London boroughs in 1963 (Robson 1965). LPAC's policy was to sustain and enhance central- London activities, especially its world city functions. Thus, LPAC launched a world city study in 1990 the purpose of which was to assess London's 'competitive performance as measured against other world cities, especially New York and Tokyo, and other European cities including Paris,

Frankfurt and Berlin, together with an evaluation of the factors which under-pin this'. Changes in the international competitive climate, including the extension of the European community, tariff reductions, deregulation, and the establishment of the EEC's single market were seen as posing a potential threat to London's international position. The pre-eminence of the City in the field of commodity and financial futures, was threatened by competition from Paris, Frankfurt and Amsterdam (LPAC 1990).

In its world city report of 1992, LPAC's consultants stressed the importance of size, income, and population within both the metropolitan and the sur-rounding regions. At the same time, the report highlighted the importance of London's cultural resources, the cosmopolitan nature of its people, its network of global linkages, and the world-leading role in the financial markets held by the City of London. These aspects of London were given further prominence by the London Pride Partnership, London First, and the City Corporation, and reflected in the central government's regional planning guidance issued through the Government Office for London.

Research reports prepared for the LPAC study focused on the strength and effectiveness of world cities' land-use planning, comparing London with Frankfurt, Berlin, Paris, New York, and Tokyo. In the case of Frankfurt and Tokyo, the national and State—or regional—governments were closely involved in planning policies; and decisions and the operations of all three levels were hierarchical in nature and highly integrated. In Paris, and in London after GLC abolition, the different levels of government were by com-parison poorly integrated and controls were focused at the local government level. In New York, in common with other US cities, there was no federal gov-ernment role in land-use planning. The effectiveness of these controls also var-ied, with land-use controls in Germany identified as highly effective (Ellis 1992). The point of these contrasts was to show up the planning vacuum at the regional level in London. Planning was not required for its own sake, nor in the interest of orderly development alone. The demand was that land-use planning and control operated in a such a fashion as to ensure that London held a competitive position among the world cities.

The emphasis on office development reflected the emergence of the business community, devoted to ensuring that the economic well-being of London as a financial centre was sustained, as a dominant voice in London policy mak-ing. City-wide strategic planning was considered necessary to guide future development and in particular to provide for transportation improvements. The voice of the London business community spoke in the accents of the large institutions and predictably favoured a vision of London's world city status that emphasized the importance of a central location and a plentiful stock of quality modern office accommodation:

In terms of the extent of the stock, the choice available and the relative cost London was, in 1992, still a highly attractive location, due in part to the massive eastward exten-sion of the CBD into Docklands and through new development in the City in response to the shortages of the mid-1980s. In 1992 there were more than 14 million square meters of office space in Central London, with a potential for another 2 million square meters in Docklands within few years. Frankfurt and Berlin, in contrast, suffered high costs as a result of continuing scarcity. (Coopers and Lybrand Deloitte 1992)

Occupier surveys showed very strong preferences for a City address. When the new planning regime came into being in July 2000, business expectations were high. Unsurprisingly, they favoured a future for London that focused upon continuous renewal and the development of high buildings in the central area.

A New Planning Regime

One of the GLA's inheritances from the interregnum was the existing Regional Planning Guidance—the revived RPG3—at any rate until such time as the Spatial Development Strategy (SDS) was formulated and approved by formal Examination in Public (EIP). The planning guidance pointed out that Unitary Development Plan (UDP) policies for the central area boroughs were 'disjointed' and called upon them to work together to resolve cross-borough issues and harmonize their UDPs. In October 1999 the boroughs, LPAC, and GOL agreed upon a boundary and on guidelines for coordinating the central area, the first time the heart of Greater London had achieved physical expression in the planning process. Another key issue was East-West 'balance'. Differences between inner and outer London and between East and West, and growth in the development corridors critical to London's economic regeneration and prosperity, were also priorities to be addressed. Four corridors running north, south, east, and west were defined. The Thames Gateway, first defined under Michael Heseltine, extended from Docklands through to Thurrock, north of the river, and the Kent Thameside. The Lee Valley ran from Hackney out through North London through the M11 corridor to Stansted and Cambridge. The western wedge extended from Hammersmith through Park Royal and Heathrow beyond London past the M25 as far as Reading, Newbury, and Basingstoke; and, finally, the southern corridor ran from Wandsworth out through Croydon to Gatwick and the Crawley-Horsham area. In each case their definitions challenged the logic of the Greater London boundary, signalling that the GLA would have to work closely with the Home Counties.

Under the GLA Act, the foremost of the Mayor's strategic responsibility was the preparation of the SDS for London. Effectively the responsibility for strategic planning now shifted from the boroughs collectively, and from the Secretary of State, to the Mayor. Accordingly, the boroughs' strategic role came to an end when LPAC was abolished and taken into the Mayor's office, and their UDPs were now required to be in general conformity with the SDS. The adoption of the strategy became a matter for the Mayor, not the Assembly, and it was he who was empowered to monitor the implementation of the SDS and of the boroughs' UDPs.

Although the SDS fulfilled a function similar to that of the earlier GLDP, it was not itself a development plan and fell outside the mainstream of the statutory planning system. It was specifically intended that the SDS would not be a revival of the GLDP but an entirely new kind of plan that set out the spatial implications of the other statutory strategies that the Mayor needed to publish, along with his other policies. This was not, then, 'developmental planning for its own sake but as the servant of other policies . . . It follows that the SDS is not a detailed development plan, but more a broad statement of ambition, focused on key development and infrastructural requirements' (PEMB 2000: 59).

Ministers resisted pressure to have the SDS declared a development plan, insisting that it was instead a new-style planning instrument. Subsequent guidance from GOL elaborated this thinking, requiring the SDS to

adopt an integrated approach, embracing all aspects of physical planning, infrastructure development and other policies affecting or affected by the distribution of activities. By doing so, it should help to secure the effective co-ordination and targeting of activities and resources, and a consistent, holistic approach to the delivery of policy objectives. It should contribute to the achievement within London of sustainable development, a healthy economy and a more inclusive society. (LPAC 2000: 3)

The SDS was novel in other respects. The document had to be produced within a short timescale—a reflection on the notoriously slow GLDP process—and was to be selectively updated and amended. The SDS was required to deal only with matters which are of strategic importance to Greater London, implying that the courts might have to determine what was and was not strategic. Specifically, section 334 (6) established that a matter did not have to affect the whole area of Greater London in order to be of strategic importance to it. Although the SDS was subject to an EIP, the procedures for this were quite different from those relating to structure plans, in that the matters to be examined were at the discretion of the inspector conducting the inquiry, and the Secretary of State had no power of direction. Furthermore, the EIP panel reported to the Mayor, not to the Secretary of State. While not being bound by it, the Mayor was required to take the report into account. Nevertheless, the Secretary of State was given power to intervene where it appeared to him that the SDS departed from the current national or regional policies or was detrimental to the interest of an area outside Greater London.

Thus, despite all the rhetoric of devolution and novelty, the SDS framework was in practice closely controlled by the central government. In that respect too, it was unlike the other strategies the Mayor was obliged to produce. In particular, the Secretary of State had reserve powers to require the SDS to be made, reviewed, and altered. He would make regulations with respect to form and content and procedures to be followed in preparing, publishing, reviewing, or withdrawing it, and these regulations closely followed those relating to structure plans. Additionally, in formulating the SDS the Mayor was required to have regard to a wide range of matters, some of which were matters of judgement by the Secretary of State: for example, the effects of the strategy on international obligations and its implications for environmental protection. Most importantly, the Secretary of State retained the power to issue regional planning guidance for London and the adjoining areas, which the Mayor was obliged to take into account.

Although the SDS was not a statutory development plan, its impact upon the boroughs was much the same as if it were, since the Town and Country Planning Act was amended to place it in a hierarchical relationship with the boroughs' UDPs. Thus, both Part I and Part II of a UDP had to be in general conformity with the SDS. A borough, when proposing a new UDP or proposing to amend the existing UDP, was obliged to apply to the Mayor for a written opinion on whether or not the proposals were in general conformity. If they were not, the borough might still proceed with the plan-making process, in which case the Mayor's views simply counted as an objection. But the plan might not be adopted unless it achieved conformity, and the Secretary of State might place time limits on this process.

The Mayor was not a development control authority for normal purposes, and those powers remained with the boroughs subject to the overriding powers of the Secretary of State. The development control provisions included an important anomaly: because SDS is not a statutory development plan, it did not constitute a 'policy framework' under section 70 of the Town and Country Planning Act 1990. Thus, there was no formal duty upon the boroughs or the Secretary of State to have regard to it in determining planning applications. Section 347 of the Act required each of the functional bodies to have regard to the SDS, but made no specific reference to the boroughs. However, the impact of SDS upon development control is likely to grow over time, albeit indirectly, due to the requirement for UDPs to conform with the SDS, and planning applications must in turn comply with the UDP. But there is no specific requirement that applications should be determined by the boroughs in accordance with the SDS itself, or even that they should take it into account.

The development control powers granted to the Mayor related to developments of particular importance to London, where he had certain limited powers to block a planning application. The Act defined four categories of planning application which the boroughs would be required to notify to the Mayor: large-scale developments; major infrastructure developments; developments which might affect key strategic policies; and those which might affect key strategic sites or views. Large-scale development referred to proposals for more than 500 residential units or for commercial developments above a floor-space limit of 30,000 square metres in the City, 20,000 in central London, and 15,000 elsewhere; and tall buildings. The bill had originally proposed that the Mayor should have the right to determine a office developments more than 50 metres in height or more than 20,000 square metres in size. The City Corporation protested that with such low limits more than one in four planning applications would need to be submitted to the Mayor, while Sir Norman Foster warned that the introduction of a new layer of planning 'may lead to companies going to Chicago or Frankfurt instead of London' (*ES*, 14 December 1998).

The government estimated that about 150–250 applications annually would fall into these categories. Once an application was notified, planning permission could not be granted until all the relevant documentation—including, for example, representations against the development, officer reports, proposed conditions—had been forwarded to the Mayor, and he had in turn notified the local authority that he was content for permission to be granted. Although the Mayor could not direct a London borough council to grant planning permission, he could veto one within 14 days, giving written reasons—which might include conflict with the SDS or being 'otherwise contrary to good strategic planning'. Applicants could appeal to the Secretary of State in the usual fashion, and the Secretary of State could direct a borough not to comply with a Mayoral refusal, as well as call in applications for his own decision. In order to deter the Mayor from making inappropriate use of his powers, the Secretary of State could award the costs of any inquiry occasioned by an unreasonable refusal against the Mayor. Here, too, central government retained important powers to curb the Mayor's capacity to act independently, although the subtleties of the new London planning system seemed to invite determination in the courts.

Preparing the Strategies

Two of the strategies which the Mayor was obliged to produce were central to the task of renewing London as a world city. The SDS was intended to function as a master plan to which all other strategies must conform. The SDS then could be seen in one of two ways: as a land-use planning document or as an overarching strategy whose principles provided the key to all other actions. The economic development strategy (EDS), though not explicitly spatial, similarly has the potential to have a profound effect on the patterns of London's economic activity. An important difference between them lay in how they were to be originated. The SDS emanated from the Mayor's own office, while the EDS was the responsibility of the London Development Agency (LDA). Both, however, were similarly scrutinized by committees set up by the Assembly.

With encouragement of the DETR, LPAC officials began work at an early stage to ensure that the Mayor would benefit from a substantial body of preliminary work on the SDS. LPAC had, since its establishment in 1996, achieved a remarkable degree of consensus. Thus, in commending their 'endowment' document to the Mayor, LPAC political leaders, representing three main parties, affirmed that

Politics has rarely intruded: decisions have generally been made cross-party. The driving-force has been integrated developments, transport and environmental policy in the best interests of London as a sustainable World city and of Londoners' quality of life. This approach has, we believe, proved productive in achieving 'highest common factor' results. (LPAC 2000: 1)

Preparing the SDS was, then, greatly facilitated by this preparatory work. The absorption of LPAC staff into the GLA enabled it to be carried forward in a fraction of the time needed had the GLA started entirely from scratch. Indeed, the aim was explicitly

to enable the Mayor to proceed quickly with its preparation. LPAC acknowledges that the form the strategy takes should be for the Mayor to decide, so it is not proposing a strategy. Instead it has put together a number of 'policy building blocks' covering key parts of the SDS's content. These building blocks result from extensive and time-consuming analysis and consultation. Doing this in advance of the GLA means that the Mayor will be able to proceed much more quickly with its preparation. (Simmons 2000: 2)

However, the LPAC endowment could go only so far, as the SDS was required to contain a statement of the Mayor's strategies not just for spatial development but for a range of other areas laid down in the act.

Nor could LPAC escape its origins as a borough-based organization. It had admittedly 'undertaken this advanced SDS work with the interests of its boroughs in mind'. LPAC's political leaders, in commending the 'endowment' document to the Mayor, stressed the need to involve the boroughs in the preparation of the SDS through 'constructive engagement'. Whether that engagement would occur was the greatest area of uncertainty during the transition, for the GLA was set up in such a way as to ensure that it could not be dominated by 'parochial'—that is, borough—interests. Fearing a break with this established pattern of consensual working, the LPAC leaders' final statement was to stress as forcibly as they could their belief that it was

essential that the Mayor continues LPAC's working relations with the boroughs as key partners in the SDS. Not only would this facilitate the Act's requirement for UDP conformity, but it would establish the GLA's role in providing strategic co-ordination for borough activities and promulgating best practice. (LPAC 2000: 25)

Predictably, however, Livingstone's SDS did break with the past pattern of consensus-seeking. The Mayor was emphatic that London's strategies should flow from his own will and not from that of the boroughs. On taking office, he quickly built up his own SDS steering group to bring together the different groups of people directly involved in drawing up the strategy, including his Deputy Mayor and advisers. The Deputy Mayor, Nicky Gavron, was expected to play a key role as the SDS champion. The steering group met fortnightly and was coordinated by a secondee from KPMG. The Mayor also held a separate fortnightly planning and SDS meeting in which planning applications were to be discussed with his advisers and planning staff. Apart from these working groups, the Mayor appointed Lord (Richard) Rogers to work two days a week in the GLA as a consultant in the GLA's Architecture and Urbanism Unit to assist with implementing the SDS and 'delivering the urban renaissance in London'. The chairman of the government's Urban Task Force, the report of which had been largely ignored by ministers, Lord Rogers was expected to bring the Task Force's principles into the SDS. He would also work on issues of urban design, working with key stakeholders to develop urban strategies and guidance for key areas and sites around London in order to promote high quality buildings and public spaces.

The all-inclusive approach adopted by the Mayor ensured that a wide range of stakeholders were able to make their voices heard on planning issues. In the short term, this approach complicated and slowed down the decision process. Complaints were heard that the GLA, far from simplifying the planning process by bringing everything together in a streamlined regional strategic authority, was causing additional muddle and confusion by bringing new people and organizations into the debates about planning applications. Developers found themselves dealing with the boroughs, English Heritage, voluntary organizations, community groups, and the London Development Agency, which had inherited its land and property section from English Partnerships. They were also subject to the determinations of the Mayor, as well as the views of the Assembly and its planning advisory committee, and the Deputy Mayor. In the longer term, planning applications would be handled in the context of the approved SDS, but the interim period was one of special difficulty.

The consultation requirements on the draft strategy were bound to introduce further uncertainties. Business groups were at the forefront of consultation proposals, but once again the commitment to inclusiveness meant that it would be difficult to draw a boundary between who could, and who could not, have a seat at the table. In particular, early draft proposals seemed to suggest that significant community and minority groups had been overlooked. Although the Mayor had allocated a part of his budget to fund consultation and promotion of the SDS, it was unclear whether this would be for the initial proposals document, in which case the sums allocated were small, or for the SDS, which would be subject to the lengthy and expensive process of an EIP.

Whereas responsibility for formulating the SDS rested with the Mayor, that for economic development was located at one remove with the LDA. The LDA was accountable to the Mayor who appointed its board. Business-led, the board also included a number of other key GLA members, while other board members, and the chairman in particular, had a long history of involvement in orchestrating London's renewal. While the LDA was formally one of nine Regional Development Agencies established in 1999, its origins lay in the interregnum period. At that time, the promotion of development was led by a coalition of private sector and government-led agencies such as London First. During the run-up to the establishment of the GLA, an interim organization, the London Development Partnership, was set up by bringing together 17 organizations, including the London First Centre and the ALG to do the preparatory work for developing economic strategy. The LDP's role in the interim period was to coordinate inward investment—superseding the London First Centre—improve the skill base and business competitiveness, and promote social and physical regeneration. The City Corporation provided an office and a range of businesses, voluntary groups, trade unions, universities, and tourism agencies joined together to support the project. When Eric Sorenson, former chief executive of the London Docklands Development Corporation, was put in charge of the LDP he was quick to stress its transitional character. Nevertheless, the concerns he set out had not been met. 'We have discovered how much there is still to learn about London', he told *Property Week*. 'We know a lot about key deprivation factors, but the figures are out of date. We have also discovered how little we know about business drivers' (*Property Week Supplement*, May 2000: 15).

Described as a shadow LDA, the LDP was expected to transform itself seamlessly. It did so, with many familiar faces reappearing in new seats. LDP chair George Barlow, Chief Executive of the Peabody Trust, was appointed chair of the LDA, sending a strong message that the private sector-led and City-focused approach would be carried forward in the LDA and in the preparation of an economic strategy for London. Barlow had authored a key LDP document on *Building London's Economy* on which the LDA was expected to base its initial policies. Mike Ward, a former-GLC councillor colleague of Livingstone's and latterly Director of the influential Centre for Economic Strategies, took over as chief executive.

The LDA declared a number of key objectives as the basis for an agreed economic policy for London. Central to these objectives was the promotion of London as a sustainable world city. To this end, the LDA sought to improve business competitiveness and sustain the City region by encouraging economic diversity. This growth orientation was, however, conditioned by social objectives, including transport, schooling, and housing, and supporting the development of the social enterprise sector. In pursuit of its aims of empowering London's communities and supporting disadvantaged people into work, the LDA is required to work closely with the private and public investors and with the GLA on its spatial development proposals, and with the Learning and Skills Councils—the former Training and Enterprise Councils—and with the Small Business Service—formerly Business Links.

Apart from its strategic role, the LDA was given executive responsibility for the delivery of the government's main regeneration programme, the Single Regeneration Budget, involving the allocation of £250 million to a variety of local organizations and partnerships. In this role it could target very large sums of public investment for regeneration purposes in accordance with its own distinctive priorities. At the same time, the LDA runs executive programmes for the Department of Trade and Industry—which it inherited from English Partnerships—as well as for the Department for Education and Employment. It is also responsible for a major programme of physical development, primarily in East London, including such major opportunity sites as the Royal Docks and the Woolwich Arsenal.

The special statutory context of the SDS was such that the other strategies—transport, economic development—would have to be harmonized with it. However, the LDA proved much speedier in the production of its strategic document than the Mayor's office, so the draft economic strategy was formulated, presented, and referred back before any sign emerged of what the SDS might contain. This did not make any easier the Assembly's task when it set about scrutinizing the draft strategies.

Scrutinizing the Strategies

A scrutiny panel of six members, led initially by the former LPAC chair, Sally Hamwee, then by Bob Neill, a Conservative, was set up to investigate the initial SDS proposals document. At root, the Assembly's responsibility was to scrutinize, not to suggest alternative planning stances. But the temptation to produce a counter-strategy proved hard to resist, and the Mayor's document provoked fierce criticisms and alternative proposals from Assembly members, revealing sharply divergent views of the future of London.

Producing the SDS was a long-drawn-out business, involving some 15 drafts. The Mayor's view was that the earlier drafts had ducked difficult issues. The final version did not, but it polarized the Assembly. Commentators noted the apparent discomfort of Labour's Nicky Gavron, who had ostensibly led the preparation of the SDS yet appeared to have been sidelined from the key decisions over its policy content. One Assembly member observed that she had 'played a role very similar to that of ministers who have lost the argument within the Cabinet but decided to stay in, restating her own views and presenting them as though they were the official policy'. All six of the scrutiny committee members, from their different viewpoints, had criticized various aspects of *Towards the London Plan* (GLA 2001). Although the GLA Greens had been generally supportive of the Mayor, they parted company over the SDS and planning policies generally.

The principal axis on which these disagreements turned was whether London's future lay in playing to international market forces—as the Mayor, surprisingly, seemed now to believe—or in planning, directing, and regulating for social result. For example, when the SDS investigative committee examined transport and economic developments in the Mayor's plan for East and West London, it objected to a bias in favour of developments in West London. Plans to expand transport services and business developments in the west, to cater for the new terminal at Heathrow airport, and to exploit the potential of this growth corridor conflicted with long-established social commitments to redress the imbalances by investing in the Thames Gateway corridor to the east (GLA minutes, 13 July 2001).

The Assembly also established an economic development investigative committee (EDIC) to focus on the draft strategy. An all-party committee of nine members, the EDIC made an initial assessment of the draft strategy, held two public hearings, and consulted the Assembly's transport and environment committee in order to achieve consistency between strategies. Despite the presence of Assembly members on the LDA board, the EDIC's response to the draft was uncompromising, criticizing the LDA, in particular for providing a 'pick and mix' approach to economic development and for failing to offer a balanced approach to issues across London. Fifteen key recommendations were made, and the LDA was asked to bear them in mind when redrafting the strategy. A series of undertakings was exacted from the LDA under questioning at the oral hearings, and the EDIC insisted that the Agency would be held to account on these. The committee warned that they expected to contribute to the process of prioritizing and finalizing the Strategy once all the consultation responses have been received and considered, and also expected 'a continuing involvement' in the development and implementation of the follow-up action plans.

At the end of the process, EDIC issued its own report, which registered its dissatisfaction with the LDA's orientation to the London problem. The committee mapped out in its place a strategic, pan-London perspective, drawing heavily, in so doing, on the statutory cross-cutting themes of sustainable development, equality of opportunity, and health. It offered this in the spirit of 'assisting' the LDA in determining the priorities for economic development within London.

A 'more challenging long-term vision' was called for, and this would require a full analysis of the state of the regional economy. A key issue in the metropolitan structure that had been recognized for some years was the need to support the important role of London's suburbs and local employment centres, while encouraging local living and working patterns: in particular, the role of important sub-regional employment centres, such as Croydon. The treatment of town centres in the strategy was 'simplistic, with no consideration of issues of size, functions and the varying needs and opportunities of these centres'. At the same time, it was necessary to balance tensions arising from the development pressures in the east and west of London, something which the SDS would be attacked for neglecting.

Coming from the Assembly, the EDIC criticisms partly reflected a contrast of style. The two reports were different in tone, the LDA's indicative and exhortatory, the Assembly's redolent of firm project management with more than an echo of the language of the former GLC. But the disagreements between the two viewpoints ran deeper. The EDIC report paid far more attention to shaping the economic face of London and to the role of major metropolitan sub-centres than did the Mayor's strategy, which centred on a particular view of London as a world city.

Retaining London as a World City

The 'world city' idea had a natural appeal in the Mayor's office, where schemes that placed the Mayor on an international stage held out the tempting prospect of a higher profile. Hence, Livingstone was eager from the outset to build on the work of LPAC and private business groups. He warmly supported the notion of the capital as 'a command post of the global economy' in which the central area was 'the material/urban manifestation of international control over finance and commerce in a global environment' (Ellis 1992: 3). 'London's content is stupendous', he argued, and was something

on a scale to challenge one's imagination. It is far from being a question of historic sites and ceremonials . . . It plays the role of the great city throughout the ages—to being together in one place a critical mass of economic, scientific, cultural and intellectual possibilities . . . The melting pot feature of the capital—diversity coupled with the most modern forms of communications—is integral to London character. (*Independent*, 15 August 2000)

Picking up a well-honed concept, the Mayor inflected it with his own distinctive vision of social and ethnic mix and 'an evolving 24 hour city culture'. At the same time, there was an opportunity to link the socially progressive aspects of his policies, such as his support for a multicultural and multi-ethnic London, with 'pro-business' support for the single European currency and for the building of tall office blocks. As Livingstone put it a few months after taking office, 'London is a world city because most of the world's nationalities are represented here. More than 300 languages are spoken in London and our city is recognised the world over as a major centre of culture, innovation and, of course, the global economy' (GLA Mayor's questions, February 2001).

Here was a significantly different language from that of the GLC leader of the 1980s. Indeed, there had been a seismic shift. One of Livingstone's first statements set out his view of the relations he expected between his office and the business community. It could scarcely have been warmer or indeed more evidently designed as an olive branch:

London competes with cities around the world. In some cases different sectors compete with different locations. The financial services and banking industry competes with New York, Frankfurt and Tokyo. Manufacturers compete with a range of locations, both in other regions of the UK and Europe and low-cost manufacturing sectors in South East Asia. New knowledge and internet based industries compete directly with Amsterdam, San Francisco and Bangalore. Its fashion and creative industry stand head to head with New York, Paris and Milan. Tourism competes globally. Overall, London's key competitors include New York (for certain of the biggest companies), Paris and Frankfurt. (GLA 2000c: 3)

Nevertheless, despite occasional references to London's multiculturalism, the Mayor offered a contestable view of what constitutes a world city. His vision focused on the established central business district (CBD) and new office centres adjacent to it, where demand for global business activities was concentrated. The stress was on development opportunities in and around central London—an emphasis reflected in the LDA's argument that London's growth was increasingly being driven by high-value activity for which the central area was the necessary location (LDA 2000). In his view, Westminster's draft UDP was a case in point: London's boroughs pursued their local interests at the expense of London's role as a world city. Such local concern with maintaining existing heritage was not strategically helpful, and was likely to impede demand for westward office expansion from the city.

Some felt that this concern to retain world city status by accommodating office growth in the central area, sat less well with the political concerns of London's elected local government. The boroughs, the other parties, and the defunct LPAC had been committed to social objectives as well as to a broader, more inclusive view of the London economy. Their views clashed with the idea of London's world position as a overriding concern, creating a tension that was bound to become manifest once the other policy commitments were made explicit through the formulation of the strategies.

The draft economic development strategy had given a prominent place to the idea of London as a world city, drawing its strength from the CBD. The Assembly, on the other hand, drew attention to the need for a policy to meet the needs of London's suburbs and local employment centres and not just the central area. Members took the view that the LDA in pursuing world city functions risked overlooking the importance of local economic functions and, in particular, the role of London's suburbs.

In this criticism the Assembly committee was also reflecting expert opinion on the need to achieve a broader base of office development in London. Twelve months before the GLA came into being, the London office review panel, an advisory group, had stressed the need to reserve space in key central London locations for office development, placing high priority on the GLA 're-establish[ing] the concept of office centres in outer London as viable locations for the customer'. These would be just a 'few centres and locations which have, or may have, the level of infrastructure, labour market and development capacity necessary to support critical masses of office-related activity which individually are of strategic, regional significance'. In outer London, according to the panel, office policy had spread itself too thinly in promoting development, other than in Croydon. The demand for office space was at its most brisk in the north-west sector, including the M1 and M4 corridors and the 'brand alley' of the Great West Road. Thus, the panel had warned that:

The SDS must grasp this policy nettle and make the difficult decision to identify [alternative centres] and play to their strengths. In doing this, it need not rule out office provision in other, smaller centres or locations, but it must recognise that this will be of a different order and may require different local policy responses. (LORP 1999: 22)

Judged against the broader policy context, the Mayor was thus open to the charge that he was stressing global economic functions to the detriment of important regional priorities. Arguably, a failure to develop outer London's town centres with significant concentrations of office space could place London's business future in jeopardy. Much of London's economic activity took place in other centres, but there were few proposals in the economic development strategy for town centres and sub-regions. Indeed, the LDA's espousal of the world city concept could also be seen as overlooking the negative implications of London's high-cost/high-value trajectory, in which the focus on high-value land uses and international linkages ignored the implications for survival and retention rates of existing local firms.

These were indeed some striking indications of Livingstone's preferences. The Mayor's espousal of a world city concept, featuring international economic functions, was indicated by his attitude to tall buildings in the central area. When an application was submitted for a controversial Norman Foster design for a 41-storey tower for Swiss Re on the Baltic exchange site, to be the third tallest building in London, it was condemned as a dangerous precedent, likely to lead to other high-rise proposals. The Mayor took a different view. The proposal, he declared,

is for the type and quantity of high quality office floor space that the City needs in order to maintain and enhance its position as a world city, and to enable its international role in the business and financial sectors to flourish. The quality of design is of the highest order. It certainly has my full support. (GLA minutes, 20 July 2000)

Giving evidence on tall buildings in relation to the Mayor's London Plan, representatives of English Heritage and the Royal Institute of British Architects, told the SDS investigative committee that there was no firm evidence anywhere that London needed tall buildings. Building high could have negative impacts on the city's historical environment, while high densities could be achieved without building upwards (GLA minutes, 28 June 2001). The LPAC's own 1998 study acknowledged that while 'experience in Singapore and Chicago might lead to a view that it is "a shame" that London does not have a very high building', the fact that a high building can be an icon for a city 'should be a consequence and not a purpose for building it'. In relation to the need for office supply, the study argued that such buildings were not essential; and while occupiers might choose a high building when it was available, most would be content to occupy the same grade of space in a lower building. Moreover, there was 'no evidence to support arguments that London would lose jobs to other world cities if high buildings are not developed' (Building Design Partnerships *et al.* 1998: 41, 42).

The Mayor's new affection for globalization was perhaps the most surprising feature of London's planning regime, given his ideological position and his past sympathy for anti-capitalist protestors. The world city concept had been common currency in London's policy circles since the early 1990s. In one sense, therefore, the Mayor was simply adopting an accepted definition of the London problem. In another sense, however, his mayoralty marked a break with a consensus established among the boroughs by LPAC's policy analysis during the decade. Thus, the tall buildings issue signalled a rejection of the conventional wisdom and a shift in favour of unbridled development. There was a political logic. As the *Economist* (4 August 2001: 26) pointed out:

The city has run out of office space . . . [it] can no longer accommodate all the multinationals flocking to London. Vacancy rates are at a historic low and the price of office space higher than any comparable location in the world. Canary Wharf has land left to expand. The city does not. It can only go up, with skyscrapers, or north-east over its boundaries.

On this analysis, the Mayor had skilfully exploited the rivalry between the City and the Canary Wharf and supported demands for tall buildings in return for planning gains that would enable him to achieve his social objectives in the poor boroughs bordering the City. The cost, however, of the Mayor thinking globally and acting locally in this way was to distance himself from his wider constituency and from the wealthy peripheral boroughs in particular. Certainly, the 'world city' concept, despite its business and global attractions, seemed unlikely to do much for the alternative concept of an all-inclusive, mutually supporting, metropolitan community.

10

The Mayor and Metropolitan Government

NO verdict can yet be reached on the new Greater London Authority. A body whose *raison d'être* depends heavily on a strategic planning role cannot be judged until its plans are further advanced. Our aim here has been to show how the GLA came into being, setting it in the context of past attempts to govern the capital, with—and without—a London-wide body, and to identify key issues for the future. The concept of London as a world city, which resonated through the decade of the interregnum, will in due time provide a good measure of achievement. A test will be the extent to which this new authority can help to sustain the prosperity of the capital in the face of international competition, while at the same time meeting the domestic needs of its cosmopolitan people.

In this final chapter, we examine the style of the first Mayor in the opening months of the new GLA. New constitutions take time to settle down: their *modi operandi* are shaped by the way rules and relationships work out when first put to the test. In the case of London, the working of the capital's reformed government depends crucially on the developing relationships between the Mayor and the Assembly, between the Mayor and the boroughs, individually and collectively, and between the Mayor and Whitehall. Any system of metropolitan government rests on just such a set of relationships between local, area-wide, and national bodies. The issues of policing, transport, and regeneration of the London economy highlight the ways in which these relations have worked out so far. Early debate over all these has inevitably involved an initial exploration of boundaries by potential rivals. With so many players jockeying for position, there was bound to be an initial impression of friction and disagreement. So much was foreseen:

There obviously will be disagreements and trials of strength as the Authority learns to orchestrate public and private sector organisations in tackling London's problems. There are many potential sites of conflict, particularly the interface between the political mandates of the new institution and the boroughs. The challenge is to design a structure that encourages the authority to seek and develop consensus and co-operation rather than confrontation. (IPPR and KPMG 1997: A.15)

The test of any metropolitan government is how well it manages and reconciles these conflicts.

Living with the Assembly

The White Paper *A Mayor and Assembly for London* identified the need to achieve 'the right balance' between the Mayor and the Assembly in order to avoid 'frivolous or destructive intervention' on the part of members, while allowing the Assembly to scrutinize the Mayor's proposals and, if it so chose, to amend his budget (DETR 1998a). The Mayor's powers, duties, and responsibilities were designed to ensure that the programme on which he was elected could be delivered. Meanwhile the Assembly's primary duty is not to determine the direction of mayoral strategy but to secure the accountability of the Mayor by scrutinizing all his activities and those of the bodies responsible for transport and economic development.

With only weeks to settle into place after the mayoral election, the Livingstone team had little opportunity to develop ground rules and procedures before the system 'went live' in July. In the longer term, the relationship between the Mayor and the Assembly will doubtless depend on the success or failure of attempts to establish a political concordat. In the short term both were bound to explore the nature and limits of their respective powers. In the event, while from the outset the Mayor's role was relatively clear, the first year was one in which Assembly members struggled to find theirs. Two issues highlighted likely difficulties in the Mayor-Assembly relationship. The first concerned the Mayor's co-option of a significant proportion of Assembly members by using his patronage powers, appointing them as his advisers or to key positions on the functional bodies or both. The second, related, issue arose from the scrutiny role of the Assembly itself, established to restrain a Mayor on whom it was bound to become, to a large extent, dependent.

As Mayor, Livingstone had enjoyed the unique status of being a powerful elected executive, independent of party, in a governmental system that was based on partisan alignments. Whatever his personal inclination, he had no choice but to create a new politics based on coalitions around issues. This had indeed been the intention of the GLA's creators: the electoral system chosen for the Assembly, based on an elegant theory of political choice, had been designed to make a party majority unlikely and coalition-building necessary. In these circumstances the Mayor had the incentive, and the opportunity, to appeal across parties to establish a framework for support.

This he did by drawing in as many as possible of his potential critics with a view to neutralizing their opposition, setting up for this purpose a broad-based, if enigmatically titled, 'advisory cabinet'. The Mayor was criticized for using the Assembly as 'a patronage quarry' for his cabinet and for the boards of the functional bodies, ensuring that the Assembly had better things to do than attack him, while being implicated if things went wrong. In fact, the included parties had accepted responsibility without gaining power for, as one insider commented, 'the Mayor and his kitchen cabinet of personal advisers are the only real administration'. 'Cabinet' was in any case a misnomer, for, despite its official title of executive board, the mayoral group had no executive power. Members were not bound by collective responsibility and could in no way tie the Mayor's hands.

The tactic of selective inclusion did much to shape initial relations between Mayor and Assembly. First, the leading members of the parties of the left were effectively compromised by their association with the Mayor's policies. For example, Labour's Nicky Gavron, as Deputy Mayor, was given notional responsibility for overseeing the development of the spatial development plan, the most important policy instrument available to the Mayor. Yet she was not on that account the most influential in shaping it, and when the SDS was finalized it was apparent that her voice had not prevailed on some important issues. She had originally been permitted to take up the post only on the condition that the Mayor shelved his opposition to the Underground PPP. In the event, she remained in office even as Livingstone took his battle with the government to the High Court.

Meanwhile, the government, which had unequivocally opposed Livingstone's bid for selection and then his candidacy, approached the victorious Mayor with a combination of sulky *hauteur*, dark suspicion, and *Realpolitik*. In the run-up, Blair's declaration that a Livingstone victory would be a disaster seemed to rule out the possibility of a working relationship between Downing Street and Romney House. Some even predicted that the outcome of the contest would split the Labour Party and begin to unravel the Blair premiership. In fact, the two camps rapidly settled into the new reality.

During the initial year, Labour members of the Assembly, aware of the strength of Livingstone's following in the unions and constituency parties, yet anxious to avoid exposing the government to his tirades, quietly supported many of his policies. They were in, but not of, the Mayor's coalition. The Conservatives, on the other hand, were entirely excluded. Despite the professed intention that the Assembly should be a new type of institution, free from inter-party wrangling, keeping out the Conservatives ensured that they would operate in a traditional manner as an official opposition. Livingstone's way of handling the Assembly bore directly upon the Assembly's effectiveness in its principal role, that of scrutiny. Neither a cabinet nor a parliament, the 25-strong body, especially the non-Tory part of it, was scarcely able to protect its political virtue. The Mayor's patronage had the effect of drawing a high proportion of its members into his own executive orbit. The potential for compromising the Assembly's independence of the executive became clear. Scrutiny of the functional bodies was complicated by the presence on their boards of a number of leading members, who had chosen to share the responsibility for preparing the strategies and policies. Yet they were part of an Assembly whose principal role was to scrutinize and criticize the ways in which policing, transportation, and economic development were carried out.

Critically, it was the Assembly—both the Livingstone-influenced and Tory parts of it—that discovered the nature and limitations of 'scrutiny' as opposed to the traditional oppositional criticism of local and Westminster representative bodies. Oppositions seek to undermine the executive while offering policy alternatives to the electorate. Scrutineers, to be effective, must make detailed but constructive, as well as critical, comment. Unfortunately, the local government background of many Assembly members made them instinctively inclined to an oppositional approach, for which the system provided little scope. Their experience did little to prepare them for the harsh reality of the new system: that scrutiny does not amount to control. There was no statutory requirement for the executive parts of the Authority to incorporate opposing views, merely to provide for their expression and reception. When the Assembly produced a trenchant critique of the first draft of the economic development strategy, a chastened team withdrew, undertaking to take account of the Assembly's comments. A subsequent draft, however, reverted to the original position on a number of issues, and successive drafts diverged still further from the Assembly's view. Frustrated Assembly members found there was nothing they could do short of the 'nuclear option' of overturning the Mayor's budget in favour of one of their own.

These difficulties were compounded by the Assembly's decision to shape its own organization largely around the Mayor's statutory strategies and so mirror the executive form. The transport policy and spatial planning committee and the environment and sustainability committee, focused on the relevant strategies and expected to monitor their implementation. The transport operation scrutiny committee monitored the performance of TfL as well as the implementation of the Mayor's transport policy. The economic development committee, in addition to reviewing the economic development aspects of the Mayor's strategies , monitored the London Development Agency and sought to ensure consistency in the promotion of the London economy, nationally and internationally.

This approach seemed to have the effect of gearing the Assembly's activities too closely to the Mayor's agenda, linking it to the preparation of his strategies. The transition team's advice—that the Assembly would have a more proactive agenda-setting role if it organized itself around cross-cutting themes based on client groups—was ignored. As a result, twelve months into the life of the GLA a number of Assembly members expressed concerns about the effectiveness of their scrutiny role. Matching the structure of scrutiny too closely to the strategies locked the Assembly committees into a cyclical process with a finite life. Thus, the scrutiny role seemed likely to operate in a vacuum: 'the strategies are keeping us going', commented one member. It remained unclear how the continuation of scrutiny would be provided for from 2002 onwards.

A New Concordat with the Boroughs?

Meanwhile, the re-invention of a London-wide authority revived the potential for conflict with the boroughs. Indeed, the post-GLC interregnum had done little to reduce the danger. On the contrary, since GLC abolition the London boroughs, already powerful bodies, had developed highly effective structures of joint action in order to take on a more central role in metropolitan government. As a result, the new Mayor had to come to terms with a more vigorous borough spirit than he had faced as GLC leader. Moreover, during the 1990s the boroughs themselves mended the breach provoked by the proposed abolition of the GLC, which had brought a single London-wide association to an end in 1982. At that time, the majority of the Labour-controlled authorities withdrew from the London Boroughs Association (LBA) and joined with the embattled GLC to form the Association of London Authorities (ALA), leaving the boroughs divided mainly on partisan lines. Despite periodic overtures during the interregnum, the division remained until 1995, when the two associations came together to form the Association of London Government (ALG).

The creation of the Greater London Authority in 2000 prompted a further consideration of how borough interests should be consolidated, represented, and protected. With its effective control over the new functional bodies, the GLA believed itself to be well placed to win battles in key policy areas. But by the same token the boroughs were naturally concerned not to be usurped, and did their utmost to arm their association to balance the GLA. The Greater London Employers' Association, London Boroughs Grants—formerly the London Boroughs Grants Committee, an important residue of GLC abolition—the London Housing Unit, and the Transport Committee for London were brought under the ALG umbrella to create a more substantial body than the LBA had ever been. Led by a cross-party committee of leaders, much of the ALG's work was done through panels covering housing, education, culture, and health and social services, which sought—and seek—to provide 'a strategic pan-London voice'. This was an important new aspiration for a borough-based organization; and when panels were set up on policing and community safety, research, Europe, and regeneration, it became clear that the ALG could be an important counterweight to the Mayor on London-wide issues.

At the same time, the establishment of the ALG in its new form raised questions about the nature of its relationship with the Mayor and Assembly. In London's new politics the rhetoric of 'inclusion' and Livingstone's references to a 'broad tent' persuaded some borough politicians that there should be a single body in which London-wide and local interests were united. The integration of the several pan-London functions into the ALG seemed to strengthen their case, although others subscribed to the traditional view of the ALG as a 'boroughs-only club'. In the event, the ALG opted for inclusiveness, and the Mayor, representing the new Authority, was invited to join. Livingstone's constitutional position, however, presented the new ALG with something of a conundrum. While the GLA could become a member of the Association, the Mayor himself could not be a voting member, and the Act did not permit him to delegate functions—including representation—to the members of the Assembly. Livingstone was keen to be seen and heard at the Association's leaders' committee but was obliged to delegate the presentation of his position to an official, in this case one of his politically aligned appointees.

Having secured his position in the ALG, Livingstone soon found himself in predictable battles with the boroughs. The first episode was seemingly trivial: criticisms levelled at the Mayor over his failure to organize the New Year firework display. The effect, however, was to fracture an inherently fragile relationship and within weeks there was what one observer has called a 'cathartic split' in the united front of London government. The split widened and his budget proposals in February 2001 precipitated a major conflict between the Mayor and borough members of the ALG. In a bitter and personal confrontation—'one of the most amazing meetings I have ever been to', in the words of one officer—the Mayor accused his former party colleagues of 'being liars, Millbank stooges, traitors to socialism' in refusing to support his budget.

Back at the Assembly, members of all parties, conscious of borough concerns, rejected the budget by 24 votes to one, eliminating all but the provision for additional police officers and reducing the precept increase to about a third of that originally proposed. This and other episodes led, by the end of the GLA's first year, to a complete rupture in the relationship between the Mayor and the ALG, amidst a barrage of mutual recrimination about blocking tactics and usurped responsibilities. Exasperated by what they regarded as collective stonewalling, in April 2001 the Mayor's team proposed that he should in future work through direct contact with individual boroughs rather than through the ALG. For them, the GLA was the only city-wide government of London, a role to which the ALG should not pretend. The GLA's membership of the ALG merely confused this situation and the Mayor should withdraw from the ALG. This Livingstone did the following month, to expressions of regret on both sides and protestations about the need to maintain working relations. In noting the Mayor's withdrawal, ALG leader Sir Robin Wales pointedly referred to London issues requiring 'a combination of the GLA's strategic approach, the ALG pan-borough perspective and the boroughs' practical service delivery' (*London Bulletin*, May 2001: 5). It remained unclear how these forces might combine in resolving London issues. However, there were pointers.

A Mark II GLC?

From the outset, one fear surrounding the Greater London Authority proposal had been that it might turn out to be a rerun of the GLC. Conservative spokesmen and borough leaders, with memories of the former council's ambitions, warned against giving the GLA power to impinge upon the boroughs. Indeed, a major dilemma had dominated early discussions: how to create an effective capital-wide executive, without repeating the mayhem of 1980s. In fact, the boroughs were much more strongly placed vis-à-vis the new Authority than they had been in the days when they had struggled to resist the encroachments of the GLC. More confident and powerful than before, they enjoyed in addition the protection of the ALG which had carved out for itself a place as the third force in London politics. The structure of the Authority was such that the borough interests were weakly represented in the Assembly, with only 13 constituencies for 32 boroughs and the City. The result was to give greater representative responsibility—and legitimacy—to the local authorities themselves. For some, the GLA was an unnecessarily coercive body that would be resented by the London boroughs. 'They see it as intrusive and taking away many of their powers', according to one London MP; because 'members of the Assembly will have little in common—and little contact—with the London boroughs, there will inevitably be clash and conflict between the new authority and them' (Ottaway 1998: 28). Even after the formation of the GLA itself, the Conservative leader recalled that

One of the problems that we had with the old GLC regardless of which party controlled it, was that frequently it was seen as being burdensome and oppressive in its dealings with the London boroughs, and a body which interfered too much in matters of detail rather than matters of strategy. (GLA minutes, 29 June 2000)

Suspicion of the GLA was not confined to the political right. The Labour ALG chairman, Lord Harris, spoke vehemently of the need to restrain the Mayor, given his overwhelming personal mandate, by ensuring that the boroughs influenced his strategies. 'Borough councillors', declared Harris, 'will still be the elected representatives closest to the people and they will remain a significant voice through which Londoners will speak' (*ES*, 10 January 2000).

As under the GLC, the metropolitan authority's claim to hold sway over the boroughs rested on its strategic responsibility. The Conservatives asserted the principle that local people were the best fitted to judge local transport needs, the GLA overriding local preferences only where a genuine strategic interest existed. The Mayor, however, disagreed. 'It depends how we define overriding strategic interest', he responded. 'If we are developing a bus priority strategy [with] 17 main routes cutting across London, it would be ridiculous if one borough could opt out of that so the bus priority strategy goes to one side of the borough then resumes on the other side' (GLA minutes, 29 June 2000).

A specific issue which illustrates the ambiguity of what constitutes a 'strategic' and what a 'local' interest was the uncertain status of London's major squares. Responsibility for these was given to the Mayor by the GLA Act, with routine management left to the City of Westminster. Sir Norman Foster had produced a plan titled *World Squares for All* to revitalize Trafalgar Square for Westminster City Council, whereby traffic would be excluded and Trafalgar Square, Parliament Square, and Whitehall pedestrianized. The plan was strongly backed by John Prescott. When Westminster considered it in July 1998, however, the Conservative group split with councillors from the wards most affected succeeding in getting a blocking motion accepted, according to which the scheme would not be implemented until effective measures to cut central London traffic were in place.

Local residents, worried about the diversion of traffic from pedestrianized areas, organized their opposition through a protest group, Westminster's Residents Against Gridlock (WRAG). Supporters of the Foster scheme were furious, accusing the city council of behaving like a 'glorified residents' association' and of being unfit to manage the richest city in western Europe. Westminster's experience of pedestrianizing Leicester Square had been that, so far from easing the problems of a notoriously difficult area, it had led to an increase in crime, aggressive begging, drug dealing, and other forms of anti-social behaviour, with the police too stretched to handle the disorder that might follow from any attempt to intervene. The city council's resistance led the Mayor to threaten to take day-to-day control of Trafalgar Square and Leicester Square away from them if they failed to agree to the plan. In August, Westminster decided to wash its hands of the scheme and hand the management of Trafalgar Square to the Mayor, unmollified by a compromise which would allow traffic to continue to use the south side of the square.

Other areas of potential conflict also confronted all or most of the boroughs. One was housing. In contrast to the earlier GLC, the GLA was not a housing authority. However, the Mayor argued from the outset that his strategic role meant that that the GLA, with its overall responsibility for the SDS, would be better placed to allocate funds to housing associations across London than the Housing Corporation. It was difficult to square this claim with his denial of any intention to encroach on the housing role of the boroughs. 'So our worst fears are coming true', complained a Conservative Assembly member:

You do want a Mark II GLC. You want us to be a housing authority. Perhaps then we could go a bit further and become an education authority again, and all those other things, and take control from the boroughs. (GLA minutes, 18 October 2000)

Yet the idea of the Mayor acquiring housing powers was not a new one. The IPPR, which had played a major role in shaping the government's original proposals, argued in November 1997 that the GLA could become a strategic housing authority, with the £500 billion housing budget for London being devolved to it from the DETR (IPPR and KPMG 1997: A.58–61). This was an unpalatable prospect for the government, which would suffer a huge loss of central control and face the possibility of a threatening increase in the power of the GLA. Memories lingered of the GLC as a housing authority. Nick Raynsford, in particular, as Minister for London with extensive experience of housing, was aware of the potential for a rerun of the bitter battles between the boroughs and the old GLC over housing, and was determined that the GLA would not acquire a housing role.

Livingstone, on the other hand, did not give up easily. In fact, the Mayor already had the power, through the SDS, to set targets for affordable housing development within the boroughs. He now appointed an 18-member housing commission to advise him on how to turn the opportunity into reality. The commission recommended that half of all new homes built in London should be for those who could not afford full market price, 35 per cent for those on low incomes, and 15 per cent as part of the new 'intermediate' housing sector.

A survey by the LPAC indicated that while more than half a million new homes could be built on brownfield sites across London, the boroughs had set aside no more than one-fifth of these sites for affordable housing. The Mayor's aim was to double this figure, by using his powers to refuse permission for non-compliant development. The first occasion on which this power was used was in the case of residential development in Tower Hamlets, where the Limehouse Basin was being redeveloped for the private market. The Mayor directed Tower Hamlets to refuse permission for the scheme, on the grounds that it failed to provide the required minimum of 25 per cent affordable housing set out in the borough's own UDP. Agreement was reached between the developer, the council, the freeholder, and the GLA, which led to the developer providing Tower Hamlets with the resources equivalent to 33 per cent of the development for affordable housing off-site. The agreement enabled the Mayor to rescind the direction.

Just as the very existence of the GLA evoked the possibility of its role extending stealthily into the housing field, it also raised the question of a similar encroachment in education. All the major mayoral candidates indicated their readiness to extend the powers of the GLA or to seek to develop its influence in those areas where it had no standing under the act, with education as the prime area of political interest. Thus, Norris had proposed to appoint a schools' 'Czar' to deal with educational underachievement. Such an official, who would be acting quite outside the statutory framework for education, would build up a team of experts to act as troubleshooters and to offer their services to failing schools, though quite why any school or local education authority would tolerate such intervention was not explained. Meanwhile, Livingstone urged that that the Assembly should consider education in schools to lie within its remit, and proposed involving London teachers in an inquiry into the impact of Ofsted on schools.

The London Skills Forecasting Unit was one among a number of bodies advocating a more extended role for the Mayor, arguing that while he had no powers over education below the age of 16, 'neither have the mayors in New York or Europe, and this has not stopped them from banging on about it':

The London mayor must address the problem of the quarter of schools which are failing. The mayor will be able to devise strategies for training, and will control the London Development Agency. This will produce a regional economic strategy. He or she should make development of skills paramount, and a strategy to ensure Frankfurt does not overtake London in terms of skills, if we are to retain the city's leading edge. The mayor should set strategic goals recognising that there are two Londons. We have the most highly skilled workforce in Britain and the highest GDP in Europe, but there is almost a quarter of the population with qualifications below acceptable levels, and the low qualified are the least interested in future training. (*ES*, 20 March 2000)

When the GLA assumed its powers, the LDA chair, George Barlow, launched a scheme to link the most disadvantaged schools in London with large firms, arguing that it would better equip school leavers for the labour market.

The other side of the issue of skill shortages and labour supply was discrimination on the part of employers. Here the Mayor launched an attack on the employment practices of London firms, threatening to expose those that failed to employ a sufficient quota of women and ethnic minorities, promising to 'help' private companies to achieve these quotas, and giving notice of a policy of 'naming and shaming the bigots'. There was, he declared, 'a huge reservoir of black unemployed youth. A lot of these kids have incredible ability—if you give them a second chance they will jump at it'. The Institute of Directors responded angrily, retorting that 'this has nothing to do with him. Firms have enough problems as it is dealing with tons of extra regulations being pushed through. What is being proposed could be the final straw' (*ES*, 3 July 2000).

Health was yet another area of policy in which the Mayor was tempted to expand his role. Theoretically, his responsibility extended only to fostering public health improvement. In practice, the concerns of Londoners encouraged his ambitions to do more. During the election campaign the King's Fund, a leading health-service think tank, arranged a debate at St Thomas' hospital, where Livingstone advocated extending the GLA's powers and called for legislation to transfer the London region's responsibilities for resources and hospital planning to the GLA. In particular, he promised to establish a commission and to press the Health Secretary for more resources for London hospitals and nurse recruitment. Frank Dobson, as former Health Secretary, was quick to point out that, while health inequalities were a legitimate concern, London's health services were not. Response from within the NHS was also wary, as a director of public health reported:

Reaction has largely been 'What has the Mayor and GLA got to do with us when we've got waiting-list targets to deliver and Trusts to create and reshuffle?' A minority sees the Mayor threatening to take over health and healthcare [although] this hardly seems real when central government is increasingly bypassing local authorities. (Jacobson 2000: 18)

The NHS executive's London regional office nevertheless worked up a 'coalition for health and regeneration' comprising a few local bodies and a wide range of pan-London organizations to exploit the opportunity to get health gains from partnership with the new GLA regime.

As Mayor, one of Livingstone's first announcements detailed his short-term priority to secure increases in NHS funding for London, together with the appointment of Dr Sue Atkinson, Regional Director for Public Health in London, as public health adviser. He confidently predicted that the government would eventually devolve the NHS to regional authorities, though not within the next ten to 25 years. It was a carefully gauged gamble. According to a well-placed official who supports the Mayor's view, 'if it works, people want to add more functions in. Ken has said many times that he can't understand why he is not dealing with health, or education. So there will probably be pressure for it to expand . . . it wouldn't surprise me at all.'

One way in which the Mayor sought to extend his influence in areas that lay beyond his immediate statutory powers was through the appointment of review commissions. Thus, in October 2000 Livingstone established the London Health Commission, an independent body charged with advising him on health-related issues, including reducing health inequalities and helping ensure that health was integrated with the whole range of other GLA strategies. Apart from the GLA itself, the commission was supported by a range of 'sponsoring partners', including the NHS Executive London, the King's Fund, the ALG, and the GOL.

Inevitably, Livingstone's exploration of the boundaries of his potential influence evoked a mixed reaction. To some, his attempts to broaden the mayoral mission smacked of megalomania. However, others saw it as a natural process of muscle-flexing, making the most of available opportunities:

Mr Livingstone has driven his chariot through every loophole. He seems unconstrained by statute. On Monday he told the *Independent* that he intends to end Connex South-Central's commuter rail franchise in three years, not the best way of getting it to improve services. He has no such powers, which rest with Sir Alistair Morton of the Strategic Rail Authority. He also announced that he would be appointing a London health commission. Chris Holmes of Shelter is to investigate housing policy and Glenda Jackson is joining his cabinet to tackle homelessness. He has no powers in any of these areas. It is understandable, even good, that the new Mayor should be testing his statutory muscle. Having nobbled the Assembly, he is clearly out to nobble Whitehall and the Treasury on London's behalf. What he has not the formal powers to achieve, he can at least seek to influence through the force of his mandate and his charisma. (*ES*, 6 July 2000)

In fact, all those involved in London government were playing a waiting game, as they worked out the true significance of hitherto untested negotiations. Although the transition team foresaw that the GLA would have a major impact on the boroughs, and protocols were drawn up to manage the relationships, the initial experience was one of phoney war: there was a sense of major confrontation yet to come, while an eerie calm reigned in the meantime. Thus, one borough chief executive interviewed for this study recalled establishing an elaborate filing system in his office to manage his borough's relationship with Romney House, the GLA's temporary headquarters, only to scrap it after a period of months in which he received no communications to file.

Two factors, however, promised to transform this situation: first, the phenomenon of so-called 'mission creep', as prescribed powers were quietly extended to fill gaps in areas that had been poorly thought through; and second, the long-term architecture of the GLA-borough relationships, which had been established by the Mayor's several strategies and in particular by the overarching spatial development strategy. As long as the Mayor took executive decisions within an inherited framework, as in the case of development control within existing UDPs and regional guidance, then the experience would be one of continuity with the past. As approved strategies came into force and provided an authoritative context for mayoral decision-making, the stakes were likely to be raised dramatically and would be bound to involve central government.

As we have seen, tensions between the GLA and central government already existed. The danger that they would become worse was certainly increased by the decision to give the Mayor powers which for the past 14 years had been exercised by the central departments or by executive agencies accountable to them. Despite the high hopes that an executive Mayor would be able to bring decisive action to bear on London's problems, it was clear from early on that he would be caught between the central government powers and the interests of the boroughs. When in March 2001 the deal over the PPP appeared finally to have collapsed, it seemed that the hopes for a new beginning in London government lay in ruins. The *Economist* (3 March 2001: 40) delivered what looked like a plausible final judgement:

Mr Blair's great experiment could not have ended more wretchedly. Indeed, his blueprint for London was always a compromise too clever for its own good. He gave Londoners a Mayor but wanted his own man for the job. When he got Mr Livingstone, he could at least tell himself that the Mayor's powers have been kept deliberately weak. The trouble is that Mr Livingstone is too shrewd to take responsibility for the tube without also taking the power he needs to run it properly. And if he cannot get that, he will use the courts to show voters that devolution was a pretext for the government to pass down responsibility without power.

The ultimate test of metropolitan government was its ability to give voice to a sense of unity that could transcend diversity. In creating a new metropolitan framework that was built around a Mayor who was supposed to provide the voice for Londoners, the government was seeking to express the idea of London's underlying unity. The question remained, however, of whether such a unity existed. Before the creation of the GLC, Edward Carter (1962: 74) had remarked that 'however much one may talk of a new conception of "London as a whole", it is impossible to identify "the whole" of London as if it were a unified civic structure'. Nearly 40 years later, a new metropolitan authority was predicated on the idea that there did exist a metropolitan community whose interests it could articulate. The GLC, whose history was marked by recurrent divisions between inner and outer London, failed to define or represent such a community. During the 1986–2000 period there was no institutional expression of the metropolitan interest other than the Whitehall's Government Office for London. Now the institution of the Mayor, as a single voice for London, offered a new prospect of defining and speaking for the metropolitan community. The device that was readily to hand, thanks to such bodies as London First, was the concept of London as a world city. The form in which the Mayor espoused this concept did not, however, command universal assent.

Might such a sense of London's unity be expressed through, or possibly even inculcated by, the Assembly? The system was designed to eliminate so-called 'parochialism', as the representation of local interests was described at the time. But it was in the nature of political life that such interests would be expressed through whatever channels were available: if not in the Assembly, then through inter-authority conflict. The short-lived failed experiment of a single association for London, embracing the Mayor and the boroughs, was perhaps an indication of political alignments and divisions yet to come.

What Sort of Mayor?

It is tempting to compare Livingstone the Mayor with Livingstone the GLC leader of 1981–6. However, while the man, and perhaps the psychology, are the same, the institutional constraints are significantly different. The structure of the GLC tended to amplify rather than resolve conflicts, partly because it mirrored London's diversity. The constitution of the GLA, by contrast, was designed to promote consensus both by providing for cross-community representation in the Assembly and through the symbolic pan-metropolitan Mayor. Thus, optimists have argued that the new administration has the chance to be genuinely mould-breaking. According to Lee Jasper, 'The first year has been a magnificent achievement. The second, with all the building blocks in place, will be spectacular' (*ES*, 30 April 2001). Most observers are more cautious.

After the first year, the jury was still out. Livingstone's coalition building, in which key posts were distributed to Labour, Liberal Democrat, and Green parties, could be represented as a brave foray into consensus politics or as an effective ploy to neutralize the Assembly's potentially critical role. Certainly the power relationship between the Mayor and the Assembly seemed to have been determined in the Mayor's favour. Unable to avoid the suspicion of having been bought off and constrained by a conflict of interest, leading Assembly figures found themselves bound to a Mayor who did not, in practice, have much interest in what they had to say about his business. Within his 'advisory cabinet' they found themselves outnumbered by his allies from outside. Their position brought them little influence with the Mayor, who valued their compliance more than their contribution. At the same time, Livingstone's commitment to building a broad coalition to sustain himself in power, in the absence of a party, seemed to have hampered his ability to take decisive action on big issues. Inevitably, confronted with contradictory and incompatible demands, he found himself engaged in a delicate balancing act, satisfying one group while trying to avoid alienating another.

The contrast with Mayor Giuliani's New York was indeed striking. The new system undoubtedly imported some of the style, thrust, and contentiousness of the US model. However, by the end of the first year the heightened expectations that attended Ken Livingstone's election had to some extent faded, and the honeymoon, such as it was, had ended. Giuliani's renowned ability to face down opposition was noted by opponents of London's Mayor. His over-riding concern seemed to be to make friends rather than enemies, to choose small wins, and to avoid big issues. Nevertheless, the opening months demonstrated Livingstone's capacity for setting the political agenda, with a distinct vision and flair for publicizing it.

A Mayor and Assembly for London called for a new style of politics for the capital city—more inclusive and less confrontational (DETR 1998*a*). It has certainly been inclusive, and focused on the issues that surveys repeatedly revealed mattered to Londoners—above all, public transport. However, any hopes for a 'non-confrontational' style were quickly, if inevitably, disappointed. Here, Livingstone's head-to-head conflict with the government over the Public-Private Partnership for the Underground has been as symbolically significant as it was predictable. It dominated the first year of the new authority's existence to the exclusion of developments on other policy fronts. Meanwhile, the failure of the Mayor's legal challenge to the government's plans leaves much unresolved.

The political personalities of the world's civic leaders vary widely. As we have seen, one version is the flamboyant and articulate showman, spotlighting problems, identifying issues, and addressing them in a public and dramatic manner. Another is the reticent bureaucrat or fixer, operating mainly behind closed doors and keeping press and public at arm's length. The second kind tends to respond to problems as they arise, seeking to contain protest rather than exploit opportunities for publicity. Livingstone clearly falls into both categories, and, in terms of the typology outlined in Chapter 2, is part 'crusader' and part 'broker', with a dash of entrepreneur as well.

What Livingstone appears not to be, in the classic American sense, is a city boss. Lacking either a party or a major interest group base, the political resources of the boss are denied to him, although it is arguable whether even Herbert Morrison could marshal the necessary resources within the Labour Party today. He has yet to prove himself as an entrepreneur, although the Mayor's continual pursuit of additional powers in health, education, and housing indicates that he knows full well where he would like to position himself.

As a broker, he has shown himself relatively adept, with some ability to negotiate settlements among competing interest groups. However, he would certainly like to see himself primarily in the guise of a 'crusader' with a vision, even if lacking the power needed in the short term to attain it. But can his crusading ambition be maintained indefinitely without successes along the way? Livingstone's campaign was characterized by promises which he soon discovered were far from easy to deliver. Meanwhile, his supporters were not to be easily swatted aside. The Mayor had made a lot of promises during the election. The Tube workers had demanded that he stop the PPP. London firefighters defied their leaders to back his campaign in the expectation that he would support their pay claim. He promised gay activists a 'marriage register', and had pledged himself to provide better transport facilities for the disabled. 'It would be nice to think I could issue an edict and things would happen', he told a 'Meet the Mayor' event at the Barbican (*ES*, 21 September 2000). By then, he had already discovered he could not.

The stumbling block is the limitation in the Mayor's actual power, as defined by statute, and his de facto subservience to central government, producing a relationship between Mayor and ministers that is quite different from the one that exists between the Mayor of New York and either State or Federal authorities. There should be few illusions about the standing of any London Mayor. As an MPA official reflected:

Supposing we had [a repeat of] the desecration of the Cenotaph and the digging up of Parliament Square . . . There is absolutely no doubt that the Home Secretary would make a statement to Parliament. And that's where the action would be. [Suppose] you're an editor. Where will you go? A statement from the Mayor's office? Emergency meeting of the Metropolitan Police Authority? No. A statement by the Home Secretary!

The contrast could hardly have been made more poignant by the aftermath of the terrorist attack on the World Trade Centre on 11 September 2001, when Mayor Giuliani took direct command of the rescue operation, a symbol of New Yorkers' attachment to their city. It could not be doubted who was in charge or who spoke for New York.

As yet, we have seen only the opening chapter of the attempt to produce an Authority and a leader who would 'speak for London'. On the one hand, Livingstone has proved unable, so far, to establish the idea either of a 'community capital' or of a 'world city' with its own effective form of government. On the other hand, he has shown that the Authority, for all its lack of financial resources and legal weakness, is capable of providing a voice for Londoners that did not previously exist. Has the London problem been solved? It is inconceivable that the age-old tensions between Westminster and London government, and London government and the boroughs, will simply disappear. Nevertheless, the sense of London's most exciting experiment in self-management for more than a century remains.

REFERENCES

ALG (Association of London Government) (1996). *Reaping the Rewards of Democracy: Efficiency and the Strategic London Authority*. London: ALG.

Ackroyd, P. (2000) *London: The Biography*. London: Chatto and Windus.

Archer, J. (1999). 'Dragging the Tube Out of the Dark Ages'. *Parliamentary Monitor*, 7/9: 8–9.

Baker, K. (1984). Speech, in *Report of the Conservative Party Conference, 1984*. London: Conservative Central Office.

Baker, P. and Eversley, J. (eds) (2000). *Multilingual Capital: The Languages of London's School Children and their Relevance to Economic, Social and Educational Policies*. London: Battlebridge Publications.

Banfield, E. C. (ed.) (1969). *Urban Government: A Reader in Administration and Politics* (revised edn). New York: Free Press.

—— and Wilson, J. G.(1965). *City Politics*. Cambridge, MA: Harvard University Press.

Barlow, I. (1991). *Metropolitan Government*. London: Routledge.

Bayliss, D. (1992). 'Sorting Out the Buses'. *Municipal Engineer* (Institution of Civil Engineers proceedings), 93/December: 215–18.

Beresford, Sir P. (1998). 'A New Layer of Government Will End in Tiers'. *The House Magazine*, 23/792 (26 January): 13.

Biggs, S. and Travers, T. (1994). 'Opportunities for City-Wide Government in London: The Experience of the Metropolitan Areas'. *Local Government Policy Making*, 21/2: 25–33.

Bogdanor, V. (2001). *Devolution in the United Kingdom*. Oxford: Oxford University Press.

Borraz, O. (1994). 'Mayoral Leadership in France', in O. Borraz *et al.*, *Local Leadership and Decision-Making: A Study of France, Germany, United States and Britain*. London: LGC Communications.

Buck, N., Gordon, I., and Young, K. (1986). *The London Employment Problem*. Oxford: Oxford University Press.

Building Design Partnerships, London Property Research, London Research Centre, and Ziona Strelitz Associates (1998). *High Buildings and Strategic Views in London*. London: LPAC.

Carter, E. (1962). *The Future of London*. Harmondsworth: Penguin Books.

Carvel, J. (1999). *Turn Again Livingstone*. London: Profile Books.

Chevrant-Breton, M. (1997). 'Selling the World City: A Comparison of Promotional Strategies in Paris and London'. *European Planning Studies*, 5/2: 137–61.

CLD (Commission for Local Democracy) (1995). *Taking Charge: The Rebirth of Local Democracy* (Final Report of the Commission for Local Democracy). London: CLD.

Clifton, G. (1989). 'Members and Officers of the LCC, 1889–1965', in A. Saint (ed.), *Politics and the People of London: The London County Council, 1889–1965*. London: Hambledon Press.

Commissioner of Police (1969). *Report of the Commissioner of Police of the Metropolis for the Year 1968* (Cmnd 4060). London: HMSO.

Coopers and Lybrand Deloitte (1992). *London, World City: Report of Studies*, i. London: LPAC.

D'Arcy M. and MacLean, R. (2000). *Nightmare: The Race to Become London's Mayor*. London: Politico's.

Davis, J. H. (1988). *Reforming London: The London Government Problem 1855–1900*. Oxford: Clarendon Press.

—— (1989).'The Progressive Council, 1889–1907', in A. Saint (ed.), *Politics and the People of London: the London County Council, 1889–1965*. London: Hambledon Press.

—— (2001). 'London Government: 1850–1920: The Metropolitan Board of Works and the London County Council'. *London Journal*, 26/1: 47–56.

delle Site, P. and Filippi, F. (1995). 'Bus Service Optimization and Car Pricing Policies to Save Fuel in Urban Areas'. *Transportation Research*, 29a/5: 345–58.

DETR (Department of the Environment, Transport and the Regions) (1997). *Leadership for London–A Consultation Paper*. London: DETR.

—— (1998a). *A Mayor and Assembly for London* (Cm. 3897). London: TSO.

—— (1998b). *A New Deal for Transport: Better for Everyone* (Cm. 3950). London: TSO.

DoE (Department of the Environment) (1983). *Streamlining the Cities: Government Proposals for Reorganising Local Government in Greater London and the Metropolitan Counties* (Cmnd. 9063). London: HMSO.

Donoughue, B. and Jones, G. W. (1973). *Herbert Morrison: Portrait of a Politician*. London: Weidenfeld and Nicolson.

Eastwood, A. (1991) 'An Inevitable Nationalisation'. *Policing*, 7/3: 271–80.

Ellis, R. (1992). Annex to Coopers and Lybrand Deloitte, *London, World City: Report of Studies*, i. London: LPAC.

Foley, D. L. (1972). *Governing the London Region: Reorganisation and Planning in the 1960s*. Berkeley: University of California Press.

Forrester, A., Lansley, S., and Pauley, R. (1985). *Beyond Our Ken: A Guide to the Battle for London*. London: Fourth Estate.

Fox, K. (1977). *Better City Government: Innovation in American Urban Politics, 1850–1937*. Philadelphia: Temple University Press.

Freeman, R. (1979). 'The Marshall Plan for London Government: A Strategic Role or Regional Solution?'. *London Journal*, 5/2: 160–75.

Geddes, A. and Tone, J. (1997). *Labour's Landslide: The British General Election, 1997*. Manchester: Manchester University Press.

GLA (Greater London Authority) (2000a). *Congestion Charging: London Assembly Scrutiny Report 1*. London: GLA.

—— (2000b). *Appointments Committee, Report on Proposed Organisational Structure*, London: GLA (7 June).

—— (2000c). *The Mayor and Relations with the Business Community* (Mayor's Office). London: GLA (6 June).

—— (2001). *Towards the London Plan: Initial Proposals for the Mayor's Spatial Development Strategy*. London: GLA.

Glass, R. (1961). 'Introduction', in Centre for Urban Studies, *London: Aspects of Change*. London: MacGibbon and Kee.

GLC (Greater London Council) (1984). *Planning for the Future of London: The Greater London Development Plan as Proposed to be Altered by the Greater London Council*. London: GLC.

—— (1985). *The London Industrial Strategy*. London: GLC.

—— (1986). *The Future of London's Government: Research and Consultation Project*. London: GLC.

Goldstein, A. (1989). 'Travel in London: Is Chaos Inevitable?' (London Regional Transport Lecture). London.

Goodnow, F. J. (1969). 'The Historical Development of the City's Position', in E. C. Banfield (ed.), *Urban Government: A Reader in Administration and Politics*. (revised edn). New York: Free Press.

Greater London Group (1992). Annex, in Coopers and Lybrand Deloitte, *London, World City: Report of Studies*, i. London: LPAC.

Hall, P. (1963). *London 2000*. London: Faber and Faber.

—— (1989). *London 2001*. London: Unwin and Hyman.

Hallman, H. A. (1977). *Small and Large Together: Governing the Metropolis*. Beverley Hills, CA: Sage.

Harris Research Centre, NEDO, LPAC, and Automobile Association (1991). *A Road User Charge? Londoners' Views: Report on Survey Findings*. London: NEDO.

Hart, D. A. (1976). *Strategic Planning in London: The Rise and Fall of the Primary Road Network*. Oxford: Pergamon Press.

Hebbert, M. and Travers, T. (1988). *The London Government Handbook*. London: Cassell.

Herbert, Sir E. (1960). *Report of the Royal Commission on Local Government in Greater London, 1957–1960* (Cmnd 1164). London: HMSO.

IPPR (Institute of Public Policy Research) and KPMG (1997). *The Greater London Authority: Principles and Organisational Structure*. London: Corporation of London.

Jacobson, B. (2000). 'Co-operation Without Politics'. *Health Service Journal*, 110 (20 April): 18–19.

Jennings, W.I., Laski. H. J., and Robson, W. A. (eds) (1935). *A Century of Municipal Progress*. London: Allen and Unwin.

Kennedy, D. (1995). 'London Bus Tendering: An Overview'. *Transport Reviews*, 15: 253–64.

KPMG (1999). *Transition Arrangements for the Greater London Authority, Report*. London: Government Office for London.

Labour Party (1977). *London's Government–The Way Ahead: A Report by the Minority Labour Group on the Greater London Council*. London: Labour Party.

—— (1990). *London Pride: Policy Document for the London Borough Elections 1990*. London: Labour Party.

—— (1996a). *Regional Policy Commission, Renewing the Regions: Strategies for Regional Economic Development*. Sheffield: Sheffield Hallam University.

—— (1996b). *A Voice for London*. London: Labour Party.

—— (1997). *New Labour: Because Britain Deserves Better*. London: Labour Party.

Lagroye, J. and Wright, V. (eds) (1979). *Local Government in Britain and France: Problems and Prospects*. London: Allen and Unwin.

LDA (London Development Agency) (2000). *Draft Economic Development Strategy: A Draft Strategy Produced by the London Development Agency on Behalf of the Mayor of London*. London. LDA.

Livingstone, K. (1999). 'A Fare Deal for Londoners'. *Parliamentary Monitor*, 7/7: 20, 22.

LORP (London Office Review Panel) (1999). *1999 Report*. London: LPAC.

LPAC (London Planning Advisory Committee) (1988). 'Strategic Planning Advice for London: Policies for the 1990s' (discussion document). London: LPAC.

—— (1990), *London: A World City Moving Into the Twenty First Century: Draft Consultant's Brief*. London: LPAC.

—— (1996). *An Integrated Transport Programme for London*. London: LPAC.

—— (1999). *London Office Review Panel: 1999 Report*. London: LPAC.

—— (2000). *LPAC's Endowment to the Mayor and the Boroughs*. London: LPAC.

LRC (London Research Centre) (1998). *The Four World Cities Transport Study*. London: LRC.

LRT (London Regional Transport) (1988). *Consultation Document: 1988–1991*. London: LRT.

LSPU (London Strategic Policy Unit) (1987). *Policing London: Collected Reports of the LSPU Police Monitoring and Research Group, No. 2*. London: LSPU.

LT (London Transport) (1993). 'Memorandum to the Transport Committee' (January). London: LT.

—— (1996). *Planning London's Transport: To Win As a World City*. London: LT.

LU (London Underground) (2001). 'Unblock the Tube: Top 10 Myths Exploded'. At: http://www.thetube.com/content/unblock/top10.asp (accessed 26 October 2001).

MacGregor, S. and Pimlott, B. (eds.) (1990). *Tackling the Inner Cities: The 1980s Reviewed, Prospects for the 1990s*. Oxford: Clarendon Press.

Mackie, P., Preston, J., and Nash, C. (1995). 'Bus Deregulation: Ten Years On'. *Transport Reviews*, 15/3: 229–51.

MacPherson (1999). *The Stephen Lawrence Inquiry: Report of an Inquiry by Sir William MacPherson of Cluny*. London. The Stationery Office.

Marshall, Sir F. (1978). *The Marshall Inquiry on Greater London: Report to the Greater London Council, by Sir Frank Marshall, MA, LLB*. London: GLC.

Miles, S. (1970). 'Governing the Metropolis: A Commentary on World Opinion', in S. Miles (ed.), *Metropolitan Problems*. Toronto: Methuen.

Moran, M. (1999). 'Is Congestion Charging the Right Road to Take?'. *Parking Review*, 99/October: 29–30.

Murray, L. (1997). *Transport in London: Whose Decision?*. London: LRC.

MMC (Monopolies and Mergers Commission) (1991). *London Underground Limited: A Report on Passenger and Other Services Supplied by the Company*. (Cm. 1555). London: HMSO.

MPA (Metropolitan Police Authority) (2000). *Report on the Mayor's Draft Transport Strategy*. 9 November.

Newman P. (1995). 'London Pride'. *Local Economy*, 10: 117–23.

—— and Thornley, A. (1997). 'Fragmentation and Centralisation in the Governance of London: Influencing the Urban Policy and Planning Agenda'. *Urban Studies*, 34/7: 967–88.

Ottaway, R. (1998). 'Hindering the Mayor'. *Public Finance*, 18 December: 28.

Pimlott, B. (1994). *Frustrate Their Knavish Tricks: Writings on Biography, History and Politics*. London: HarperCollins.

PEMB (*Planning Encyclopedia Monthly Bulletin*) (2000). 'The Greater London Authority Act 1999', January: 23–74.

Rallings, C. and Thrasher, M. (2000). 'Personality Politics and Protest Voting: The First Elections to the Greater London Authority'. *Parliamentary Affairs*, 53: 753–64.

Rao, N. (2000). *Reviving Local Democracy: New Labour, New Politics?* Bristol: Policy Press.

Rhodes, G. (1970). *The Government of London: The Struggle for Reform*. London: Weidenfeld and Nicolson.

—— and Hastings, S. (1972). 'The Greater London Council', in G. Rhodes (ed.), *The New Government of London: The First Five Years*. London, Weidenfeld and Nicolson.

—— and Young, K. (1972). 'Elections and the Electoral System', in G. Rhodes (ed.), *The New Government of London: The First Five Years*. London: Weidenfeld and Nicolson.

Robson, W. A. (1948). *The Government and Misgovernment of London*. London: Allen and Unwin.

—— (1965). *The Heart of Greater London: Proposals for a Policy* (Greater London Paper No. 13). London: London School of Economics.

Savitch, H. V. (1988). *Post-Industrial Cities: Planning in Paris, New York and London*. Princeton: Princeton University Press.

Self, P. J. O. (1971). *Metropolitan Planning: The Planning System of Greater London* (Greater London Papers No. 14). London: London School of Economics.

Sharpe, L. J. (1995). 'The Abolition of the Greater London Council: Is There a Case for Resurrection?', in L. J. Sharpe (ed.), *The Government of World Cities: The Future of the Metro Model*. Chichester: John Wiley.

Sheppard, F. (1971). *London 1808-1870: The Infernal Wen*. London. Secker and Warburg.

Simmons, M. (2000). 'Introduction', *LPAC's Endowment to the Mayor and the Boroughs*. London: LPAC.

Smallwood, F. (1965). *Greater London: The Politics of Metropolitan Reform*. Indianapolis: Bobbs-Merrill.

Sofer, A. (1987). *The London Left Takeover*. London: J. Caslake.

SCLSERP (Standing Conference on London and South-East Regional Planning) (1974). *London and South-East England: Regional Planning, 1943–74*, London: SCLSERP.

Startin, N. (2001). 'Candidate-centred and Party-free Elections: Lessons from the Livingstone Mayoral Campaign'. *Representation*, 38: 31–45.

Tebbit, N. (1984). Speech to Meeting of London Conservatives (14 March). London.

Tocqueville, A de. ([1835]1994) *Democracy in America*. London: Everyman.

Transition Team (1999). *Shaping Up for the Mayor and Assembly: Responses to 'The Shape of Things to Come'*. London: Mayor and Assembly for London Transition Team.

Travers, T. (2001). 'The Years of Borough Government: 1986–2000'. *London Journal*, 26/1: 69–80.

—— and Jones, G. (1997). *The New Government of London*. York: Joseph Rowntree Foundation.

——, ——, Hebbert, M., and Burnham, J. (1991). *The Government of London*. York: Joseph Rowntree Foundation.

Warren, R. O. (1966). *Government in Metropolitan Regions: A Re-appraisal of Fractionated Political Organisation*. Davis: University of California Press.

Westergaard, J. (1961). 'The Structure of Greater London', in Centre for Urban Studies, *London: Aspects of Change*. London: MacGibbon and Kee.

Wheeler, Sir J. (1999). 'Executive Decision', *Police Review*, 13 August: 16–17.

Whitehouse, W. (2000). *GLC–The Inside Story*. Sunbury on Thames: James Lester.

Williams, O. P., Herman, H., Liebman, C., and Dye, T. R. (1965). *Suburban Differences and Metropolitan Policies*. Philadelphia: University of Pennsylvania Press.

Yates, D. (1977). *The Ungovernable City: The Politics of Urban Problems and Policy-Making*. Cambridge, MA: MIT Press.

Yeo, T. (1998). 'The Cities Await'. *The House Magazine*, 23/794 (9 February): 9.

Young, K. (1986). 'Metropolis, R.I.P?'. *Political Quarterly*, 57/1: 36–46.

—— (1994). 'The Party and English Local Government', in A. Seldon and S. Ball (eds), *Conservative Century: The Conservative Party Since 1900*. Oxford: Oxford University Press.

—— and Garside, P. L. (1982). *Metropòlitan London: Politics and Urban Change, 1831–1981*. London: Edward Arnold.

—— and Grayson, L. (1987). *Abolition: The Reform of Metropolitan Government in England, 1983–86: A Review and Bibliography*. Letchworth: Technical Communications.

Young, K. and Kramer, J. (1978). *Strategy and Conflict in Metropolitan Housing: Suburbia versus the Greater London Council, 1965–1975*. London: Heinemann.

—— and Rao, N. (1997). *Local Government Since 1945*. Oxford: Blackwell.

INDEX

Printed in the United Kingdom
by Lightning Source UK Ltd.
111752UKS00001B/60